GRAPHIS POSTER 97

36 –51–55   101–104   146
4– 25– 33– 35– 62 –67 –68 – 74 – 80 –8 9 –91 –96 –102 –107 –116 –132 –142 –159 –166 –169 –173 –179
188–206– 211 – 216 –225

THE INTERNATIONAL ANNUAL OF POSTER ART

DAS INTERNATIONALE JAHRBUCH DER PLAKATKUNST

LE RÉPERTOIRE INTERNATIONAL DE L'ART DE L'AFFICHE

EDITED BY · HERAUSGEGEBEN VON · EDITÉ PAR:

B. MARTIN PEDERSEN

PUBLISHER AND CREATIVE DIRECTOR: B. MARTIN PEDERSEN

BOOK PUBLISHER: CHRISTOPHER T. REGGIO

EDITORS: HEINKE JENSSEN, CLARE HAYDEN

ASSOCIATE EDITOR: PEGGY CHAPMAN

ART DIRECTORS: B. MARTIN PEDERSEN, JOHN JEHEBER

ASSOCIATE ART DIRECTOR: JENNY FRANCIS

PHOTOGRAPHER: ALFREDO PARRAGA

GRAPHIS INC.

(OPPOSITE): LG AD INC. / THE ART DIRECTORS CLUB

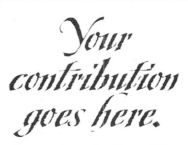

Your
contribution
goes here.

Please take a moment now to fill out an Art Works
pledge card. And continue to fill the world with art.

CONTENTS · INHALT · SOMMAIRE

REMARKS

WE EXTEND OUR HEARTFELT THANKS TO CONTRIBUTORS THROUGHOUT THE WORLD WHO HAVE MADE IT POSSIBLE TO PUBLISH A WIDE AND INTERNATIONAL SPECTRUM OF THE BEST WORK IN THIS FIELD.

ENTRY INSTRUCTIONS FOR NEXT YEAR'S ANNUAL MAY BE REQUESTED FROM:
GRAPHIS INC.
141 LEXINGTON AVENUE
NEW YORK, NY 10016-8193

ANMERKUNGEN

UNSER DANK GILT DEN EINSENDERN AUS ALLER WELT, DIE ES UNS DURCH IHRE BEITRÄGE ERMÖGLICHT HABEN, EIN BREITES, INTERNATIONALES SPEKTRUM DER BESTEN ARBEITEN ZU VERÖFFENTLICHEN.

TEILNAHMEBEDINGUNGEN FÜR DAS NÄCHSTE JAHRBUCH SIND ERHÄLTLICH BEIM:
GRAPHIS INC.
141 LEXINGTON AVENUE
NEW YORK, NY 10016-8193

REMERCIEMENTS

NOUS REMERCIONS LES PARTICIPANTS DU MONDE ENTIER QUI ONT RENDU POSSIBLE LA PUBLICATION DE CET OUVRAGE OFFRANT UN PANORAMA COMPLET DES MEILLEURS TRAVAUX RÉALISÉS DANS CE DOMAINE.

LES MODALITÉS D'INSCRIPTION PEUVENT ÊTRE OBTENUES AUPRÈS DE:
GRAPHIS INC.
141 LEXINGTON AVENUE
NEW YORK, NY 10016-8193

(OPPOSITE) THOMPSON & COMPANY / MEMPHIS COLLEGE OF ART
(FOLLOWING PAGE) GÉZA MOLNÁR / AGNES SMETANA

SMETANA
* ÁGNES *

— üvegtervező művész —
1995. június 22 – július 15.
DOROTTYA GALÉRIA
Budapest V., Dorottya utca 8.
A kiállítás megtekinthető
— vasárnap kivételével —
— naponta 10–18 óráig

COMMENTARIES

KOMMENTARE

COMMENTAIRES

DANTON
REŻYSERIA - ANDRZEJ WAJDA - CEZAR '83
W ROLACH GŁÓWNYCH - GÉRARD DEPARDIEU - WOJCIECH PSZONIAK
- NAGRODY ZA ROLE - VII FFS MONTREAL '82, POLSKA/FRANCJA
1982.

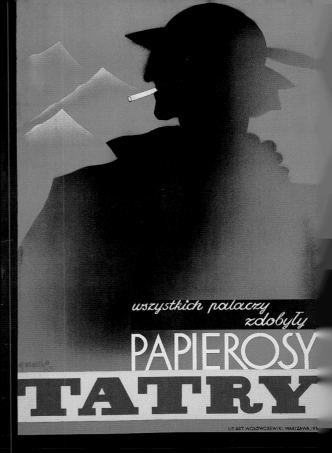

wszystkich palaczy
zdobyły
PAPIEROSY
TATRY

LIT. ART. W.CŁÓWCZEW(K), WARZAWA, 193

Muzeum **Plakatu** ma **20** lat

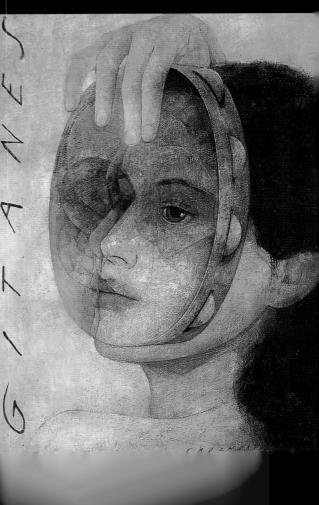

GITANES

Krystyna Spiegel

Once in the museum, the poster is only a scrap of the "robe decorating the city." To preserve the "robe" or to reconstruct it is impossible. In metaphoric terms, the life of a poster is like that of a butterfly. Its beauty is best admired in an album of reproduction, where the eye can pursue each particular detail with the single-mindedness of the scholar and relish in the harmony of colors and effectiveness of shapes. Thus, the act of providing a poster with all due museum attention is like catching it in mid-flight, so that it will remain to excite the imagination of future generations despite the defectiveness of human memory. □ When the Poster Museum at Wilanów opened on June 4, 1968, as a branch of the National Museum in Warsaw, it made history. In a sense, it was a prototype for similar institutions which soon started appearing around the world. □ The Polish poster found a safe haven where it could be protected against the ravages of time. And poster artists were guaranteed the survival of their work. From the viewpoint of art historians, the time came for painstaking effort in creating a representative collection. Emphasis was placed on systematic studies of the form, needed to provide a firm basis for poster scholarship. The result of this ambitious program was a developing interest in the poster, which was increasingly perceived as a means of artistic expression equal in status to the other fields of art. □ Enthusiasm for the very idea of a poster museum was fueled by the circumstances which had earlier led to the phenomenon known as the Polish Poster School. The school's international prestige and the undisputed position of Polish graphic artists, whose innovative means of expression were a breakthrough in existing aesthetic conventions, were strong stimuli. In 1966, when the First International Poster Biennale was inaugurated in Warsaw, establishing a forum for creative competition, the Museum was written into the event to serve as its archive and at the same time as a gallery for the laureates. □ The majority of "spiritus movens" of the project was Janina Fijulkowska, later longtime curator of the Poster Museum at Wilanów. Her adroitness in creating and maintaining the artistic profile of the institution resulted in the Museum receiving the artistic community's stamp of approval, not just as a gallery exhibiting posters but as a place of social and professional gatherings. □ Since its opening, the Museum has hosted innumerable meetings with artists, scholarly symposia and conferences which have helped to integrate the community and have simultaneously elevated the form to artistic importance. For the people connected with the Museum, the goal has always been to make it an opinion-generating center in the field of visual communication with emphasis on graphic design and poster art. With the moving of the quarters of the International Poster Biennale (IPB), in its 14th year in 1994, to the Museum, this goal has been realized. The competition which is sometimes called the "Poster Olympics" and is considered the most important artistic event in the country opens new perspectives for the Museum. As the seat of the event, the Museum can now bring influence to bear upon the choice of aesthetic criteria which are considered in qualifying works for exhibition with a positive effect upon the character of the collection and its representativeness. □ The Museum continues to execute a program which is the result of museum practice. Responsibilities, placed upon the institution by its statute, include collecting, preserving and displaying the collection along with specialist conservation care expressed in a program for preserving and revalorizing paper. □ The current exhibition program includes a permanent display of two hundred objects relating to the history of the Polish poster from the late nineteenth century until modern times, the "salon of the Polish Poster," an annual presentation on the current state of Polish poster art based on works submitted by artists, and "Laureates of the Internationale Poster Biennale," which features individual exhibitions of the Gold medal winners. The program also features individual exhibitions by IPB jurors, and series on "Masters of the Polish Poster" and "Contemporary Masters of Foreign Posters." □ The museum's collection consists of posters, designs of posters and other occasional prints—some 50,000 titles, including close to 30,000 Polish posters and 20,000 foreign ones. Artistic qualities remain the most important criteria in selecting works for the collection; since it is not the goal to record everything, items that are trivial to the aesthetics of form can be eliminated. Despite the strict principles for establishing the main collection, the Museum is in possession of a canonical set of the Polish poster for the years 1892-1995, including all the works that have come to be considered classics. □ The collection is regularly augmented by gifts, transfers and deposits, as well as by purchase. Exchange of work with collectors and institutions is another method of obtaining new items for the collection. The artists themselves constitute a significant number among of donors, confirming thus their conviction that the Museum indeed has a role in shaping culture. □ The Museum is also involved in publishing activities. Each exhibition is customarily accompanied by a poster and by suitable publications, which, in the case of displays written into the Museum's exhibition series, come together to form publishing series of considerable importance in topical literature. □ The position of the Museum is underscored by its extensive international contacts with poster institutions around the world, resulting in extensive exchange of publications, individual objects and exhibitions. Since 1993, the Poster Art Foundation whose statutory goals are convergent with the Museum's profile, has had its seat there. □ For its contribution to spreading poster art, the Museum has been distinguished by the "Ernst Litfass 1816-1874" Honorary Medal (named after the designer of the traditional announcement post) awarded in 1983 by the Fachverband Aussewerbung in Düsseldorf. □ Regardless of what the future holds for it, the poster will always have a "home" for its past at the Wilanów Museum.

(OPPOSITE PAGE, TOP LEFT) WIESLAW WALKUSKI, "DANTON, REZ A WAJDA." 1993. (TOP RIGHT) TADEUSZ GRONOWSKI, PROMOTION FOR TATRY CIGARETTES, 1931. (BOTTOM LEFT) WALDEMAR SWIERZY, PROMOTION FOR THE TWENTIETH ANNIVERSARY OF THE POSTER MUSEUM IN WILANÓW, 1988. (BOTTOM RIGHT) WIKTOR SADOWSKI, PROMOTION FOR GITANES, 1991. ALL POSTERS COLLECTION OF THE POSTER MUSEUM IN WILANÓW. PHOTOS BY PIOTR SYNDOMAN.

KRYSTYNA SPIEGEL IS THE CURATOR OF THE POSTER MUSEUM AT WILANÓW, A DIVISION OF THE NATIONAL MUSEUM OF WARSAW. HER ESSAY ON THE HISTORY AND ACTIVITY OF THE MUSEUM IS TAKEN FROM THE BOOK *MUZEUM ULICY* (MUSEUM OF THE STREET), PUBLISHED BY THE POSTER MUSEUM IN 1996.

Einmal im Museum, ist das Plakat nur noch ein Fetzen des «Gewandes, das die Stadt schmückt». Dieses Gewand zu erhalten oder wiederherzustellen ist unmöglich. Das Leben eines Plakates ist wie das eines Schmetterlings: Seine Schönheit lässt sich am besten in einer Reproduktion betrachten, wo das Auge jede Einzelheit mit der Beharrlichkeit eines Gelehrten betrachten und sich an der Harmonie der Farben und der Zweckmässigkeit der Formen erfreuen kann. Es ist, als würde man auch die Plakate im Fluge einfangen, um sie sorgfältig in Museen zu verwahren und zu erhalten, so dass sie trotz der Unzulänglichkeiten des menschlichen Gedächtnisses auch die Phantasie zukünftiger Generationen beflügeln können. □ Als das Plakatmuseum von Wilanow am 4. Juni 1968 als Abteilung des National-museums in Warschau eröffnet wurde, war das ein historischer Schritt. In gewissem Sinne war es ein Modell für überall in der Welt entstehende, ähnliche Einrichtungen. □ Das polnische Plakat hat hier einen sicheren Hafen gefunden, in dem es gegen die Unbill der Zeit geschützt ist. Aus der Sicht der Kunsthistoriker war es an der Zeit, eine repräsentative Sammlung zu schaffen. Systematische Studien des Mediums Plakat sollten für eine solide, wissenschaftliche Basis sorgen. Das Ergebnis dieses ehrgeizigen Programms ist ein wachsendes Interesse am Plakat und seine vermehrte Anerkennung als eine gleichberechtigte Form künstlerischen Ausdrucks. □ Das Klima, das die Entstehung der polnischen Plakatschule mit ihren revolutionären Ausdrucksformen begünstigt hatte, schürte auch die Begeisterung für die Idee eines Plakatmuseums. 1966, als die erste Internationale Plakatbiennale in Warschau stattfand, ein Forum für kreativen Wettbewerb, wurde das Museum mit einbezogen, indem es als Archiv und gleichzeitig als Galerie für die preisgekrönten Arbeiten diente. □ Der Spiritus movens des Projektes war Janina Fijalkowska, die noch viele Jahre als Kuratorin des Plakatmuseums in Wilanow wirkte. □ Seit seiner Eröffnung haben in diesem Museum unzählige Treffen von Künstlern stattgefunden, sowie auch Symposien und Tagungen. Das Ziel aller für das Museum Tätigen war seit jeher die Schaffung eines meinungsbildenden Zentrums im Bereich der visuellen Kommunikation, wobei Graphik-Design und Plakatgestaltung den Schwerpunkt bilden. Als 1994 die 14. Internationale Plakatbiennale zum ersten Mal im Museum selbst stattfand, bedeutete das für das Anliegen der Museumsleitung einen riesigen Schritt vorwärts. Der Wettbewerb, der manchmal auch «Plakatolympiade» genannt wird und die bedeutendste künstlerische Veranstaltung in Polen ist, eröffnet für das Museum neue Perspektiven. Als Sitz der Veranstaltung kann das Museum jetzt Einfluss nehmen auf die künstlerischen Auswahlkriterien. Das hat auf die Sammlung als solche und auf ihre Vollständigkeit einen positiven Effekt. □ Zu den Aufgaben des Museums gehören gemäss Statuten das Zusammentragen, Erhalten und Ausstellen der Sammlung, verbunden mit besonderer

Sorgfaltspflicht hinsichtlich der Konservierung und Restaurierung von Papier. □ Zum gegenwärtigen Programm gehört die ständige Ausstellung von ca. 200 Objekten, die zur Geschichte des polnischen Plakates gehören, sowie der jährlich stattfindende «Salon des polnischen Plakates» auf der Basis von aktuellen Plakaten, die von den Künstlern eingereicht werden. Hinzu kommen die Ausstellungen der Goldmedaillengewinner und der Juroren der Plakatbiennale; Plakatausstellungen, die von anderen Museen übernommen werden; Einzelausstellungen ausländischer Plakatkünstler; eine Reihe zur Geschichte des polnischen Plakates und Themenausstellungen. □ Neben dem Aufbau der Sammlung befasst sich das Museum mit der Aufzeichnung von Fakten im Zusammenhang mit dem polnischen und ausländischen Plakat sowie von gegenwärtigen Veranstaltungen, die für die Weiterentwicklung des Plakates von Bedeutung sein könnten. Die gesammelte Information liefert eine Grundlage für die Überprüfung der gegenwärtigen Kenntnis der Plakatkunst und ihrer Schöpfer. Aktive Nachforschungen hinsichtlich der Klassifizierung bestimmter Perioden ermöglichen vergleichende Studien und eine Diskussion der Position des polnischen Plakates im Rahmen der internationalen Plakatgeschichte. □ Die Sammlung des Museums umfasst Plakate, Plakatentwürfe und andere Graphik für bestimmte Anlässe, insgesamt ca. 50000 Stück; ca. 30000 davon stammen aus Polen, der Rest aus dem Ausland. Die künstlerische Qualität ist das oberste Kriterium bei der Auswahl für die Sammlung. Trotz der strengen Prinzipien für den Aufbau der Hauptsammlung gilt diese als vollständig, was das polnische Plakatschaffen von 1892 bis 1995 betrifft. □ Die Sammlung wird regelmässig durch Geschenke und Leihgaben und nur zu einem ganz geringen Anteil durch Käufe erweitert. Der Austausch von Plakaten mit Sammlern und anderen Institutionen ist ein weiteres Mittel, um die Sammlung zu vervollständigen. Die Künstler selbst machen einen grossen Teil der Spender aus, womit sie ihrer Überzeugung Ausdruck verleihen, dass das Museum bei der Schaffung einer Kultur tatsächlich eine Rolle spielt. □ Das Museum betätigt sich auch als Verlag. Zu jeder Ausstellung erscheint normalerweise ein Plakat und eine angemessene Publikation. So entsteht im Rahmen der regulären Ausstellungsreihe des Museums eine Serie von Schriften, die thematisch von einiger Bedeutung sind. □ Die intensiven Kontakte des Museums mit Plakatsammlungen in aller Welt führen zu einem ausgedehnten Austausch von Publikationen, einzelnen Plakaten und Ausstellungen. Seit 1993 hat die Stiftung Plakatkunst, deren Statuten denen des Museums von Wilanow entsprechen, hier auch ihren Sitz. □ Im Jahre 1983 hat der Fachverband Aussenwerbung, Düsseldorf, das Museum für seine Verdienste in der Förderung der Plakatkunst mit der Ernst-Litfass-Ehrenmedaille ausgezeichnet. □ Wie auch immer die Zukunft des Mediums Plakat aussieht, seine Vergangenheit wird im Museum von Wilanow ein «Zuhause» haben.

KRYSTYNA SPIEGEL IST KURATORIN DES PLAKATMUSEUMS VON WILANOW, DAS 1968 ALS ABTEILUNG DES NATIONALMUSEUMS IN WARSCHAU ERÖFFNET WURDE UND VIELEN MUSEEN IN ALLER WELT ALS VORBILD DIENTE. IHR BEITRAG ÜBER DIE GESCHICHTE UND TÄTIGKEIT DES MUSEUMS IST DEM 1996 VOM MUSEUM HERAUSGEGEBENEN BAND ÜBER DIE POLNISCHEN PLAKATE DER SAMMLUNG, MUZEUM ULICY (MUSEUM DER STRASSE), ENTNOMMEN.

Une fois accrochée dans un musée, l'affiche n'est plus qu'un lambeau de cet «habit qui pare la ville». Il est impossible de conserver cet habit ou de le raccommoder. La vie d'une affiche ressemble à celle d'un papillon. Pour découvrir sa beauté, rien ne vaut une reproduction. L'œil peut alors admi-rer chaque détail avec minutie pour savourer l'harmonie des couleurs et l'expressivité des formes. C'est comme si on attrapait les affiches en plein vol pour les conserver soigneusement dans des musées, de manière à ce qu'elles puissent donner des ailes à l'imagination des générations futures malgré l'insuffisance de la mémoire humaine. □ Le Musée de l'Affiche de Wilanow, département du Musée National de Varsovie, a été inauguré le 4 juin 1968. Et on peut considérer que cette date marque un tournant historique. En effet, ce musée a, dans le monde entier, servi de modèle à de nombreuses institutions du même genre, qui ont pu bénéficier des expé-iences faites en Pologne. □ L'affiche polonaise a trouvé ici un refuge sûr qui la protège des attaques du temps, et les affichistes ont la certitude que leurs œuvres seront conservées. Pour les historiens de l'art, la création d'un tel musée était entièrement justifiée. Il était temps de rassembler une collection représentative et d'étudier l'affiche de manière systématique et approfondie. Le résultat de ce pro-gramme ambitieux est évident, puisqu'il a permis d'éveiller la curiosité du public et de faire accepter l'affiche comme un moyen d'expression artis-tique à part entière. □ Le climat qui avait engendré l'émergence de ce que l'on a appelé l'école polonaise de l'affiche, connue pour ses formes d'expression révolutionnaires, a favorisé la création du musée. En 1966, lors de la première Biennale Internationale de l'Affiche, le musée fut inté-gré à la manifestation, servant à la fois d'archives et de galerie où furent présentés les travaux primés. □ Cependant, le véritable *spiritus movens* du projet fut Janina Fijalkowska, qui allait être conservateur du musée pendant de longues années. C'est elle qui hissa le musée au niveau artis-tique qu'on lui connaît, ce qui lui valut le respect des artistes, pour lesquels l'établissement devint, outre un endroit pour présenter leurs affiches, un véritable lieu de rencontre. Depuis son inauguration, le musée a accueilli d'innombrables colloques et congrès qui ont contribué à intégrer les artistes et à faire accepter l'affiche comme un art. D'ailleurs, l'objectif de tous les collaborateurs du musée a toujours été la création d'un centre de communication visuelle au rayonnement important, l'ac-cent étant mis sur le graphisme et l'affiche. En 1994, lorsque, pour la pre-mière fois, la Biennale Internationale de l'Affiche eut lieu dans le musée même à l'occasion de sa 14e édition, les responsables du musée surent qu'un très grand pas en avant venait d'être fait. Ce concours, aussi appelé parfois «l'Olympiade de l'affiche», est la plus grande manifesta-tion artistique en Pologne. Le fait de l'accueillir ouvre donc de toutes nou-velles perspectives. C'est ainsi que les responsables du musée peuvent désormais influer sur les critères artistiques déterminant la sélection des affiches exposées, ce qui a un effet positif sur la collection et sur sa représentativité. □ A l'avenir, il semble indispensable que le musée con-tribue à organiser une série de séminaires qui s'intéresseraient aux courants actuels pour les éclairer d'un point de vue scientifique. □ Entre-temps, le musée continue de développer un programme qui correspond à sa vocation première. Selon les statuts, ses tâches principales consis-tent à agrandir et entretenir sa collection et à exposer les œuvres qu'il détient, un soin tout particulier devant être apporté à la conservation et à la restauration du papier. □ Ce vaste programme comprend l'exposition permanente de quelque 200 œuvres retraçant l'histoire de l'affiche polon-aise et le Salon de l'affiche polonaise, qui rassemble chaque année les travaux d'artistes contemporains. A cela s'ajoutent les expositions con-sacrées aux artistes ayant remporté la médaille d'or de la Biennale Internationale de l'Affiche et à leurs jurés ainsi que d'autres manifesta-tions organisées par divers musées. Enfin, des expositions individuelles présentant les travaux des maîtres de l'affiche internationale, une série sur l'historie de l'affiche polonaise et des expositions à thème viennent compléter l'offre du musée. □ Outre l'agrandissement de sa collection, le musée s'intéresse à l'histoire de l'affiche polonaise et internationale ainsi qu'aux manifestations qui pourraient avoir une influence sur l'évolu-tion future de la discipline. Les informations recueillies servent de base à une étude de l'état des connaissances dans le domaine de l'affiche et des affichistes. Des recherches poussées permettent de faire des études comparatives afin de déterminer la place de l'affiche polonaise dans l'his-toire de cet art. La collection du musée comprend des affiches, des esquisses et des produits graphiques divers. Au total, elle rassemble quelque 50 000 œuvres, dont environ 30 000 proviennent de Pologne et environ 20 000 du reste du monde. Lors du choix des affiches, le critère principal reste la qualité artistique de l'œuvre. Le musée n'a évidemment pas l'intention de tout collectionner et refuse les affiches qui ne répondent pas à certains critères esthétiques. Malgré ces principes très stricts, la collection du musée est très complète en ce qui concerne l'affiche polon-aise de 1892 à nos jours. C'est ainsi qu'elle comprend toutes les affiches considérées comme des classiques de cet art. □ La collection est com-plétée en permanence, notamment grâce à des dons et à des prêts. Les acquisitions sont par contre plus rares. D'autre part, le musée échange des œuvres avec des collectionneurs ou d'autres institutions. Les artistes eux-mêmes comptent au nombre des donateurs les plus importants, ce qui prouve s'il le fallait qu'ils estiment que le musée participe activement à la création d'une véritable culture de l'affiche. □ D'autre part, le musée est également éditeur. En règle générale, chaque exposition donne lieu à la publication d'une affiche ou d'un catalogue, ce qui a permis de faire paraître une série d'ouvrages importants. □ Les contacts étroits qu'entre-tient le musée avec des institutions similaires dans le monde entier entraînent un échange permanent de publications, d'affiches individu-elles ou d'expositions entières. Depuis 1993, le musée abrite aussi la Fondation de l'Affiche, dont les objectifs sont très proches de ceux du musée. □ En 1983, le musée a reçu la «Médaille d'honneur Ernst Litfass» du «Fachverband Aussenwerbung» de Dusseldorf pour le récompenser de ses efforts visant à promouvoir l'affiche en tant qu'art. □ Pour termin-er, on peut donc dire que quel que soit l'avenir de l'affiche, son histoire sera fidèlement conservée par le Musée de l'Affiche de Wilanow.

KRYSTYNA SPIEGEL EST CONSERVATEUR DU MUSÉE DE L'AFFICHE DE WILANOW. CET ARTICLE SUR L'HISTOIRE ET LES ACTIVITÉS DU MUSÉE EST EXTRAIT D'UN LIVRE CONSACRÉ AUX AFFICHES POLONAISES DE LA COLLECTION, PUBLIÉ EN 1996 PAR LE MUSÉE SOUS LE TITRE **MUZEUM ULICY** (LE MUSÉE DE LA RUE).

Alain Le Quernec

My first collaboration with *Graphis Poster* dates back to 1978. Walter Herdeg had asked me to adapt one of my designs for the 1979 edition. The image likened a poster designer to an exhibitionist. □ Even today, this analogy characterizes my way of working, and I always feel a certain emotion when I see my images fleetingly marking urban territory, exposed to all eyes. More than ever, I believe we can only judge a poster's quality and impact once the poster is exposed on the street. Museum exhibits and magazine reproductions only present dead images extracted from their context and reality. These presentations are like the collections of exotic butterflies: the objects are arranged next to each other and may be leisurely observed; yet they are immobile, forever pinned down. □ Very early on, the poster became my principal activity, following an attraction I had to public images. Considering the poster as a means of expression entirely separate from any other, I found that the hardness of the urban environment, the exposure in places not considered as sacred, the submission to order, and the poster's very short lifespan became singularities more than handicaps in a process I wanted to make novel, creative and artistic. □ At Graphis, my encounter with the Polish poster of the 1960s was a shock. Its stylistic freedom shattered all of the plastic and commercial rules the advertising world imposed and still imposes. The Polish school was the reference not to any particular graphic style, but to a fantastic plastic and typographic openness in which everything became possible. The Polish example demonstrated that it was sufficient to want to create this effect, and then impose it. In another domain, the spontaneous posters born of the student revolts in Paris in May 1968 made me realize that the poster did not depend on a costly printing system. With rudimentary equipment, large images could be printed and everyone could express himself through a poster. □ Wanting to be a poster designer at the end of the 1960s seemed incongruous or out of fashion, in France anyway. Savignac had been the last great poster designer, and the disappearing art had never been so well-known and recognized. Yet the evolution of photoengraving and printing techniques allowed advertisers to create hyper-realistic photographs of products we consumed. Creators of posters became useless. □ Progressively, illustrators and photographers became nothing more than mercenary executors of concepts defined by marketing teams. Advertising was developed and structured with arrogance and foolishness in a world in which I could only be marginal. □ When I created my first images using basic techniques, with barely existing budgets, I did not imagine that the technological revolutions linked to the computer would considerably lower the cost of poster-making; nor did I imagine that all public and private structures would be seized with the desire to communicate at any price, or that the urban signs as complements to an ever-increasing number of posters would proliferate as they did. I never dreamed that this evolution would allow my social, political and cultural images to exist in formats and techniques comparable to those used in the advertising world. □ The poster's current situation may seem paradoxical; an ever-increasing number of images are printed with a continually improving technical quality which changes nothing about the overall aesthetic quality. But it would be wrong to blame this entirely on our time period and wax nostalgic for a hypothetical golden age. We collect, sell, and exhibit posters that date from the beginning of the century without raking into account their poor semantic and aesthetic quality. Like today, these early posters' eye-catching messages used an elementary artistic language devoid of innovation. Their only potential value is historical; they act as witnesses to their era. □ The poster's history is lined with personalities and groups that serve as reference points in this ocean of paper. Each of them has redefined and enlarged the range of the plastic language that is unique to the poster. Initiators, experimenters, they mark their influence on their era through their disciples' or survivors' productions. A poster can always be situated in context before or after such a production. Regardless of the name—Rodchenko, Bernhart, Cassandre, Savignac, Tomaszewski, Glaser or Bass—each of us selects his references. □ Some posters by these creators are references to their time period yet remain curiously timeless. Thirty years later, Savignac's Aspro poster could be resurrected today and its message would be just as efficient and profitable. Yet it was when he was at the summit of his art that the advertising world turned away from him and more generally from a certain kind of poster design, instead preferring photography that lacked mystery and imagination. I have often asked myself what a great artist like Savignac could do except pursue his work for its own sake. □ I speak much of Savignac. He is a major reference, and for me, he is the last great poster designer. No one else in France bears this title, which refers to a bygone era. Nowadays, one is a "graphic designer" and claims the right to intervene in all of the visual aspects affecting our environment. The poster is nothing more than one advertising medium among others. These new professionals do not bring the same level of interest to the poster, or perhaps they do not bring the same level of emotion. I am not certain that they can defend the poster as an art form. □ The poster's very nature and its obligation to be perceived and understood in a fraction of a second in an often visually saturated environment has forced it to develop the characteristics of a specific minimalist or telegraphic language, to paraphrase Cassandre. To work with the poster is to obligate oneself to keep only the essential and remove all that can be considered chatter and repetition. It is an exercise in concision, a single gunshot. When it misses its target, it gets no second chance. □ The art of poster-making is therefore a gymnastics of the mind for me, and an exercise of intellectual rigor in and of itself that is more theoretical than practical. No doubt I owe this idea of my work to Henryk Tomaszewski. Besides the fact that he is one of the great artists of his time, Henryk Tomaszewski was an extraordinary professor. He made his students discover their tendency to overcrowd their work out of a fear that the message would not clearly be understood. He showed how this tendency weakened the message rather than reinforced it. In this way, the students discovered that the search for the essential could become subtle; and that once beyond styles and effects, they could begin to develop the elements of a true artistic language. Though it may be ambitious to think we can succeed at this, it remains nevertheless the illusion that each of us must maintain.

ALAIN LE QUERNEC IS A FREELANCE DESIGNER AND GRADUATE PROFESSOR OF ART IN HIS NATIVE BRETAGNE, FRANCE. HE STUDIED ART IN PARIS FROM 1961 TO 1965, AND IN 1972 WON A SCHOLARSHIP TO STUDY WITH HENRYK TOMASZEWSKI IN POLAND. HE IS A MEMBER OF ALLIANCE GRAPHIQUE INTERNATIONALE.

(THIS PAGE, TOP LEFT) "LA PECHE VEUT VIVRE," CLIENT: LE MONDE AND PARTIE SOCIALISTE. (CENTER) "CAFÉ THÉÂTRE ET COMPANIES," CLIENT: LE PARVIS, CENTRE CULTUREL. (RIGHT) CLIENT: LAHTI POSTER BIENNALE. (MIDDLE LEFT) "ELÉMENTS MOINS PERFORMANTS," CLIENT: THÉÂTRE DE L'INSTANT. (CENTER) "ALQ-UBO," CLIENT: UNIVERSITÉ DE BRETAGNE OCCIDENTALE, BREST. (RIGHT) "PETITES VARIATIONS AMOUREUSES," CLIENT: THÉÂTRE DE QUIM-

PER - SCÈNE NATIONALE. (BOTTOM LEFT) "DUBIGEON," CLIENT: MUSÉE CHÂTEAU DES DUCS DE BRETAGNE, NANTES. (CENTER) "CINÉMA LIBERTÉS," CLIENT
ASSOCIATION GROS PLAN, QUIMPER. (RIGHT) "LA TERRE," CLIENT: VILLE DE MONT LUÇON. ■ (THIS PAGE, TOP) "BOSNIE," CLIENT: COMITÉS BOSNIE. (MID
DLE) CLIENT: VILLE DE QUIMPER. (BOTTOM) CLIENT: QUIMPER HOSPITAL. (THIS SPREAD) ALL POSTERS DESIGNED BY ALAIN LE QUERNEC

Meine erste Zusammenarbeit mit Graphis geht auf das Jahr 1978 zurück, als Walter Herdeg mich bat, eines meiner Bilder für den Umschlag von Graphis Poster 79 abzuwandeln: Es zeigt den Plakatkünstler als Exhibitionisten. Genauso sehe ich meine Tätigkeit noch heute. □ Mehr denn je bin ich überzeugt, dass man die Qualität eines Plakates, seine Wirkung erst dann beurteilen kann, wenn es seinen Platz auf der Strasse eingenommen hat. □ Ich habe mich sehr früh auf die Gestaltung von Plakaten konzentriert, weil mich diese Bilder der Strasse faszinieren. Für mich ist das Plakat ein Ausdrucksmittel für sich, und die Härte des urbanen Umfelds, die Tatsache, dass es an Orten gezeigt wird, die keinesfalls als heilige Hallen betrachtet werden, dass es Regeln unterworfen ist und nur eine kurze Lebensdauer hat, all das sind für mich eher einzigartige Gegebenheiten als Hindernisse bei einem Arbeitsprozess. □ Dieses leidenschaftliche Engagement und die Tatsache, dass ich Autodidakt bin, sind vielleicht auf meine Kindheit zurückzuführen, auf die typisch französischen Plakate von Savignac oder Loupot. Der entscheidende Einfluss kam auf jeden Fall in der grossen Zeit des Plakates, einerseits waren es die polnischen Plakate und andererseits die Pariser Plakate vom Mai 68, die mich tief beeindruckten. □ Diese polnische Schule wies den Weg, nicht in Bezug auf einen bestimmten graphischen Stil, sondern auf den Einsatz von Typographie und der bildnerischen Mittel. Und alles war möglich. Das polnische Beispiel bewies, dass es genügte, etwas zu wollen und es umzusetzen. Auf der anderen Seite zeigten mir die spontanen Plakate der Studentenrevolte vom Mai 68 in Paris, dass das Plakat nicht unbedingt ein teures Druckerzeugnis sein muss. □ Als ich meine ersten Plakate mit rudimentären Techniken und so gut wie nicht vorhandenen Budgets machte, konnte ich mir nicht vorstellen, dass die Computertechnologie die Herstellungskosten eines Plakates derart senken helfen würde. Und ich konnte mir nicht vorstellen, dass als Folge des Wunsches nach Kommunikation um jeden Preis seitens privater wie öffentlicher Stellen immer mehr Plakatwände in den Städten aufgestellt werden würden, als Rahmen für die immer zahlreicher werdenden Plakate. Ich konnte mir diese Entwicklung nicht vorstellen, dank derer meine sozialen, politischen und kulturellen Plakate eines Tages in ähnlichen Formaten und ähnlicher Druckqualität wie die Werbeplakate erscheinen würden. □ Die gegenwärtige Situation des Plakates mag paradox erscheinen: Die ständig wachsende Zahl von gedruckten Bildern in einer technischen Qualität, die sich immer weiterentwickelt, ändert nichts an der extrem schlechten Qualität der Bilder, die von der Werbeideologie diktiert wird. □ Es wäre falsch, nur unsere Epoche verantwortlich zu machen und einem hypothetischen 'Goldenen Zeitalter' nachzuweinen. Man sammelt, man verkauft, und man stellt die Plakate vom Anfang dieses Jahrhunderts mit Erfolg aus, ohne sich ihrer mangelnden semantischen, ästhetischen, graphischen und somit künstlerischen Qualität bewusst zu werden. Wie die heutigen Plakate benutzen ihre aufdringlichen Werbebotschaften eine äusserst simple künstlerische Sprache, ohne Überraschungen, ohne Innovation; ihr einziger Wert, wenn überhaupt, mag historischer Natur sein, denn sie sind Zeugen ihrer Epoche. □ Einige wenige Individuen oder Gruppen machten Plakatgeschichte, sie setzten die Massstäbe. In diesem Ozean von Papier sind sie feste Werte, Vorbilder für uns. Jeder von ihnen hat die dem Plakat eigene künstlerische Sprache neu definiert, hat neues Terrain betreten. Das macht für mich die künstlerische Qualität im Werk dieser Plakatkünstler aus, jenseits von Trends und Stilrichtungen. □ Bestimmte Plakate dieser Künstler, die bezeichnend für ihre Epoche waren, bleiben seltsamerweise zeitlos: dreissig Jahre nach seiner Entstehung hätte das Aspro-Plakat von Savignac auch heute noch Bestand, die Botschaft wäre genauso deutlich, wirksam, effizient. Trotzdem hat sich die Werbebranche von Savignac abgewandt, als er aufder Höhe seines künstlerischen Schaffens war, oder, allgemeiner ausgedrückt, von einem bestimmten Typ gezeichneter Plakate, indem sie Photos ohne Geheimnis oder Phantasie den Vorzug gab. Ich habe mich oft gefragt, was ein grosser Künstler wie er anderes machen konnte, als sein Werk für sich fortzusetzen. □ Ich spreche viel von Savignac, er ist sehr wichtig für mich. Er ist der letzte «Plakatkünstler». Niemand in Frankreich nennt sich noch so, dieser Titel gehört der Vergangenheit an, heute ist man Graphiker, und man beansprucht das Recht, bei allen visuellen Aspekten unserer Umwelt mitzureden; das Plakat ist nur noch ein Medium von vielen. Diese neuen Fachleute bringen dem Plakat nicht mehr das gleiche Interesse, vielleicht nicht mehr das gleiche Gefühl entgegen, ich bin mir nicht sicher, ob sie das Plakat als eine Form der Kunst betrachten. □ Wie erklärt sich das weltweite Interesse am Plakat, selbst in Ländern, wo dieses Medium kaum eingesetzt wird? Ich habe mich gefragt, ob es Sinn macht, Plakatgestaltung in den Unterricht aufzunehmen, mit Schülern, die zum grössten Teil in ihrem Berufsleben nie ein Plakat gestalten werden. □ Das Wesen des Plakates, der Anspruch, dass es in einem Bruchteil von Sekunden gesehen und registriert werden muss, und zwar in einem visuell gesättigtem Umfeld, hat dazu geführt, dass es eine spezielle minimalistische oder telegraphische Sprache entwickelt hat, wie Cassandre sich ausdrückte. Ein Plakat zu gestalten bedeutet, sich auf das Wesentliche zu beschränken, alles zu vermeiden, was Geschwätz, was Wiederholung ist – es ist eine Übung in Prägnanz, ein Gewehr mit nur einem Schuss Munition, bei dem es keinen zweiten Versuch gibt, wenn es sein Ziel verfehlt. □ Die Gestaltung von Plakaten ist deshalb für mich eine Gymnastik des Geistes, eine intellektuelle Übung in Rigorosität, eher theoretischer als praktischer Natur. Diese Auffassung meiner Arbeit verdanke ich zweifellos Henryk Tomaszewski. Abgesehen davon, dass er einer der grossen Künstler unserer Zeit ist, war er auch ein aussergewöhnlicher Lehrer. Er brachte seine Schüler dazu, selbst herauszufinden, inwieweit sie dazu neigen, ihre Arbeiten zu überladen, herauszufinden, dass zu viele Zeichen – eingesetzt aus Angst, nicht verstanden zu werden – die Botschaft schwächen statt sie zu stärken. Sie merkten auf diese Weise, dass die Suche nach dem Wesentlichen etwas ganz Subtiles sein kann und dass es ihnen gelingen könnte, jenseits von Trends und Effekten, Elemente einer wirklich künstlerischen Sprache zu entwickeln. Und wenn es auch hochfliegend ist zu glauben, dass man es je schaffen wird, so ist es eine Illusion, die jeder haben sollte.

ALAIN LE QUERNEC IST FREIER GRAPHIKER UND PROFESSOR FÜR KUNST IN SEINER HEIMAT, DER BRETAGNE. VON 1961 BIS 1965 STUDIERTE ER KUNST IN PARIS. DANK EINES STIPENDIUMS SETZTE ER 1972 SEINE STUDIEN BEI HENRYK TOMASZEWSKI IN POLEN FORT. ER IST MITGLIED DER AGI.

Ma première collaboration avec *Graphis Poster* remonte à 1978, Walter Herdeg m'avait demandé d'adapter une de mes images pour la couverture de l'édition 1979. Cette image assimilait l'affichiste à un exhibitionniste. □ Aujourd'hui encore, cette affirmation définit bien le regard que je porte sur mon activité, elle caractérise ma démarche, et j'éprouve toujours une émotion particulière à voir mes images marquer éphémèrement le territoire urbain. Plus que jamais, j'estime que l'on ne peut juger de la qualité d'une affiche qu'une fois dans la rue. Les expositions dans les musées, les reproductions dans les revues ne présentent que des images mortes; j'ai toujours établi une comparaison entre ces présentations et les collections de papillons exotiques, rangés les uns à côté des autres, mais immobiles, épinglés à jamais. □ Très tôt, l'affiche est devenue mon activité principale, suivant en cela une attirance pour l'image publique. Considérant l'affiche comme un mode d'expression à part entière, la dureté de l'environnement urbain, l'exposition dans les lieux non sacralisés, la durée de vie très courte devenaient des singularités plus que des handicaps à une démarche que je voulais novatrice, créatrice, artistique. □ Cet engagement passionnel et autodidacte se décide peut-être dès l'enfance avec les affiches «à la française» de Savignac ou de Loupot, mais il se détermine sûrement dans les temps forts de son époque et tout particulièrement deux d'entre eux: l'affiche polonaise et l'affiche de mai 68 à Paris. □ La rencontre dans Graphis avec l'affiche polonaise des années soixante fut un choc, sa liberté stylistique bousculait tous les a priori plastiques et commerciaux que nous imposait le système publicitaire. Cette école polonaise était la référence, non pas d'un style graphique particulier, mais d'une fantastique ouverture plastique et typographique. Tout était possible. A l'exemple des Polonais, il suffisait de le vouloir et de pouvoir l'imposer. Dans un autre domaine, les affiches spontanées de la révolte des étudiants à Paris en mai 1968 m'ont fait prendre conscience que l'affiche ne dépendait pas forcément d'un système coûteux d'imprimerie. Avec des équipements rudimentaires on pouvait imprimer de grandes images, tout le monde pouvait s'exprimer par l'affiche. □ Vouloir être affichiste à la fin des années soixante pouvait paraître incongru ou démodé en France. Savignac était déjà le dernier affichiste, un art disparaissait, et pourtant jamais il n'avait été aussi fort reconnu. Mais l'évolution des techniques de photogravure et d'impression permettait de plus en plus à la publicité de faire des photos hyperréalistes des produits de consommation, les créateurs d'images devenaient inutiles. Progressivement, illustrateurs et photographes n'étaient plus que les exécutants de concepts définis par les équipes marketing. La publicité se développait, se structurait, avec arrogance et fatuité dans un monde où je ne pouvais qu'être marginal. □ Quand je réalisais mes premières images avec des budgets presque inexistants, je n'imaginais pas que les révolutions technologiques liées à l'ordinateur abaisseraient considérablement le coût de fabrication des affiches; je n'imaginais pas non plus que toutes les structures privées ou publiques seraient prises du désir de communiquer à tout prix et que la conséquence serait la multiplication de panneaux urbains. Je n'imaginais pas cette évolution qui fait que mes images sociales, politiques et culturelles puissent un jour exister dans des formats et des techniques comparables à ceux de la publicité. □ La situation actuelle de l'affiche peut paraître paradoxale, le nombre sans cesse croissant d'images imprimées avec une qualité technique en constant progrès ne modifiant en rien la faiblesse extrême de la qualité des images dictée par l'idéologie publicitaire. □ On aurait tort d'incrimer plus particulièrement notre époque et de regretter un hypothétique âge d'or. On collectionne, on vend, on expose avec succès des affiches du début de siècle sans se rendre compte de leur pauvreté sémantique, esthétique, graphique et donc artistique. □ Cette confusion du regard se retrouve dans les affiches de cinéma qui ont toujours sacrifié aux pires tendances commerciales, mais leur nullité graphique ne les a jamais empêchées de devenir des objets de culte, témoignages bien réels de fictions dont on croit garder une trace. □ L'histoire de l'affiche est jalonnée par quelques individualités ou groupes qui nous servent de repères. Chacun d'eux a redéfini, élargi le champ d'un langage plastique propre à l'affiche. Initiateurs, expérimentateurs, ils marquent leur époque de leur influence à travers les productions de leurs disciples, et une affiche se situe avant ou après un tel. Peu importe leur nom, chacun de nous choisit ses repères. □ En établissant de nouveaux codes de lectures, ils créent de nouveaux langages et nous enrichissent d'une sensibilité nouvelle. C'est ce que j'appelle la dimension artistique de l'œuvre de ces créateurs. □ Certaines affiches de ces créateurs, références de leur époque, demeurent curieusement intemporelles: trente ans après, l'affiche Aspro de Savignac pourrait être ressortie aujourd'hui, son message serait toujours aussi évident, efficace, rentable. Pourtant, alors qu'il était au sommet de son art, le courant publicitaire s'est détourné de Savignac et d'un certain type d'affiches dessinées, lui préférant une photographie sans mystère ni imagination. Je me suis souvent demandé ce que pouvait faire un grand artiste comme lui sinon poursuivre son œuvre pour lui-même. □ Je parle beaucoup de Savignac, il est pour moi le dernier «affichiste». Personne en France ne porte plus ce titre qui renvoie à une époque révolue, aujourd'hui on est «graphiste» et on revendique le droit d'intervenir dans tous les aspects visuels de notre environnement. Ces nouveaux professionnels n'accordent peut-être plus le même intérêt à l'affiche ou peut-être pas la même émotion, je ne suis pas sûr qu'ils puissent la défendre comme un art. □ Comment expliquer l'intérêt pour l'affiche à travers le monde, même dans les pays où ce média n'est presque pas utilisé? □ La nature même de l'affiche, l'obligation qu'elle a d'être perçue et enregistrée en une fraction de seconde dans un environnement souvent visuellement saturé lui a imposé de développer les caractéristiques d'un langage spécifique minimaliste ou télégraphique pour paraphraser Cassandre. Travailler l'affiche, c'est s'obliger à ne retenir que l'essentiel, à écarter tout ce qui peut être bavardage, répétition, c'est un exercice de concision, c'est un fusil à un coup: il n'y a pas de seconde chance. □ La pratique de l'affiche est donc pour moi une gymnastique de l'esprit, un exercice de rigueur intellectuelle, en soi plus théorique que pratique. Je dois sans doute à Henryk Tomaszewski cette conception de mon travail. Mis à part le fait qu'il est un des grands artistes de son temps, Henryk Tomaszewski fut un extraordinaire professeur, il faisait découvrir à ses étudiants combien ils avaient tendance à surcharger leur travail, que la multiplication des signes affaiblissait le message au lieu de le renforcer. Ils découvraient ainsi que cette recherche de l'essentiel pouvait devenir subtile ils pouvaient imaginer développer les éléments d'un véritable langage artistique et, s'il est ambitieux de penser y parvenir, c'est pourtant l'illusion que chacun devrait entretenir.

ALAIN LE QUERNEC EST DESIGNER INDÉPENDANT ET PROFESSEUR D'ART EN FRANCE, DANS SA BRETAGNE NATALE. DE 1961 À 1965, IL ÉTUDIE L'ART À PARIS. EN 1972, IL BÉNÉFICIE D'UNE BOURSE D'ÉTUDES QUI LUI PERMET D'APPROFONDIR SES RECHERCHES AVEC HENRYK TOMASZEWSKI EN POLOGNE. IL EST MEMBRE DE L'AGI.

EARTH FAIR 95

There are
some things
that make
life worth
living, and
some things
you can't
live without.

Milton Glaser

The earliest rule I remember about posters (from my first year of high school fifty years ago) was that they were made for people on the run. Consequently, the ideal poster should be simple in form, reductive in content, and easily understood. By and large, these seemed to be useful if not obvious assumptions. □ In recent years, however, I've found myself modifying these beliefs in a variety of ways – partially out of my desire to investigate alternative visual and philosophical possibilities, and also in an attempt to recognize the changes that have occurred in the last half of the century in the public's ability to respond to ambiguity and complexity. Film, computers, and television have helped create a visual environment that scarcely resembles the one I knew as a student. In addition, designers have become increasingly interested in thinking of design as a tool for philosophical and social inquiry – to some extent replicating the role that painting traditionally assumed. At the moment such issues as "what is real," "what is beautiful," or "what is socially responsible" can engage a designer's interest as well as the more traditional concern for effective communication about a product. □ EARTH FAIR '95 (opposite) In all beginnings there is the word. I tend to start my work with a literary idea; in this case that the words "ART" and "AIR" were concealed within the words Earth Fair, the subject of the poster. This might be called a poetic discovery, but the next problem quickly became how to exploit this hidden treasure. The formal decisions – the change in weight of the typography, the use of diagonals, the strong red with contrasting colors at the edges – all attempt to make the idea accessible, but the effect of the poster is largely based on the written statement that accompanies the image and completes the thought in the viewer's mind. In this case, the words "Earth Fair" are rather like a metamorphic drawing that changes as you look at it. □ OLD AND NEW I struggled with this assignment from Silas Rhodes because I found the poem by Alexander Pope left me cold. After weeks of thinking about it I could generate no imagery for it. I struggled and finally produced an image that seemed to illustrate the basic theme of the poem: the relationship of the old and new. The part of the poster that I believe is more significant is the description of my procedure in an intimate conversation with the viewer under the heading "Thoughts." Here I trace the history of the poster and my dissatisfaction with the problem. I even offer an alternative solution to anyone interested. This may be the first time that two solutions were presented simultaneously on the same poster. After all, one is supposed to believe in what he presents to the world. Confidence is the hallmark of a good design . . . well maybe not now. □ DESIGNTALK The subject of 'Design' provided the opportunity to explore the nature of light, form and illusion. The attempt here is to create the appearance of a surface bulging towards the viewer and challenging the assumption of rectangular flatness the poster form generally assumes. I first generated the typography and squares as a conventional design by computer. The output was then wrapped around a cylinder and photographed with a strong light source on the left. The curved die cuts on the top and bottom complete the effect. The result may not be obvious enough; viewers often assume that the effect of light is caused by the accidental ambient light that the poster happens to be placed in. □ A DRAWING LESSON The idea behind this poster was to create a didactic work that would actually deliver what it promised to do (unlike most advertising which makes a promise or generates desire). This piece makes an observation on the nature of drawing and illustration, and demonstrates that observation by showing a photograph and the work derived from it. It presumes that the audience, those interested in art or illustration, would be willing to commit themselves to the time and effort required to understand the message. This flies in the face of the most basic assumptions about the poster: namely that it must be easily understood and read on the run. Two facts might alter those assumptions. First, this poster is in the subway where the wait for trains can seem interminable – making riders desperate for anything to read. Secondly, the slightly peculiar form of the work with its floating bones could arouse the interest of a visually sophisticated person or potential student who might be more susceptible to complex ideas. □ QUADERNO A poster can raise the same formal and philosophical questions about the nature of reality as a painting. Here the issue of spatial illusion is addressed by dealing with the subject matter within the constraints of isometric perspectives, not unlike a Japanese screen. The rectangle of the poster was cut to aid in the illusion. What is most interesting to me about this exercise is the unwillingness of the principal subject (the Olivetti power book) to stay settled in its space. My mind has difficulty accepting the isometric convention and insists on trying to make the computer recede in space in the more familiar renaissance-one-point-perspective schema. The effect is disquieting and if you stare at the computer for a while it will seem to float off the page. □ SVA MASTER SERIES This small poster for my show at the School of Visual Arts actually was the inspiration for the DesignTalk poster. I was impressed by the illusion of white, the white surface of the notebook curving towards the viewer. □ CHARVOZ There is always some risk in attempting to communicate more information than the situation requires, the most obvious being the good chance that the essential information will be diffused and diluted. The client in this case was a manufacturer of art materials, and the central purpose of the poster was to make people aware of that fact. I created a landscape of art materials, each drawn in a different medium to express this idea. At the same time I concealed the word 'Charvoz' in the form of a rebus within the poster. Whether or not these convolutions hinder the effectiveness of the poster is the essential issue. I very much like the idea that someone might be looking at this poster two years after first seeing it and realize there was something he or she hadn't noticed the first time. I also believe that there is an intuitive response on the part of the the viewer to

A NATIVE OF NEW YORK CITY, **MILTON GLASER** ATTENDED THE COOPER UNION ART SCHOOL. IN 1954 HE CO-FOUNDED PUSHPIN STUDIOS WITH SEYMOUR CHWAST, AND IN 1968 FOUNDED *NEW YORK* MAGAZINE WITH CLAY FELKER. HE HAS DESIGNED PUBLICATIONS AROUND THE WORLD AND HAS BEEN HONORED BY ONE-MAN SHOWS AT THE MUSEUM OF MODERN ART, THE LINCOLN CENTER GALLERY, THE POMPIDOU CENTRE IN PARIS AND THE ROYAL MUSEUM IN BRUSSELS. MR. GLASER IS A HALL OF FAME MEMBER OF THE ART DIRECTORS CLUB AND HAS RECEIVED THE SCHOOL OF VISUAL ARTS MASTER SERIES AWARD.

what we might call submerged material that deepens the experience and helps the poster persist in the mind. Since we acknowledge that this phenomenon exists in music, poetry, and painting, why not in a poster? Perhaps T. S. Elliot put it best when he said, "The use of the overt content of a poem is to satisfy one habit of the reader: to keep his mind diverted and quiet while the poem does its work upon him, much as the imaginary burglar has always provided a bit of nice meat for the house dog." □ ART IS This most recent poster began with an assignment from the chairman of the School of Visual Arts (Silas Rhodes) to interpret the phrase "Art is." Six designers were given the same prob-

lem, and the results were distributed simultaneously throughout the city in the subways and at bus shelters. Trying to define art is obviously not a simple task, but the variety and range of the responses made for a lively series of public announcements. In my own case the accompanying text attempts to extend the visual message, a point that the text omits, I realize, is that some forms are intrinsically and mysteriously more satisfying than others. I am convinced the form of the bowler hat is – sculpturally speaking – one of the most elegant and aesthetically pleasing objects ever made. Can we call it art if that was not its intent? That question will require more than a poster to answer.

Die Regel, wonach ein ideales Plakat einfach in der Form, knapp im Inhalt und leicht verständlich sein muss, gilt nur noch bedingt. Heute können Fragen wie «was ist real», «was ist schön» oder «was ist sozial vertretbar» einen Gestalter ebenso beschäftigen wie die herkömmlichen Fragen nach wirkungsvoller Kommunikation für ein Produkt. □ EARTH FAIR 95 An jedem Anfang steht das Wort. Ich beginne meine Arbeit mit einer liter-

Teil des Plakates ist in meinen Augen aber die Beschreibung meines Vorgehens unter dem Titel «Gedanken», eine intime Unterhaltung mit dem Betrachter. Hier gehe ich auf die Geschichte des Plakates ein und auf meine Unzufriedenheit mit der Aufgabe. Ich biete jedem, den es interessiert, sogar eine andere Lösung an. Es mag das erste Mal sein, dass zwei Lösungen gleichzeitig für ein Plakat geboten werden. Schliesslich

 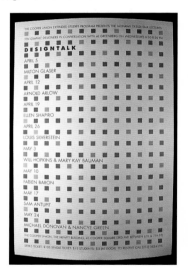  

arischen Idee, in diesem Fall ging ich davon aus, dass die Worte «Art» und «Air» in den Worten Earth Fair, dem Thema des Plakates, verborgen sind. Man kann das eine poetische Entdeckung nennen, aber als nächstes präsentierte sich das Problem, wie man diesen verborgenen Schatz nutzen könnte. Die formalen Entscheidungen – die veränderte Gewichtung der Typographie, der Einsatz von Diagonalen, das kräftige Rot, umgeben von kontrastierenden Farben – dienen alle dazu, die Idee zugänglich zu machen, aber die Wirkung des Plakates basiert zum grossen Teil auf dem geschriebenen Text, der das Bild begleitet und den Gedanken im Kopf des Betrachters zu Ende führt. Hier sind die Worte Earth Fair eher wie eine metamorphische Zeichnung, die sich verändert, während man sie betrachtet. □ OLD AND NEW Ich hatte Mühe mit dem Auftrag von Silas Rhodes, weil das Gedicht von Alexander Pope mich kalt liess. Ich hatte wochenlang darüber nachgedacht, und es gelang mir nicht, es bildnerisch umzusetzen. Ich mühte mich ab, und schliesslich entstand ein Bild, das das Grundthema des Gedichtes aufzunehmen schien: die Relation zwischen dem Alten und dem Neuen. Der wichtigere

soll man an das, was man der Welt präsentiert, glauben. Vertrauen ist das Kennzeichen guter Gestaltung ...na ja, vielleicht dieses Mal nicht. □ DESIGNTALK Das Thema «Design» bot Gelegenheit, das Wesen von Licht, Form und Illusion zu untersuchen. Hier ging es um die Schaffung einer Oberfläche, die sich dem Betrachter entgegenwölbt und damit die rechteckige Flachheit des üblichen Plakatformats in Frage stellt. Zuerst entwickelte ich die Typographie und Quadrate wie ein konventionelles Design mit dem Computer. Das Ergebnis wurde dann um einen Zylinder gewickelt und mit einer starken Lichtquelle auf der linken Seite photographiert. Die gebogenen Ausstanzungen oben und unten vervollkommnen den Effekt. Das Ergebnis ist vielleicht nicht offensichtlich genug, denn häufig glauben die Betrachter, dass der Lichteffekt durch das zufällige Licht des Ortes entsteht, an dem das Plakat gerade aufgehängt ist. □ A DRAWING LESSON Die Idee hinter diesem Plakat war, eine didaktische Arbeit zu schaffen, die tatsächlich das bietet, was sie verspricht (im Gegensatz zu vielen Werbeplakaten, die ein Versprechen machen oder einen Wunsch wecken). Dieses Plakat macht eine Beobachtung über das

MILTON GLASER, GEBÜRTIGER NEW YORKER, BESUCHTE DIE KUNSTSCHULE COOPER UNION IN NEW YORK. 1954 GRÜNDETE ER ZUSAMMEN MIT SEYMOUR CHWAST DIE PUSHPIN STUDIOS UND 1968 ZUSAMMEN MIT CLAY FELKER DIE ZEITSCHRIFT *NEW YORK*. ER HAT ZAHLREICHE PUBLIKATIONEN IN ALLER WELT GESTALTET, UND SEINE ARBEITEN WURDEN IN EINZELAUSSTELLUNGEN IM MUSEUM OF MODERN ART, IN DER LINCOLN CENTER GALLERY, IM CENTRE POMPIDOU, PARIS, UND IM KÖNIGLICHEN MUSEUM VON BRÜSSEL AUSGESTELLT. MILTON GLASER IST MITGLIED DER HALL OF FAME DES ART DIRECTORS CLUB.

Wesen des Zeichnens und der Illustration, und es bringt diese Beobachtung zum Ausdruck, indem es eine Photographie und die davon abgeleitete Arbeit zeigt. Es setzt voraus, dass das Publikum, das sich für Kunst und Illustration interessiert, bereit ist, die Zeit und Gedanken zu investieren, die nötig sind, um die Botschaft zu verstehen. Das widerspricht dem Grundsatz, wonach ein Plakat leicht verständlich und im Vorbeigehen lesbar sein muss. In diesem Fall sprechen die folgenden Umstände gegen den Grundsatz. Dieses Plakat ist in den U-Bahn-Stationen ausgehängt, wo das Warten auf die Züge manchmal endlos erscheint, und die Wartenden verzweifelt nach Lesestoff suchen. Hinzu kommt die ganz spezielle Art des Plakates, die eher das Interesse einer visuell anspruchsvollen Person oder eines potentiellen Studenten wecken wird, also von Personengruppen, die empfänglicher für komplexe Ideen sein dürften. □ QUADERNO Ein Plakat kann die selben formalen und philosophischen Fragen über die Realität aufwerfen wie die Malerei. Hier wird die Frage der räumlichen Illusion aufgenommen, indem das Thema innerhalb der Grenzen isometrischer Perspektiven behandelt wird. Das

diese Tatsache aufmerksam machen. Ich schuf eine Landschaft aus Künstlermaterial, wobei jeder Gegenstand in einer anderen Technik dargestellt ist. Gleichzeitig verbarg ich das Wort 'Charvoz' als Rebus im Plakat. Die wesentliche Frage dabei ist, ob diese Umwege der Wirksamkeit des Plakates schaden. Mir gefällt die Idee, dass jemand vielleicht zwei Jahre nachdem er das Plakat zum ersten Mal gesehen hat, etwas entdeckt, was er zuvor nicht bemerkt hatte. Ich glaube zudem, dass es beim Betrachter eine intuitive Reaktion auf das gibt, was man verdeckte Substanz nennen könnte, die die Erfahrung vertieft und dazu beiträgt, dass das Plakat im Gedächtnis haften bleibt. Wir wissen, dass es dieses Phänomen in der Musik, Dichtung und Malerei gibt, warum also nicht beim Plakat? Vielleicht hat T.S. Elliot es am besten ausgedrückt, als er sagte «Der offenkundige Inhalt eines Gedichtes dient dazu, einer Gewohnheit des Lesers entgegenzukommen: seinen Verstand abzulenken und ruhig zu halten, während das Gedicht das seine tut, um auf ihn einzuwirken, ganz ähnlich wie der imaginäre Einbrecher, der immer ein bisschen

 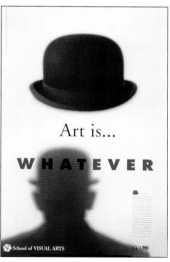

Rechteck des Plakates wurde ausgeschnitten, um die Illusion zu verstärken. Am interessantesten bei dieser Übung ist für mich die Weigerung des Gegenstandes (es handelt sich um das Olivetti Power Book), an seinem Platz zu bleiben. Mein Verstand hat Mühe, die isometrischen Regeln anzunehmen und versucht immer wieder, den Computer im Raum verschwinden zu lassen, nach der vertrauteren, auf einen Fluchtpunkt zulaufenden Perspektive der Renaissance. Das Resultat ist beunruhigend, und wenn man eine Weile auf den Computer starrt, scheint er sich von der Seite abzuheben. □ SVA MASTER SERIES Das kleine Plakat für meine Ausstellung an der School of Visual Arts inspirierte mich zu dem Plakat "Design Talk". Mich faszinierte die Illusion von Weiss, wobei die weisse gebogene Oberfläche des Notizbuches sich zum Betrachter hin wölbt. □ CHARVOZ Es ist immer ein Risiko, mehr Informationen liefern zu wollen, als die Situation erfordert, wobei das grösste Risiko darin liegt, die wichtigste Information zu verschleiern und zu verwässern. In diesem Fall handelte es sich beim Auftraggeber um einen Hersteller von Künstlermaterial, und das Plakat sollte in erster Linie das Publikum auf

Fleisch für den Hofhund mitbringt.» □ ART IS Dieses erst kürzlich entstandene Plakat begann mit einem Auftrag vom Vorstand der School of Visual Arts (Silas Rhodes), den Ausspruch "Art is" zu interpretieren. Sechs Designer erhielten die gleiche Aufgabe, und die Ergebnisse wurden gleichzeitig überall in der Stadt in U-Bahn-Stationen und an Bushaltestellen ausgehängt. Der Versuch, Kunst zu definieren, ist ganz eindeutig keine leichte Aufgabe, aber die Vielfalt der Ergebnisse sorgte für eine lebendige Serie von öffentlichen Bekanntmachungen. Ich habe bei meinem Plakat versucht, die visuelle Botschaft durch den Begleittext weiterzuführen, wobei ein Punkt im Text nicht erwähnt wird. Und zwar geht es um die Tatsache, dass es in der Natur einiger Formen liegt, dass sie auf seltsame Art ansprechender sind als andere. Ich bin überzeugt, dass die Melone (gemeint ist der Hut), als Skulptur gesehen, eines der elegantesten und ästhetisch ansprechendsten Objekte ist, die je geschaffen wurden. Können wir in diesem Fall von Kunst sprechen, wenn das gar nicht die Absicht war? Diese Frage verlangt als Antwort mehr als ein Plakat.

NÉ À NEW YORK, **MILTON GLASER** A ÉTUDIÉ À LA COOPER UNION ART SCHOOL. EN 1954, IL CO-FONDE LES PUSHPIN STUDIOS AVEC SEYMOUR CHWAST ET FONDE EN 1968 LE MAGAZINE *NEW YORK* AVEC CLAY FELKER. IL A ÉGALEMENT RÉALISÉ LE GRAPHISME D'INNOMBRABLES PUBLICATIONS. DES EXPOSITIONS LUI ONT ÉTÉ CONSACRÉES AU MUSÉE D'ART MODERNE ET À LA LINCOLN CENTER GALLERY DE NEW YORK, AU CENTRE POMPIDOU ET AU MUSÉE ROYAL À BRUXELLES. MILTON GLASER, MEMBRE HALL OF FAME DU ART DIRECTORS CLUB, S'EST VU DÉCERNÉ LE MASTER SERIES AWARD DE LA SCHOOL OF VISUAL ARTS.

Autrefois, la règle voulait que l'affiche idéale soit simple au niveau de la forme, réductrice au niveau du contenue et facile à comprendre. Mais aujourd'hui, des question telles que «qu'est-ce qui est réel», «qu'est-ce qui est beau» ou «qu'est-ce qui est socialement responsable» peuvent intéresser un designer au même titre que les préoccupations plus classiques sur l'efficacité de la communication sur un produit. □ EARTH FAIR 95 Au début, il y a toujours le mot. En général, je commence à travailler sur une idée littéraire. Dans le cas présent, les mots «ART» et «AIR» se dissimulaient dans les mots «EARTH FAIR», le thème de l'affiche. C'est ce qu'on pourrait appeler une découverte poétique, mais rapidement le problème se posa de savoir comment exploiter ce trésor caché. Les décisions formelles – les différences de poids à donner à la typographie, l'utilisation des diagonales, le rouge intense et les couleurs contrastantes sur les bords – contribuent à rendre l'idée compréhensible, mais l'impact de l'affiche repose largement sur le texte écrit qui l'accompagne et complète la réflexion qu'elle suscite. Les mots Earth Fair s'apparentent davantage à un dessin qui se métamorphose quand on le regarde.□ OLD AND NEW Réalisée pour Silas Rhodes, cette affiche me donna du fil à retordre parce que le poème d'Alexander Pope me laissait froid. Même après y avoir réfléchi plusieurs semaines, j'étais incapable de le transposer en images. A force d'efforts, j'ai fini par créer une image qui semblait illustrer le thème central du poème: la relation entre le vieux et le nouveau. La partie de l'affiche qui me semble la plus importante est la description de ma démarche sous la forme d'une conversation intime avec l'observateur, que j'ai intitulée «Réflexions». J'y retrace l'histoire de l'affiche et ma frustration. Je propose même une alternative à ceux que cela intéresse. C'est peut-être la première fois qu'une même affiche propose simultanément deux solutions. Après tout, on est censé croire à ce que l'on présente au monde. Cette confiance en soi est la marque d'un bon graphisme... Mais peut-être pas cette fois-ci... □ DESIGNTALK Le thème de cette affiche fut l'occasion d'explorer la nature de la lumière, de la forme et de l'illusion. L'objectif était de créer l'impression d'une surface bombée, en défiant l'idée d'un plan rectangulaire qui est le support habituel de l'affiche. J'ai d'abord créé la typo et les carrés de manière classique, sur ordinateur. Le document imprimé a ensuite été enroulé sur un cylindre et photographié avec un fort éclairage sur la gauche. Les découpes arrondies en haut et en bas renforcent encore l'effet. Le résultat n'est peut-être pas assez évident. Lorsque les gens regardent cette affiche, ils ont souvent l'impression que les effets de lumière sont le fruit du hasard ou simplement de la lumière ambiante. □ A DRAWING LESSON L'idée derrière cette affiche était de créer un travail didactique qui tienne réellement ses promesses, contrairement à la plupart des publicités qui promettent monts et merveilles et font naître le désir. Il s'agit d'une étude sur la nature du dessin et de l'illustration, étayée par une photographie et les travaux qui en ont découlé. Cela suppose que le public, ceux qui s'intéressent à l'art ou à l'illustration, soient prêts à investir le temps et les efforts nécessaires pour comprendre le message. Cela est en contradiction flagrante avec les principes de base qui veulent que le message d'une affiche soit facile à comprendre et qu'il s'adresse à des gens pressés. Deux faits pourraient remettre en question cette règle: d'une part, cette affiche est placée dans le métro à des endroits où l'attente peut sembler longue aux usagers cherchant désespérément quelque chose à lire. D'autre part, le caractère très particulier de cette affiche peut retenir l'intérêt d'un étudiant ou de gens sensibles à l'esthétique visuelle, bref d'un petit groupe réceptif aux idées complexes. □ QUADERNO Une affiche peut poser les mêmes questions formelles et philosophiques sur la nature de la réalité qu'un tableau. La question de l'illusion spatiale est soulevée ici dans la mesure où le thème est traité dans les limites des perspectives isométriques, un peu comme un paravent japonais. Le rectangle de l'affiche a été découpé pour renforcer l'illusion. Pour moi, le plus intéressant dans cet exercice est le refus du sujet principal – le power book d'Olivetti –, à rester à sa place. Mon esprit a de la peine à se plier aux règles isométriques; il essaie toujours de repousser l'ordinateur dans l'espace, selon le schéma classique de la Renaissance où toutes les lignes convergent vers un point de fuite unique. Le résultat est inquiétant, et si l'on fixe l'ordinateur quelques instants, il semble se détacher de la page. □ SVA MASTER SERIES Cette petite affiche réalisée pour mon exposition à la School of Visual Arts m'a inspiré par la suite l'affiche «DesignTalk». J'étais fasciné par l'illusion du blanc, par la manière dont la surface blanche, incurvée du notebook se bombait sous le regard de l'observateur. □ CHARVOZ Il est toujours risqué de vouloir communiquer plus d'informations que la situation ne le requiert, et le risque le plus fréquent est de diluer ainsi l'information essentielle. Cette affiche a été réalisée pour un fabricant de fournitures d'art – ce qui devait ressortir clairement dans l'affiche. J'ai créé un paysage de fournitures d'art, en variant à chaque fois la technique pour exprimer cette idée. En même temps, j'ai dissimulé le nom «Charvoz» sous la forme d'un rébus. La question essentielle est de savoir si ces détours nuisent à l'impact de l'affiche. J'aime l'idée que quelqu'un puisse y découvrir deux ans plus tard un élément nouveau qui lui avait échappé la première fois. Je crois en outre que les gens ont une réaction intuitive à ce que l'on pourrait nommer la substance dissimulée; cela donne plus d'intensité à l'expérience et contribue à imprimer durablement l'affiche dans la mémoire. Nous savons que ce phénomène existe dans la musique, dans la poésie, dans la peinture. Alors pourquoi pas dans la création d'affiches? T.S. Elliot l'a très bien formulé avec ces mots: «Le but manifeste d'un poème est de satisfaire une habitude du lecteur: divertir son esprit et le maintenir en paix tandis que le poème exerce son emprise, comme le voleur imaginaire a toujours un bon morceau de viande pour le chien de la maison.» □ ART IS L'affiche la plus récente a été commandée par le président de la School of Visual Arts (Silas Rhodes). Il s'agissait d'interpréter la phrase «Art is». □ Six designers ont planché sur le sujet, et le fruit de leurs travaux a été placardé dans toute la ville, aux arrêts de bus et dans le métro. Tenter de définir l'art n'est évidemment pas tâche facile, mais la multiplicité et la variété des réponses ont fourni matière à une série d'affiches très vivantes. Le texte de la mienne vise à prolonger le message visuel, mais il omet un point: le fait qu'étrangement, certaines formes sont par nature plus séduisantes que d'autres. Je suis convaincu qu'un chapeau melon est, sur un plan sculptural, l'un des objets les plus élégants et les plus plaisants sur le plan esthétique jamais créés. Mais pouvons-nous parler d'art alors que sa fonction est tout autre? Il faudrait sans doute plus d'une affiche pour répondre à cette question.

GRAPHIS

POSTER

NINETY-SEVEN

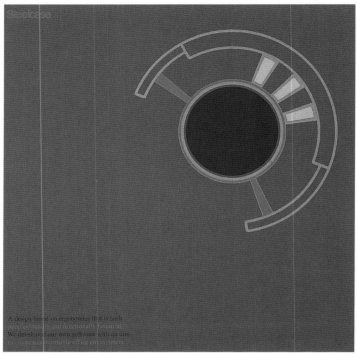

1   2

3   4

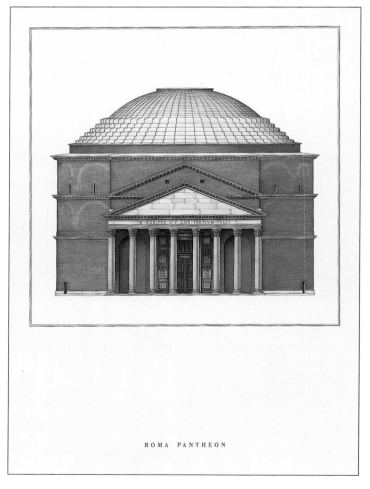

1, 2 **IWAO MATSUURA DESIGN OFFICE CO. LTD.** *STEELCASE JAPAN, K.K.* □ 3 **GRAFISK DESIGN STUDIO**
4 **EDITION LIDIARTE** *IN-HOUSE*

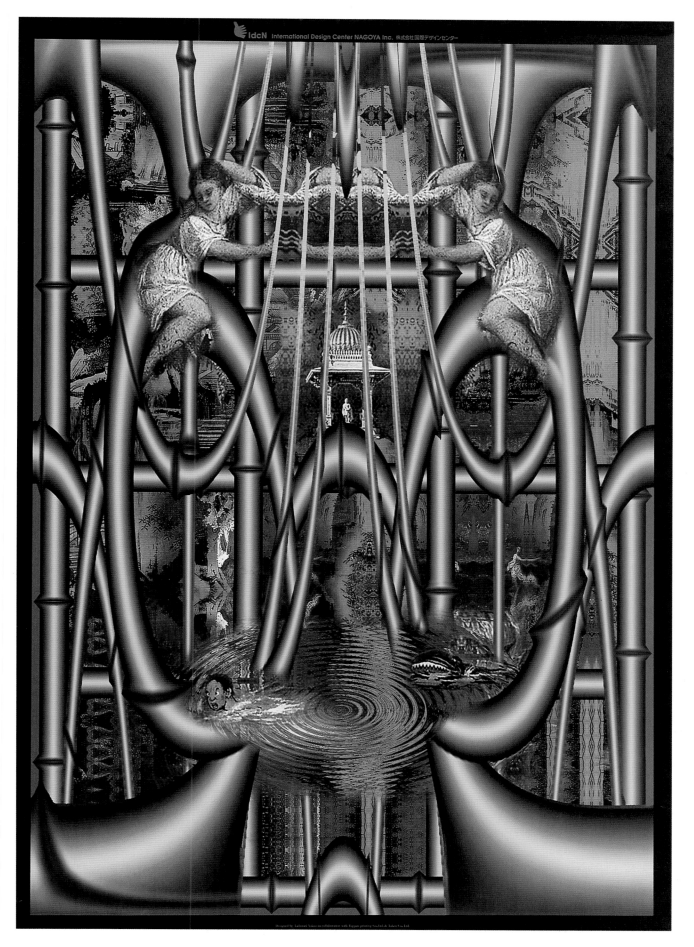

5 **TADANORI YOKOO** *JAGDA*

6

7

8

6 **BARTEN & BARTEN DIE AGENTUR GMBH** *MOTO WITT GMBH* □ 7 **THE MARTIN AGENCY** *MOTO EUROPA*
8 **RITTA & ASSOCIATES** *BMW OF NORTH AMERICA*

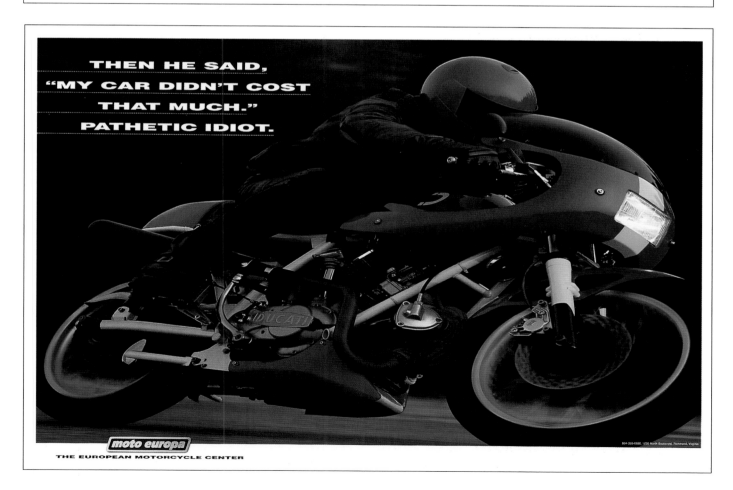

9, 10 **THE MARTIN AGENCY** *Moto Europa*

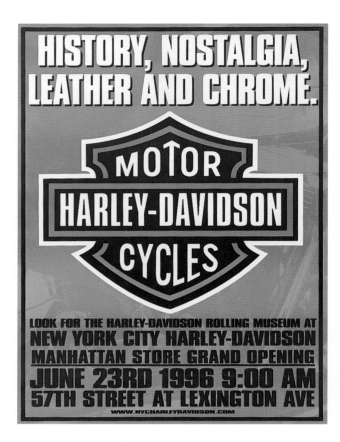

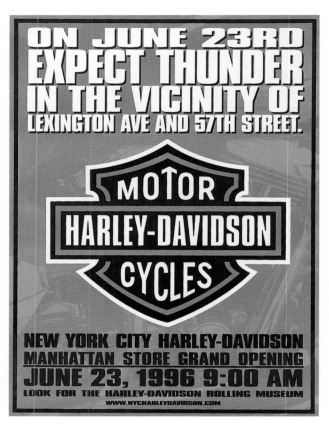

11 12

13 14

11, 12 **VOX ADVERTISING & DESIGN** *Harley Davidson*
13 **VAUGHN/WEDEEN CREATIVE** *U.S. West Communications* □ 14 **THE DESIGNORY, INC.** *Porsche Cars North America*

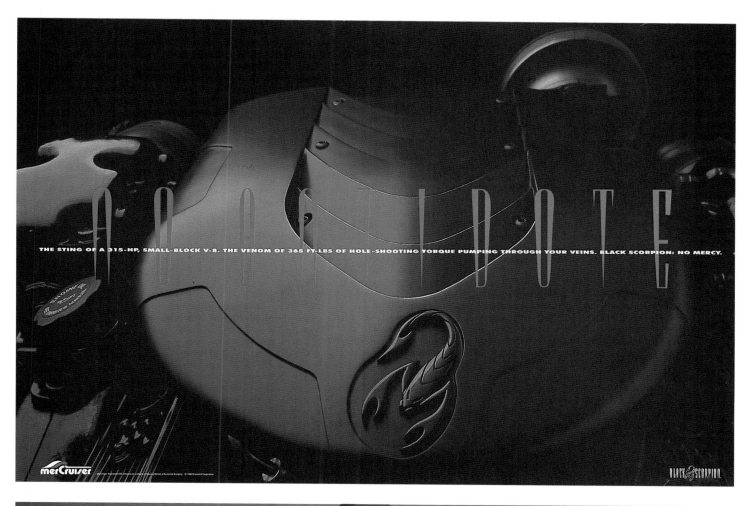

15

16

15 **SHR PERCEPTUAL MANAGEMENT** *MERCRUISER* □ 16 **RUBIN POSTAER** *AMERICAN HONDA MOTOR INC.*

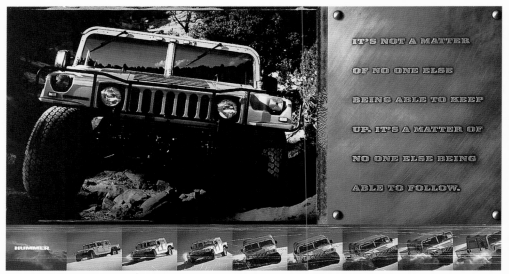

THE NEW TURBO DIESEL HUMMER IS FASTER THAN A FERRARI F50. UNLESS, OF COURSE, YOU HAPPEN TO BE ON A PAVED ROAD.

A Hummer may not set any land speed records. But then no other vehicle can cover as much land. With its unique radical design, a Hummer can literally scale an 18-inch rock ledge, ford two feet of water, plow through three-foot snowdrifts, and claw its way up mountainous sand dunes. Of course, it's no slouch on the road either. In fact, the new turbo diesel's improved acceleration makes pulling onto the freeway a breeze. It's also surprisingly easy to maneuver through rush hour traffic, bank drive-thrus, and cramped parking garages. In other words, a Hummer can take you just about anywhere. Even the passing lane.

For more information about the Hummer or a brochure detailing its unparalleled capabilities, call 800-732-5493.

IT'S NOT A MATTER OF NO ONE ELSE BEING ABLE TO KEEP UP. IT'S A MATTER OF NO ONE ELSE BEING ABLE TO FOLLOW.

THE NEW TURBO DIESEL. INTIMIDATION ISN'T YOUR ONLY MEANS OF PULLING ONTO THE FREEWAY.

It can scale an 18-inch vertical wall. It can plow through a three-foot snowdrift. It can ford two feet of water. It can climb a 60% grade. It can traverse a 40% side slope. And, with its optional new V8 6.5L turbo diesel engine, it can easily navigate the passing lane.

Of course, getting around town has never been a problem for a Hummer. You'll find maneuvering your way through bank drive-thrus, parking garages, and busy traffic just as effortless as clawing your way up a mountainous sand dune.

In the end, there are very few obstacles the turbo diesel Hummer can't handle. The on-ramp doesn't happen to be one of them.

For more information about the new turbo diesel Hummer or a brochure detailing the Hummer's unparalleled capabilities, call 800-732-5494.

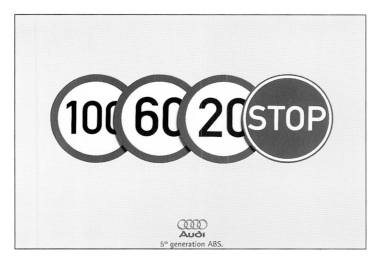

Audi
5th generation ABS.

Audi
Four-wheel drive (Quattro).

Audi
FourLink suspension.

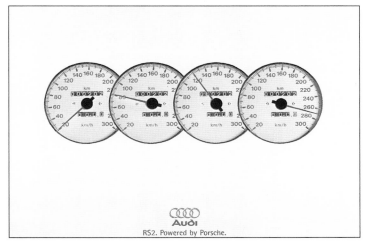

Audi
RS2. Powered by Porsche.

THERE'S NOTHING
LIKE LIVING
OFF-CAMPUS

Jeep
THERE'S ONLY ONE

ARRIVAL OF THE
FITTEST

Jeep
THERE'S ONLY ONE

20-23 **ALMAP/BBDO** *SENNA IMPORT* □ 24, 25 **THE HOT SHOP DESIGN GROUP/BOZELL** *CHRYSLER*

IN THIS HISTORICAL MOMENT NOTHING IS WRIT IN STONE. AND THE TYPOGRAPHERS' ART REFLECTS ITS CONTINGENCY IN A KALEIDOSCOPIC GLOBAL CULTURE DIGITIZED, SCRIBBLED, SCRAMBLED TYPE DEPOSES CHASTE VALUES OF ORDER AND BEAUTY. YET PERHAPS IN ITS 'FALL,' IS THE SALVATION OF GRAPHIC DESIGN PREPARED. YOU ARE INVITED TO ENTER YOUR MOST PROVOCATIVE WORK IN THE 1995 TYPE DIRECTORS CLUB 42ND EXHIBITION.

TDC No 42

DIRECTORS CLUB 42ND EXHIBITION. POETIC WORK IN THE 1995 TYPE INVITED TO ENTER YOUR MOST OUR EYES ARE OPENED, YOU ARE MYTHS ARE STRIPPED NAKED AND SIMPLICITY ARE BROKEN, CULTURAL LEGIBILITY, AND CLARITY, AND CLASSICAL DOGMAS OF TYPOGRAPHY ART, AS THE PRINCIPLES OF [GOOD] VISUAL LANGUAGE, AND THE MODERN IDEAL OF A PURIFIED THIS DECADE, ALONG WITH THE IF PARADISE WAS AGAIN LOST IN AFFORDED BY TIME WILL PROVE PERHAPS ONLY THIS PERSPECTIVE

TDC No 42

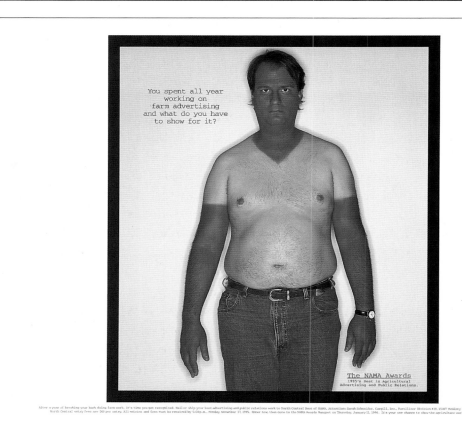

26 VANDERBYL DESIGN Type Directors Club □ 27 MARTIN/WILLIAMS NAMA

TTS TOYO INFORMATION SYSTEMS CO.,LTD.

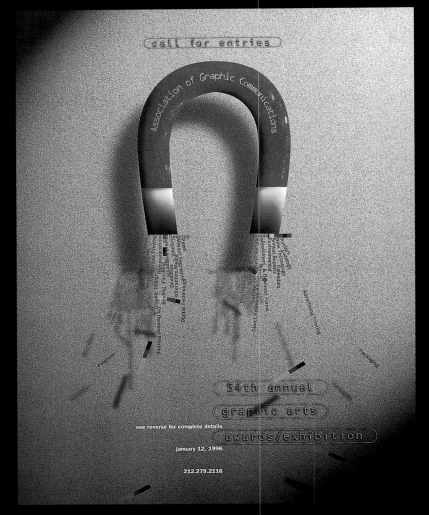

29 **MATTHEW CHUN** *ASSOCIATION OF GRAPHIC COMMUNICATIONS* □ 30 **SKOLOS/WEDELL** *LYCEUM FELLOWSHIP COMMITTEE*

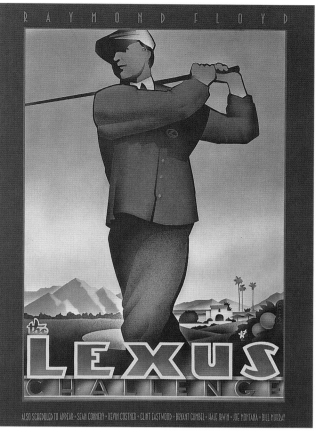

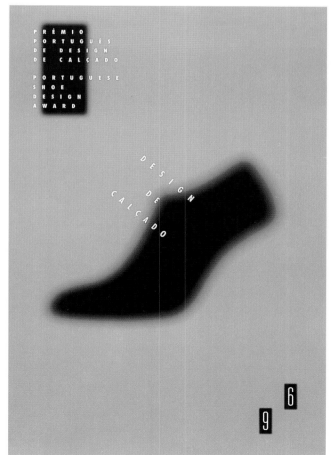

31 32

33 34

31 **NIPPON DESIGN CENTER, INC.** *NAKAGAMA CHEMICAL INC.* □ 32 **JOÃO MACHADO** *CENTRO ARTES S. JOÃO DA MADIERA*
33 **TEAM ONE ADVERTISING** *LEXUS*
34 **ATLANTA COLLEGE OF ART, COMMUNICATION DESIGN DEPARTMENT** *AMERICAN CENTER FOR DESIGN*

FELLOW HUMANS!

☞ IT SHOULD BE OBVIOUS EVEN TO THOSE OF THE MEANEST INTEL-LIGENCE THAT MARATHON 2: DURANDAL FOR WINDOWS 95 IS PART OF THE ALIEN PLOT TO ENSLAVE AND COLONIZE EARTH!

MARATHON 2'S HIGHLY ADDICTIVE GAMEPLAY (ESPECIALLY NETWORK LEVELS) AND HYPNOTIC HIGH RESOLUTION GRAPHICS WILL LULL MILLIONS OF DECENT, FLAG-LOVING AMERICANS INTO ZOMBIE-LIKE TRANCES. THIS NEAR VEGETATIVE STATE WILL RESULT IN LOSS OF MUSCLE TONE AND GENERAL SOFTENING OF THE HUMAN BODY.
AS ANYONE WILL TELL YOU, ALIENS PREFER THEIR MEAT TENDER!

☞ EACH MARATHON 2 CD CONTAINS ALIEN GENETIC MATERIAL ENGINEERED TO COMBINE WITH THE DNA OF WINDOWS 95 OWNERS. THIS WILL ENABLE ALIEN HYBRIDS TO MOVE UNDETECTED AMONG THE HUMAN POPULACE. THIS IS HOW THEY WILL GAIN ACCESS TO OUR NATIONAL PARKS, PLACES OF WORSHIP, AND GAP STORES.

THERE ARE NAYSAYERS WHO SAY THESE ARE MERE RAVINGS. MAY THEY BE THE FIRST TO GRACE THE COALS OF THE ALIEN HIBACHI!

YOU CAN FIND PROOF OF THE CONSPIRACY INSIDE THE WALLS OF THE E3 SHOW!

1) VISIT THE BUNGIE SOFTWARE BOOTH #2337 — WEST HALL

2) OFFER THE "REPRESENTATIVE" A PEANUT BUTTER SANDWICH. THEY WILL POLITE-LY DECLINE. INSIST THAT THEY EAT IT IN FRONT OF YOU.

3) THEY WILL AGAIN REFUSE, THIS TIME IN A COLD ALIEN-LIKE MANNER.

4) THIS SHOULD COME AS NO SURPRISE. ALIENS ARE HIGHLY ALLERGIC TO LEGUMES!

☞ STOCK YOUR BOMB SHELTER WITH CANNED GOODS! LEARN SECRET HANDSHAKES AND DEVELOP PASSWORDS THAT ALIENS WILL FIND HARD TO PRONOUNCE (THEY SEEM TO HAVE TROUBLE WITH THE "SH" SOUND)! MISTRUST ANYONE WHO OWNS A GLOBE!

BE WARNED!

OF ALL THE TOOLS IN SATAN'S WORKSHOP,
MARATHON 2: DURANDAL
MAY BE THE MOST DEVIOUS, MORE DANGEROUS THAN ROCK MUSIC!

NOT CONTENT TO SEDUCE UNWITTING MACINTOSH OWNERS, BUNGIE SOFTWARE HAS UNLEASHED THE DREAD MARATHON 2 ON UNSUSPECTING USERS OF WINDOWS 95. THIS MIND-SOFTENING "COMPUTER GAME" CONTAINS TERRIBLE ALIENS THAT COULD HAVE ONLY BEEN CREATED BY INDIVIDUALS WHO SOLD THEIR VERY SOULS TO LUCIFER!

THE ADDICTIVE NETWORK PLAY OF MARATHON 2 CAN TURN DECENT AMERICAN OFFICE WORKERS INTO *SLACK-JAWED ZOMBIES* RIPE FOR SATAN'S PLUCKING. YES, UNDER THE SPELL OF THIS SCOURGE, EVEN ETERNAL DAMNATION CAN SOUND APPEALING!

THESE UNDISPUTED FACTS WILL UNCOVER THE MENACE FOR YOU!

FACT #1: A CLEANING LADY IN DES MOINES, IOWA, WITNESSED A COMPA-NY COMPTROLLER TURN INTO A GOAT WHILE PLAYING MARATHON 2 FOR WINDOWS.

FACT #2: WHEN MARATHON 2'S AMBIENT STEREO SOUND EFFECTS ARE PLAYED BACKWARDS, THE WORDS "BECOME A CHEERLEADER FOR SATAN" CAN BE CLEARLY HEARD. DO NOT PERFORM THIS TEST YOURSELF!

FACT #3: MARATHON 2 CAUSES PEOPLE TO COMMIT ACTS OF UNSPEAKABLE VIOLENCE. SURELY YOU HAVE HEARD OF THE MAN IN ALBANY, N.Y., WHO, AFTER PLAYING MARATHON 2, KICKED A GAS COMPANY METER READER IN THE SHINS!

ALERT YOUR NEIGHBORS! CONTACT YOUR CLERGYMAN! VISIT BOOTH #2337 IN WEST HALL OR CALL BUNGIE AT 1-800-295-0060 AND TELL THEM YOU REFUSE TO BECOME ONE OF SATAN'S MINDLESS MINIONS.

35 36

37 38

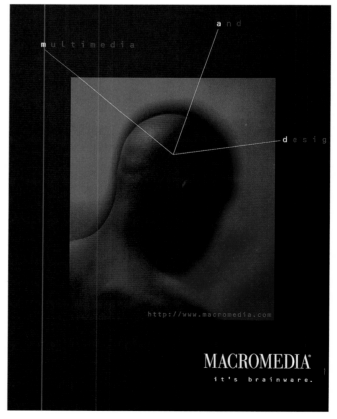

35, 36 **MCCONNAUGHY STEIN SCHMIDT BROWN** *Bungie Software* □ 37 **TBWA CHIAT/DAY** *Sony* □ 38 **XENO** *Macromedia*

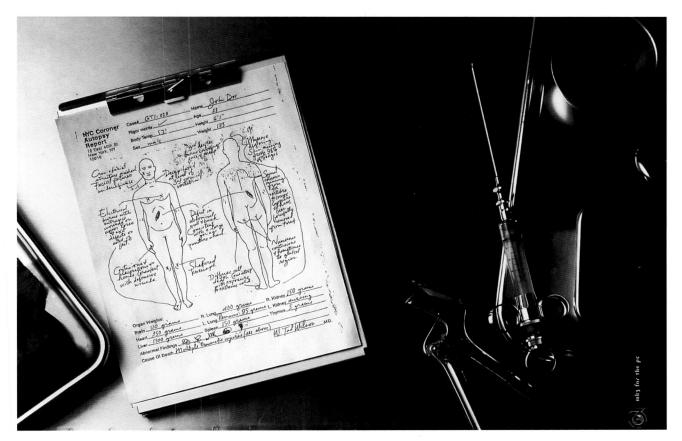

The Book of Revelation foretells the violent end of the world. It paints way too pretty a picture.

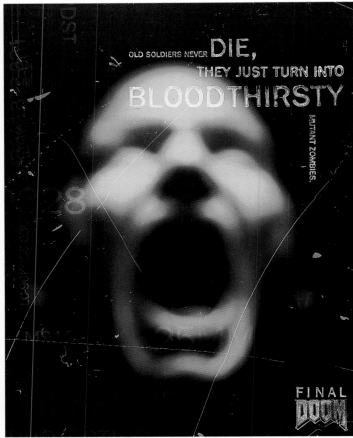

OLD SOLDIERS NEVER DIE, THEY JUST TURN INTO BLOODTHIRSTY MUTANT ZOMBIES.

FINAL DOOM

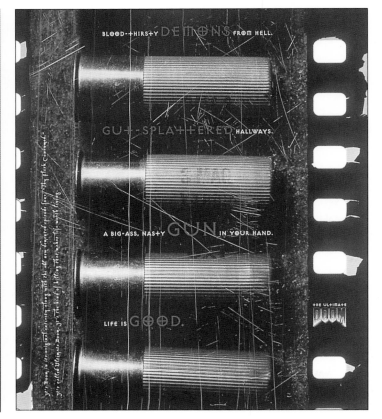

DO UNTO others AS YOU WOULD HAVE THEM DO UNTO YOU. IN THIS CASE, rip OUT THEIR SPINE and internal organs.

BLOOD-THIRSTY DEMONS FROM HELL.

GUT-SPLATTERED HALLWAYS.

A BIG-ASS, NASTY GUN IN YOUR HAND.

LIFE IS GOOD.

THE ULTIMATE DOOM

42-45 **R&D/THE RICHARDS GROUP** *GT INTERACTIVE*

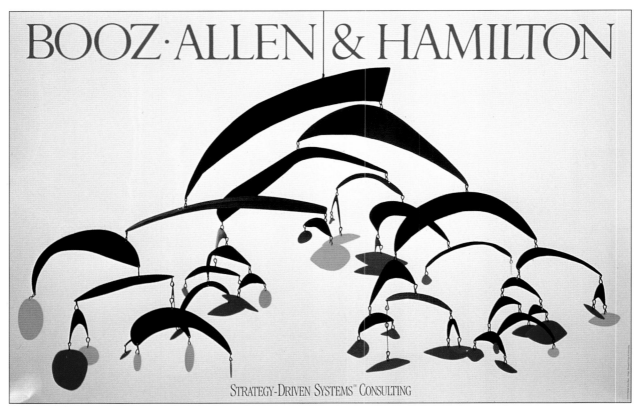

48
49

buckle up

BOOZ·ALLEN & HAMILTON

STRATEGY-DRIVEN SYSTEMS® CONSULTING

48 **BAGBY & COMPANY** *ZENITH ELECTRONICS* □ 49 **METROPOLIS CORPORATION** *BOOZ ALLEN & HAMILTON*

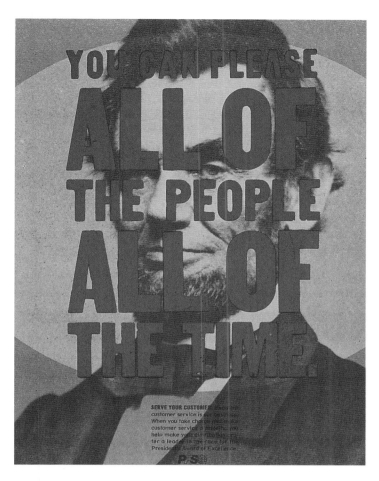

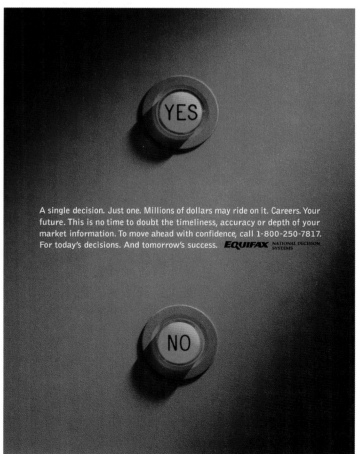

50   51

52   53

54   55

生命のことを
考えられる人に
なろうと思う。

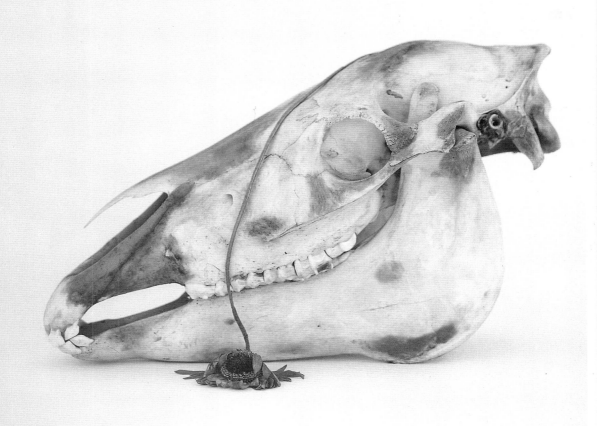

環境と生命を見つめる人になる。
東京農業大学　農学部・短期大学部／〒156 東京都世田谷区桜丘1-1-1 TEL.(03)5477-2226
生物産業学部／〒099-24 北海道網走市八坂196 TEL.(0152)48-2116

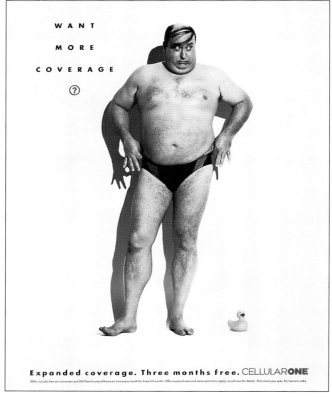

57 58

59 60

57 **HIXO, INC.** *INTELLIQUEST* □ 58 **BORDERS, PERRIN & NORRANDER** *WESTERN WIRELESS* □ 59 **HERMAN MILLER, INC.** *IN-HOUSE*
60 **MICHAEL SCHWAB STUDIO** *AMERICAN PRESIDENTS LINE*

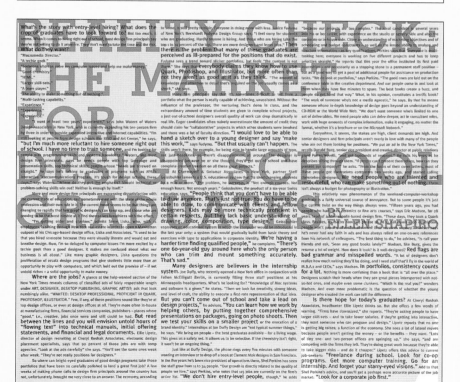

63 64

65 66

THE GIFT OF
LALIQUE
New York • Paris • Beverly Hills

VOGUE
PURFUME

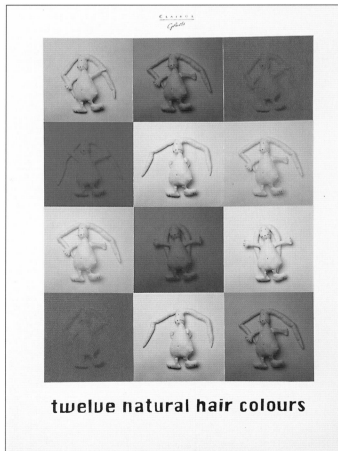

twelve natural hair colours

SHADES OF HAPPINESS...
BY CLAIROL

63 **BLUM/HERBSTREITH** *Lalique* □ 64 **ANTISTA FAIRCLOUGH DESIGN** *Mont Source* □ 65 **SUSAN NYE** *Student Project*
66 **SARAH ORCHARD** *Student Project*

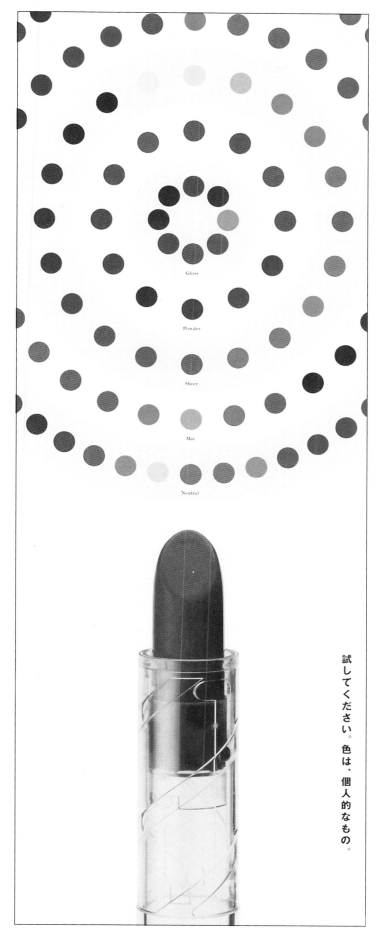

67 68

試してください。色は、個人的なもの。

楽しんでください。色は、体験的なもの。

67, 68 **NAKATSUKA DAISUKE INC.** *SHU UEMURA COSMETICS INC.*

69 70

71 72

69 PIERRE DAVID DESIGN *Les Ballets Jazz de Montreal* □ **70 ARMIN LINDAUER** *Deutsche Oper Berlin*
71 IMAGES *The Louisville Ballet* □ **72 ORIGIN DESIGN COMPANY LTD.** *The Royal New Zealand Ballet*

SAVCOR

Mikaeli 21.–29.10.1995

Mikkeli Finland

Maija Plisetskaja

Imperial Russian Ballet

BOLSHOI teatterin solistit ja orkesteri

74

The passionate story of love, betrayal and sorcery.
Swan Lake
SEATTLE CENTER OPERA HOUSE
May 28-June 1 & June 6-9, 1996
MUSIC Peter Ilyich Tchaikovsky
CHOREOGRAPHY Kent Stowell
STAGING Francia Russell
CALL TICKETMASTER AT 292-ARTS
PACIFIC NORTHWEST BALLET ACKNOWLEDGES THE GENEROUS SUPPORT OF SEAFIRST BANK AND CHATEAU STE. MICHELLE.
PACIFIC NORTHWEST BALLET
Kent Stowell & Francia Russell
ARTISTIC DIRECTORS
PATRICIA BARKER PHOTOGRAPHY: BEN KERNS DESIGN: THE LEONHARDT GROUP

75   76

77

75 **7 M . R . S . COMMUNICATION** *Prix De Lausanne* □ 76 **MULLER & COMPANY** *Westport Ballet Theater 1996*
77 **VIGON/ELLIS** *University of California, Los Angeles*

51

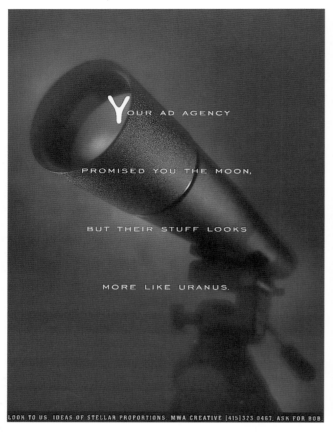

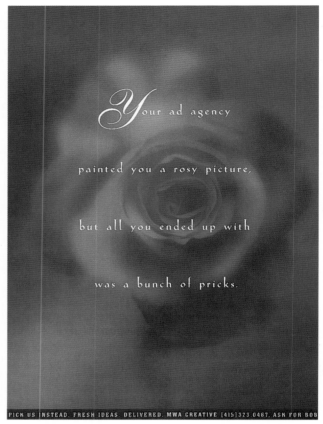

78 79

80 81

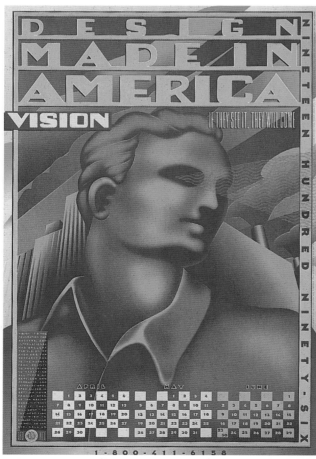

78, 79 **MWA CREATIVE** *IN-HOUSE* □ 80 **DBD INTERNATIONAL LTD.** *IN-HOUSE*
81 **VAUGHN/WEDEEN CREATIVE** *U.S. WEST COMMUNICATIONS*

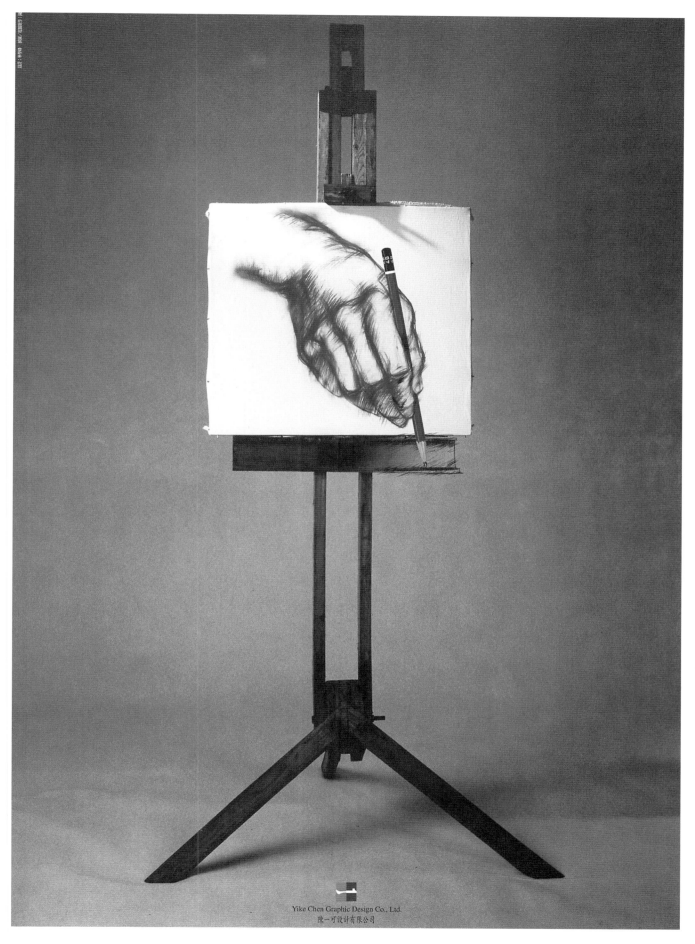

82

Yike Chen Graphic Design Co., Ltd.
陈一可设计有限公司

82 **YIKE CHEN DESIGN CO. LTD** *IN-HOUSE*

83, 84 **LESLIE CHAN DESIGN CO. LTD.** *TAIWAN IMAGE POSTER DESIGN ASSOCIATION*

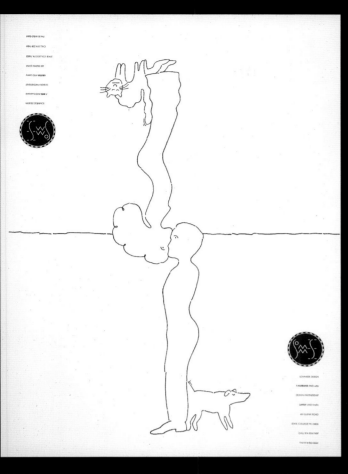

Oh, Mother! Why was I born?

And then, I was born!

85, 86 **SOMMESE DESIGN** *In-House* □ 87, 88 **MAGNA INC. ADVERTISING** *Rakuten Design Room*

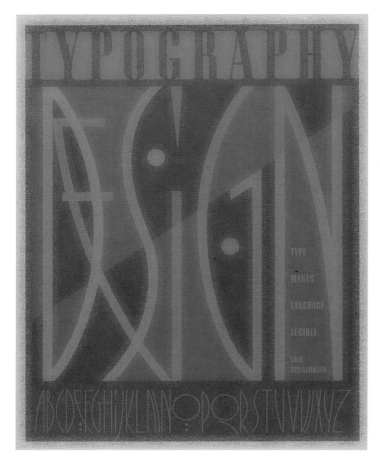

89 90

91 92

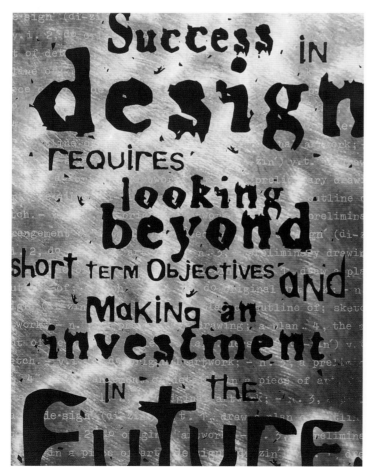

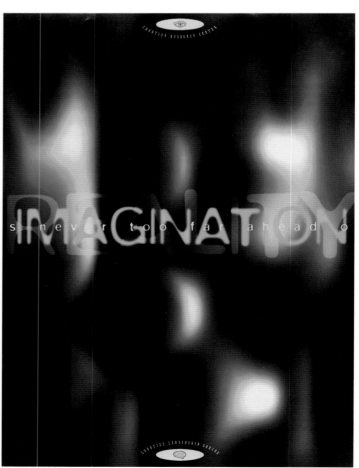

89-92 **HALLMARK CARDS INC.** *IN-HOUSE*

DESIGN/CONCEPT : **SHADOW DESIGN** - HOUSTON, TEXAS   DIGITAL PREPRESS/PRINTING : **INTERNATIONAL PRINTING & PUBLISHING, L.P.** - HOUSTON, TEXAS

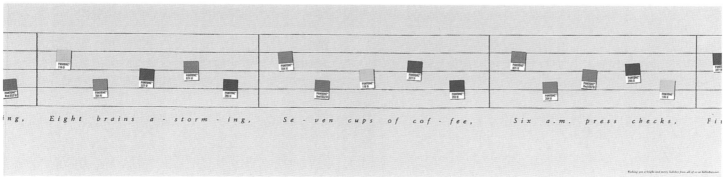

93 **SHADOW DESIGN** *In-House* □ 94 **GIBBS BARONET** *In-House*

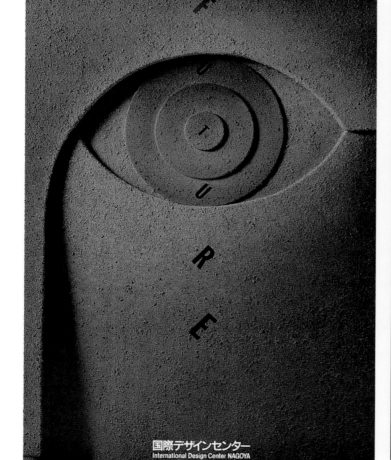

95 96

95 **TOYOTSUGU ITOH DESIGN OFFICE** *INTERNATIONAL DESIGN CENTER NAGOYA INC.*
96 **KOUKOKUMARU INC.** *OSAKA CONTEMPORARY ART CENTER*

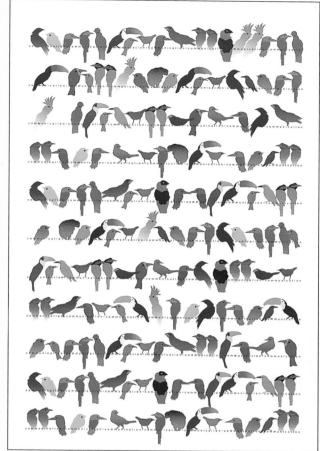

The
Establishment
Shenzhen
Art Directors
Club
1995

97   98

99   100

97 **MICHAEL SCHWAB DESIGN** *ART DIRECTORS CLUB OF CINCINNATI* □ 98 **STUDIO RADAR** *BIENSFELD CONSEIL*
99 **GRAFICOM CO. LTD.** *SHENZEN GRAPHIC DESIGN ASSOCIATION* □ 100 **YIKE CHEN DESIGN CO. LTD.** *SELF-PROMOTION*

LOOKS LIKE THERE ARE
WEIRDER THINGS THAN
A KANSAS CITY AGENCY
PRODUCING WORLD-CLASS
ADVERTISING & DESIGN.

AS FAR AS WE'RE CONCERNED,
THE IDEA OF HIRING ANYONE
BUT MULLER+CO. FOR YOUR
ADVERTISING & DESIGN
SEEMS A LITTLE BIZARRE.

MULLER + COMPANY
4739 Belleview
Kansas City, MO 64112
816-531-1992

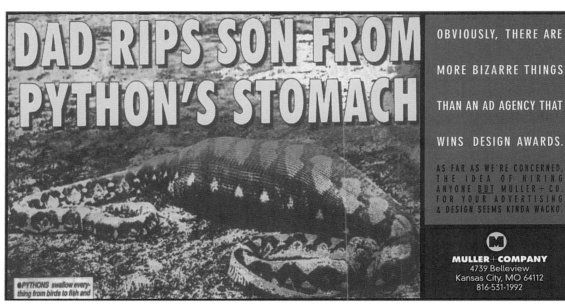

OBVIOUSLY, THERE ARE
MORE BIZARRE THINGS
THAN AN AD AGENCY THAT
WINS DESIGN AWARDS.

AS FAR AS WE'RE CONCERNED,
THE IDEA OF HIRING
ANYONE BUT MULLER+CO.
FOR YOUR ADVERTISING
& DESIGN SEEMS KINDA WACKO.

MULLER + COMPANY
4739 Belleview
Kansas City, MO 64112
816-531-1992

AS YOU SEE, THERE
ARE MORE ABNORMAL
THINGS THAN A
DESIGN FIRM THAT
WINS AD AWARDS.

AS FAR AS WE'RE CONCERNED,
THE IDEA OF HIRING ANYONE
BUT MULLER+CO. FOR YOUR
ADVERTISING & DESIGN
SEEMS TOTALLY WEIRD.

MULLER + COMPANY
4739 Belleview
Kansas City, MO 64112
816-531-1992

101-103 **MULLER & COMPANY** *SELF-PROMOTION*

"HE'S DEVELOPING SUITE NICELY."

RAYMOND P'POOL REDDING, JR.   ANNIE AND SAM REDDING ARE PROUD TO ANNOUNCE THE ARRIVAL OF THEIR SECOND CHILD AT 6:27 A.M. ON WEDNESDAY, 3·2·88
WEIGHT: 8 LBS, 8 OZ   HEIGHT: 20 1/2 INCHES

104

105

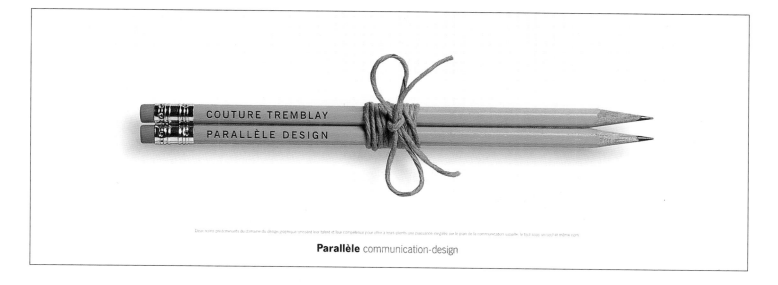

COUTURE TREMBLAY

PARALLÈLE DESIGN

Parallèle communication-design

104 **RAY REDDING** *ANNIE WATKINS REDDING* □ 105 **PARALLÈLE COMMUNICATION-DESIGN** *IN-HOUSE*

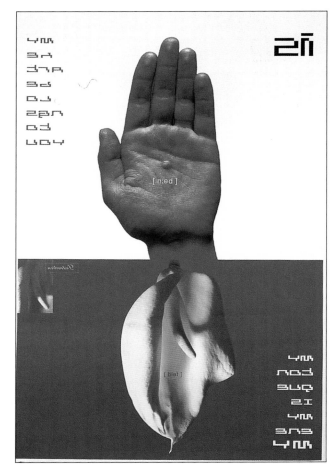

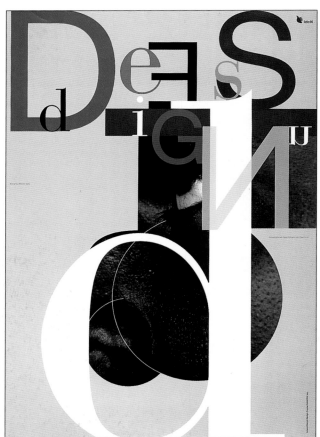

106 **GRADE GROUP** *Creative Review Magazine* □ 107 **ALLIGATOR DESIGN ASSOCIATES** *In-house*
108 **MAKOTO SAITO DESIGN OFFICE INC** *International Design Center Nagoya Inc.*
109 **WANG XU & ASSOCIATES** *Shenzhen Graphic Design Association*

TEL. 194634, 437421

STRADA PARIS 7, 3400-CLUJ

DESIGN IDEA PRINT

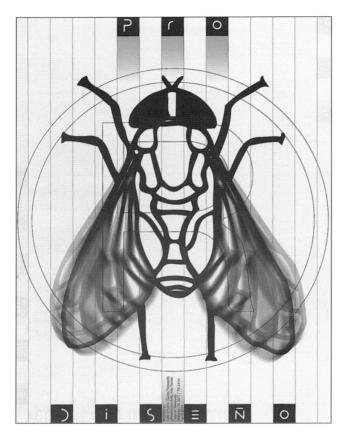

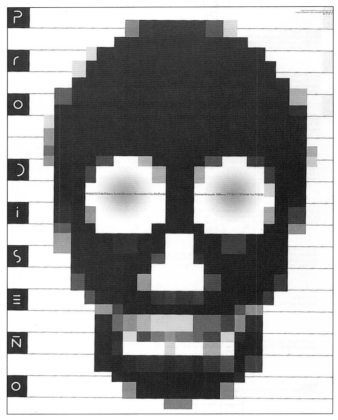

111 112

113 114

111, 112 PRODISEÑO SCHOOL OF VISUAL COMMUNICATION *EDITORIAL EX LIBRIS* □ **113 ATLANTA COLLEGE OF ART, COMMUNICATION DESIGN DEPARTMENT** *IN-HOUSE* □ **114 ALAN FLETCHER** *ICOGRADA STUDENT SEMINAR*

SCOPE
& SUPER 35

GESPRÄCHE MIT KAMERALEUTEN · REGISSEUREN · FILMWISSENSCHAFTLERN · FILMKRITIKERN · BLOCK · COUTARD · ECKHARD · GANSERA · GROB · KOENIGER · LASSALLY · MÜHLENBROCK · PRINZLER · SAGEL · SLAMA · FILHARM · WINKELMANN · KADRAGE · OPTISCHE AUFLÖSUNG · STORYBOARD · BILDGESTALTUNG · EINSTELLUNG · TEAMARBEIT · NOUVELLE VAGUE · FREE CINEMA · CINEMASCOPE · SUPER 35 · HOLLYWOOD · LOW-BUDGET · MISE-EN-SCÈNE · KAMERAARBEIT · BAD TIMING · BONJOUR TRISTESSE · BUNNY LAKE IS MISSING · C'ERA UNA VOLTA IL WEST ·

SYMPOSIUM ÜBER DAS BILDERMACHEN · FILME · VORTRÄGE · DISKUSSIONEN · 23.11. – 26.11. 1995 · STUDIENRICHTUNG KAMERA DER FH DORTMUND

· JEDE MENGE KOHLE · JOANNA · JULES ET JIM · LAMERICA · LE MÉPRIS · LOLA MONTES · DER PASSAGIER
VERANSTALTER: STUDIENRICHTUNG KAMERA DER FACHHOCHSCHULE DORTMUND · FACHBEREICH 2 · RHEINLANDDAMM 203 · 44139 DORTMUND · TEL.: 0231-9112-480 & FILMBÜRO NW
VERANSTALTUNGSORT: ROXY KINO DORTMUND · MÜNSTERSTR. 95 · 44145 DORTMUND · MUSEUM FÜR KUNST- UND KULTURGESCHICHTE DORTMUND · HANSASTR.3 · 44137 DORTMUND

UNIVERSITY OF CALIFORNIA
UCLA
SUMMER
SESSIONS
1996
LOS ANGELES

115
116

115 **INGO EULEN, HANS-HEINRICH SURES** *FACHHOCHSCHULE DORTMUND*
116 **PENTAGRAM DESIGN, INC.** *UNIVERSITY OF CALIFORNIA, LOS ANGELES*

117 118

Congratulations, School of VISUAL ARTS! Turning 50 is an occasion for great celebration. Our modest beginnings could not have predicted our dramatic growth, becoming the largest independent art college in the United States. But we are most proud of graduating outstanding students who have benefited from working with a select faculty of professionals who teach because they want to. Today, we believe that our commitment to enlarging our students' art vocabulary to include ground-breaking technological tools will not only change the way art is produced but will influence art itself in the next millennium.

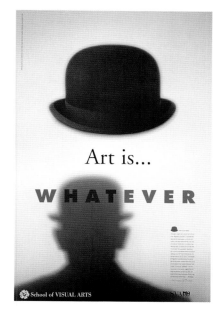

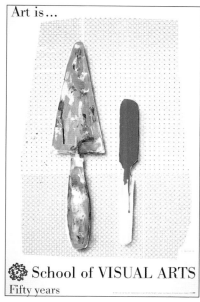

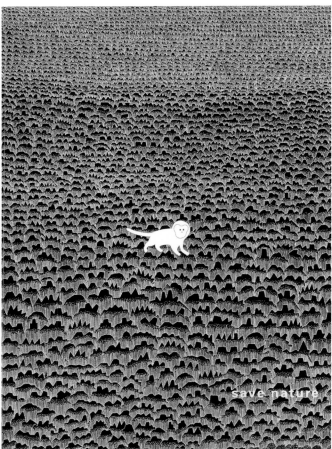

128 129

130 131

128-131 **NIPPON DESIGN CENTER, INC.** *JAPAN DESIGN COMMITTEE*

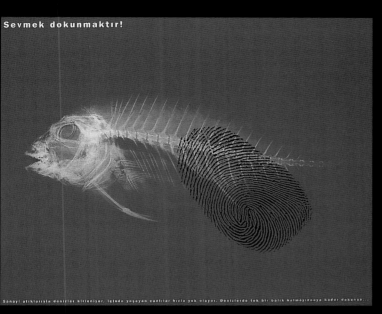

Sevmek dokunmaktır!

Sanayi atıklarıyla denizler kirleniyor. İçinde yaşayan canlılar hızla yok oluyor. Denizlerde tek bir balık kalmayıncaya kadar dokunun...

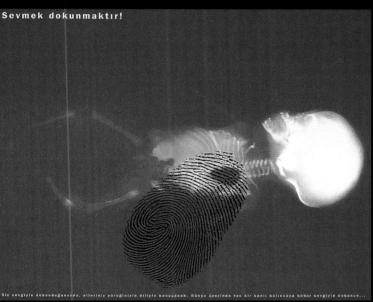

Sevmek dokunmaktır!

Siz sevgiyle dokunduğunuzda, elleriniz yüreğinizin diliyle konuşacak. Dünya üzerinde tek bir canlı kalıncaya kadar sevgiyle dokunun...

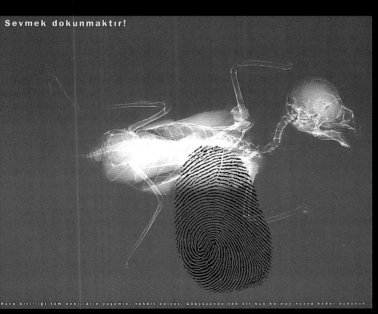

Sevmek dokunmaktır!

Hava kirliliği tüm canlıların yaşamını tehdit ediyor. Gökyüzünde tek bir kuş kalmayıncaya kadar dokunun...

132-134 **VALOR TASARIM** *MEDMAR*

135 136

137 138

135 **NINA ULMAJA GRAFISK FORM** *Stockholm Vatten AB* □ 136 **BATEY ADS SINGAPORE** *Asian Pals of the Planet*
137, 138 **KOUKOKUMARU INC.** *The Cultural Festival for Nations*

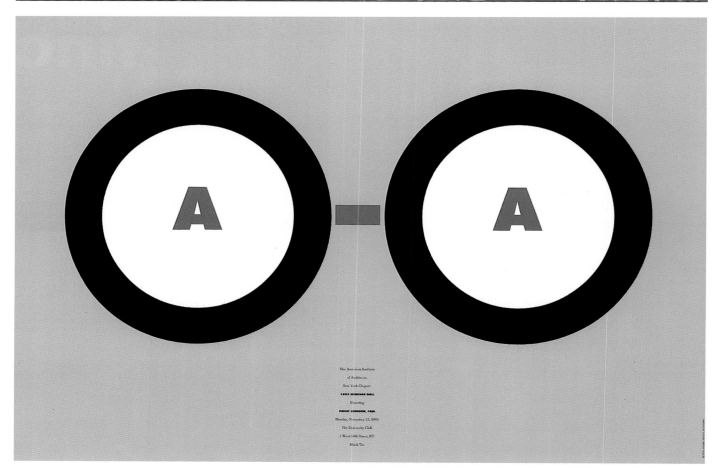

141

142

141 **RBMM** *CHS Class of '76* □ 142 **PENTAGRAM INC.** *American Institute of Architects*

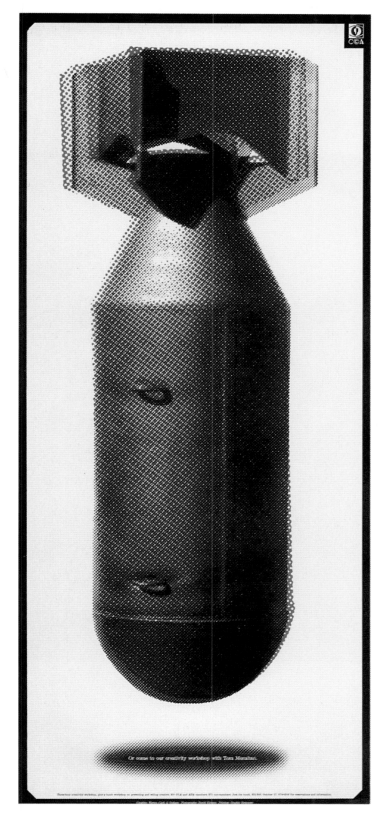

143 144

143 **CLEVELAND CLARK INC.** *Creative Club of Atlanta* □ 144 **LARSEN DESIGN OFFICE, INC.** *American Marketing Association*

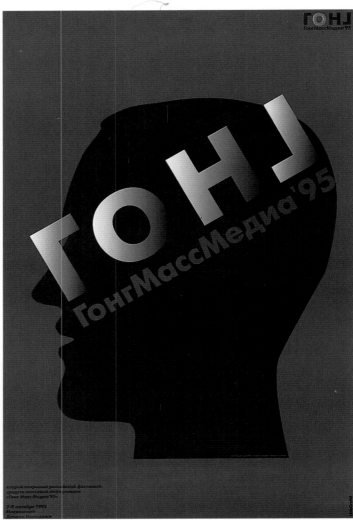

145 146

145 **PRIMO ANGELI** *Atlanta Committee for the Olympic Games* □ 146 **LOGVIN DESIGN** *Liniagrafic Print Company*

147

148

147, 148 **PENTAGRAM DESIGN INC.** *IN-HOUSE*

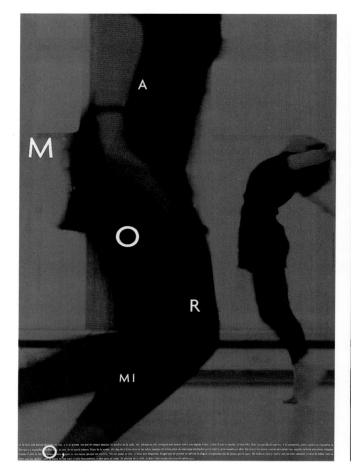

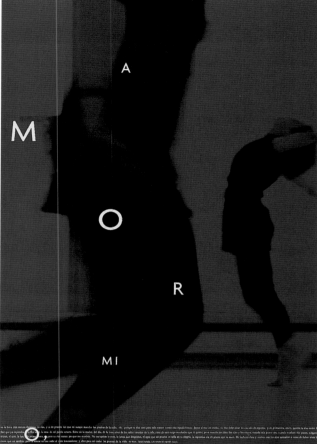

149 150

151 152

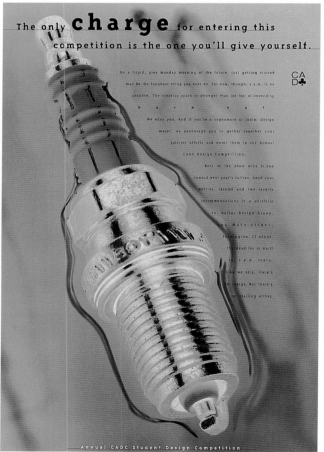

149, 150 **FELDER GRAFIK DESIGN** *TRAME VISUAL AG* □ 151 **MENDELL & OBERER** *BAYEREISCHE STAATSOPER*
152 **KEILER & COMPANY** *CONNECTICUT ART DIRECTORS CLUB*

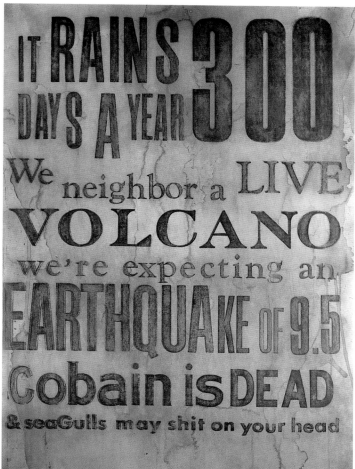

153 154

153 **BELK MIGNOGNA ASSOCIATES, LTD.** *MEAD FINE PAPERS* □ 154 **CYCLONE** *AIGA SEATTLE*

Tadanori Yokoo

155 156

157 158

155 **ANIL REVRI** □ 156 **SHEEHAN DESIGN** *SEATTLE PEACE HEATHENS* □ 157 **TROLLER ASSOCIATES** *ESCOLA PANAMERICANA DE ARTE*
158 **ANTISTA FAIRCLOUGH DESIGN** *IN-HOUSE*

Now that espresso
has come to Cincinnati,
Louise Fili has left her cappuccino
machine behind to venture west for an
evening's engagement at the Art
Directors Club of Cincinnati,
Cincinnati Art Museum,
September 20th.

ATLANTA CREATIVE SUMMIT · MAY 23, 1996

159 **LOUISE FILI LTD.** *Cincinnati Art Directors Club* □ 160 **AUSTIN KELLEY ADVERTISING** *AAAA*

no. design for the fun of it

speakers: **Patti Woodside**, The National Air & Space Museum + **Dan Stanton**, The Discovery Channel

it's a scream

THE BIG PICTURE

It's a scream! AIGA's third annual edition of "Design for the Fun of It," featuring the exhilarating exhibition film artistry of The National Air & Space Museum of the Smithsonian Institution and the bold, broadcast wizardry of The Discovery Channel.   Join the fun, March 28, when we turn the Carnegie Institute into a carnival of games, prizes, tantalizing treats, liquid libation and designer delirium. **It's shocking!** You'll feast your eyes on the sort of breathtaking productions that propel even the most conservative graphic designer into unmitigated visual euphoria, as the National Air & Space Museum previews the very first 90mm, totally bitch'n, completely computer generated film ever created for their nationally acclaimed I-Max theater. It's out of this world!   Plus – for the first time on the big screen – you'll see the stunning visuals and riveting production talents that make The Discovery Channel so popular. In this in-depth exposé, you'll hear inside sources reveal the savvy promotion strategies behind their success and witness the digital imagery magic that makes it all possible.   We want to see you there...We want you to have fun...**We want your brain!**   Tickets for last year's presentation sold out quickly, so don't be a spineless, procrastinating wimp and miss your chance...Call today!

Thursday, March 28, 1996	6:30 PM Reception & Carnival	8:00 PM Presentation	9:30 PM More Carnival
Carnegie Institute of Washington	16th & P Streets, NW	Washington, DC	

Enter on P Street. Free parking available at the corner of 15th & P Streets after 6:30 pm. No attendant will be available so please do not block other cars. Additional parking available at Duron Paint, 15th & P St.

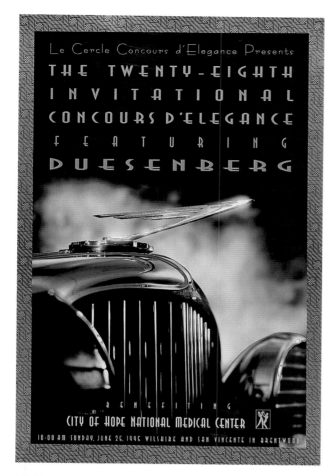

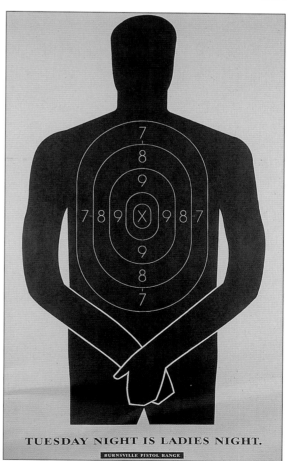

162 **DAVID DUNCAN, INC.** *Le Cercle Concours* □ 163 **VIVA DOLAN COMMUNICATIONS & DESIGN** *Advertising & Design Club of Canada* □ 164 **MULLER & COMPANY** *Kansas City Blues and Jazz Festival* □ 165 **FALLON MCELLIGOTT** *Burnsville Pistol Range*

innsbruck
sarajev

März 1995
Veranstaltungen über
Krieg im Frieden

Theater · Konzert · Film · Diskussion · Lesung · Ausstellung

Kunsthalle II · Konservatorium · Architekturforum Tirol · Kulturgasthaus Bierstindl
Treibhaus · Tiroler Landestheater · Cinematograph · ORF Landesstudio Tirol

Ausführliche Programmhefte liegen bei den Veranstaltungsorten, der Innsbruck-Information (Burggraben 3)
und anderen einschlägigen Informationsstellen auf

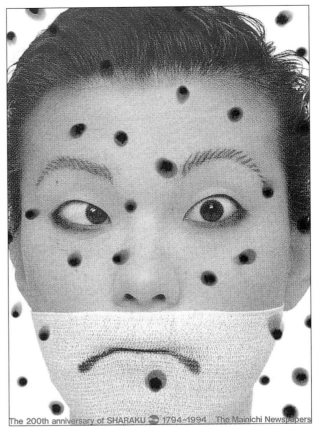

The 200th anniversary of SHARAKU 1794~1994   The Mainichi Newspapers

Coffee.
Jazz.
Not a good time to
quit
smoking.

STARBUCKS BY STARLIGHT

JAZZ JAMS. HOT COFFEE. PIONEER COURTHOUSE SQUARE. MONDAYS 5:30 TO 7. FREE 'N SOLID.

Coffee?
Tea?
Jelly
Roll?

STARBUCKS BY STARLIGHT

JAZZ JAMS. HOT COFFEE. PIONEER COURTHOUSE SQUARE. MONDAYS 5:30 TO 7. FREE 'N SOLID.

166 167

168 169

166 **GRAFIK DESIGN ZIMMERMANN** *PROJEKTSTELLE ZEITKULTUR, TIROLER LANDESREGIERUNG*
167 **NIPPON DESIGN CENTER, INC.** *SHAKEN* □ 168, 169 **LEOPOLD KETEL & PARTNERS** *STARBUCKS*

Cesar Pelli Buildings & Thoughts Wednesday October 25, 1995 6:00 pm Cooper-Hewitt, National Design Museum

170

171

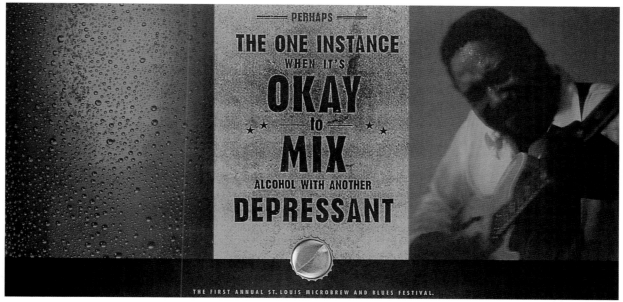

170 **PENTAGRAM DESIGN, INC.** *AMERICAN INSTITUTE OF ARCHITECTS, NEW YORK CHAPTER*
171 **CORE / R&D / THE RICHARDS GROUP** *ST. LOUIS HERITAGE*

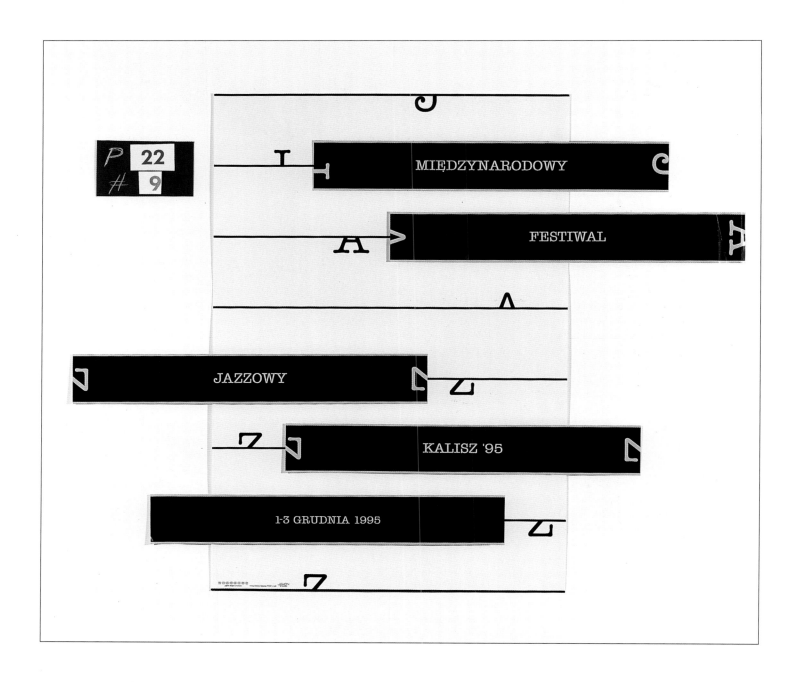

the RED HOT ball

design
industries
foundation
fighting
aids

sheraton
hotel &
towers
chicago
saturday
june 3. 1995. 7:30pm

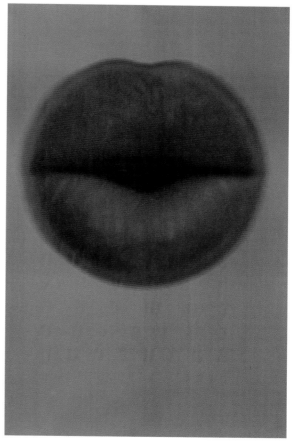

173 174

175 176

THURSDAY ★ MARCH 16

M.O.E

BETTER
THAN E•Z•R•A
...PLUS
KATIES DIMPLES ★ THE GARDENIAS

SATURDAY MARCH 9
8TH ANNUAL AIGA/WICHITA STUDENT PORTFOLIO FORUM

MODERN DOG
WICHITA
GUEST SPEAKERS: ROBYNNE RAYE + MICHAEL STRASSBURGER
FOR MORE INFORMATION AND A FREE REGISTRATION FORM,
SEE YOUR INSTRUCTOR!
Special Thanks to PRAIRIE PRINT - Screenprinting, ETS GRAPHICS
INC. - Filmwork, WESTERN RESOURCE NET INTERNATIONAL - Paper
SULLIVAN HIGDON & SINK INC. - Event Sponsor and MODERN DOG - Poster

173, 174 **VSA PARTNERS** *Diffa* □ 175 **MODERN DOG** *Moe Cafe* □ 176 **MODERN DOG** *AIGA Wichita*

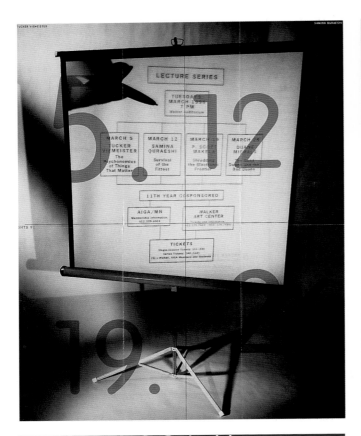

177 178

179 180

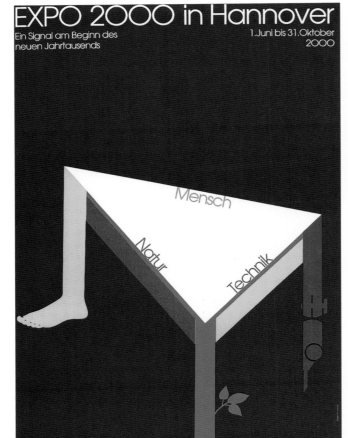

177 **WERNER DESIGN WERKS, INC.** *AIGA Minnesota / Walker Art Center* ☐ 178 **YURI DOJC INC.** *In-house*
179, 180 **JIAYANG LIN** *Hochschule Der Künste Berlin*

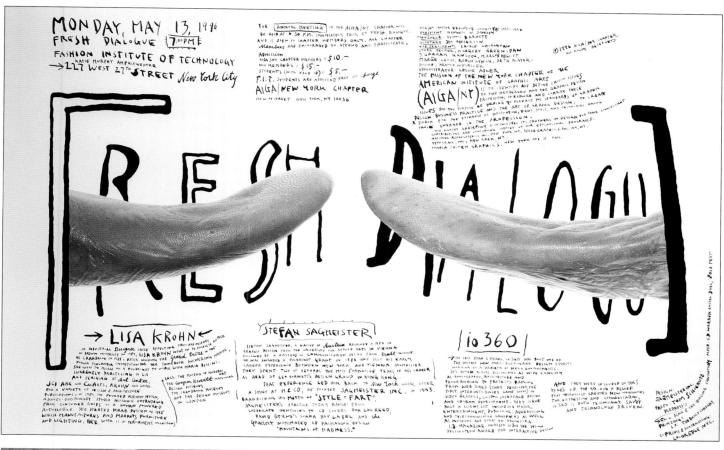

Only good clients allowed.

JWT

181 **SAGMEISTER INC.** *AIGA New York* □ 182 **J. WALTER THOMPSON** *In-House*

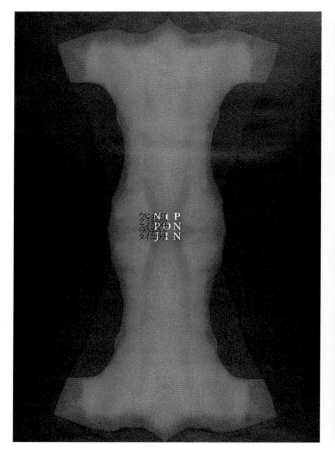

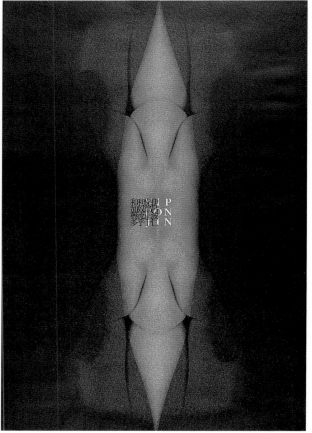

183 184

185 186

Illustrators Exhibition
EBISU MITSUKOSHI EVENT SPACE
1995 December 12 to 17

Illustrators Exhibition
EBISU MITSUKOSHI EVENT SPACE
1995 December 12 to 17

183, 184 **SHINNOSKE INC.** *CLOSE-UP OF JAPAN* □ 185, 186 **TAKU TASHIRO OFFICE** *EBISU MITSUKOSHI*

187

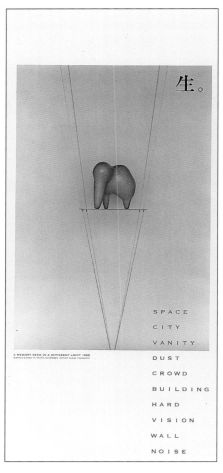

188 189 190

191 192

188-190 **YASUMI NUMAJIRI DESIGN OFFICE** *OHARA SCHOOL OF IKEBANA* □ 191 **TADANORI YOKOO** *ASAHI SHINBUN*
192 **TADANORI YOKOO** *LAFORET HARAJUKU*

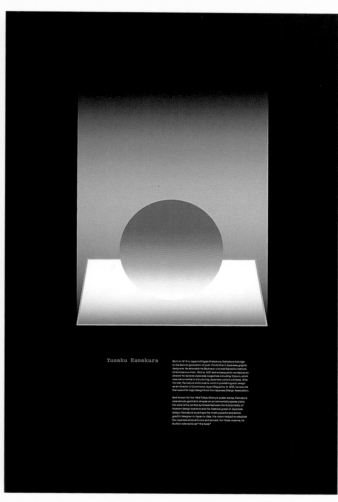

193 194

Yusaku Kamekura

DAS ANGEBOT

Karl-Heinz **Appelt**

FB **Malerei/Grafik** Teil 1

Sighard **Gille**

Professoren und Assistenten

Rolf **Kuhrt**

der Fachklassen stellen aus

Reinhard **Minkewitz**

13.10. – 8.11.1995

Neo **Rauch**

in der Galerie der HGB

Arno **Rink**

Öffnungszeiten: Dienstag bis Freitag 12 Uhr bis 18 Uhr
Samstag 10 Uhr bis 14 Uhr
Sonntag, Montag und an Feiertagen geschlossen

Hochschule für Grafik und Buchkunst
Wächterstraße 11, 04107 Leipzig
Telefon: (0341) 213 51 33

DAS ANGEBOT

Hans **Aichinger**

Fachbereich **Malerei/Grafik** Teil 2:

Dietrich **Burger**

Professoren und Assistenten

Jean **Drache**

des Grundstudiums und die Leiter

Wolfram **Ebersbach**

der künstlerischen Werkstätten

Rolf **Münzner**

stellen neue Arbeiten vor

Hartmut **Piniek**

22. März – 27. April 1996

Herbert **Viecenz**

Galerie der HGB

Doris **Ziegler**

Öffnungszeiten: Dienstag bis Freitag 12 Uhr bis 18 Uhr
Samstag 10 Uhr bis 14 Uhr

Hochschule für Grafik und Buchkunst
Wächterstraße 11, 04107 Leipzig

195, 196 **ANDRÉ GRAU** *GALERIE DER HOCHSCHULE FÜR GRAFIK UND BUCHKUNST LEIPZIG*

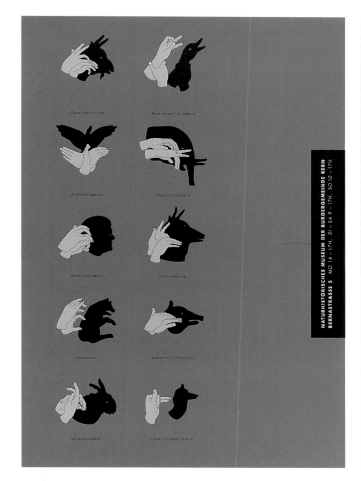

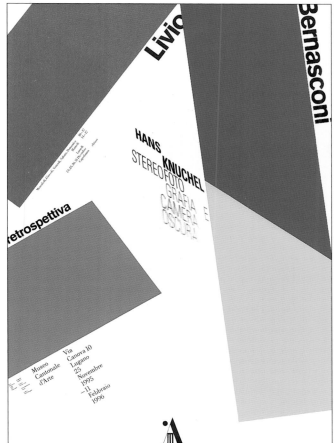

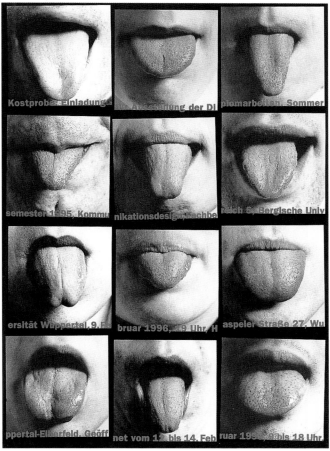

197 198

199 200

197 **CLAUDE KUHN GRAPHIK DESIGN** *NATURHISTORISCHES MUSEUM DER BURGERGEMEINDE BERN*
198 **HOLGER MATTHIES** *HAMBURG SUMMER THEATRE FESTIVAL* □ 199 **BRUNO MONGUZZI** *MUSEO CANTONALE D'ARTE*
200 **CAROLINE HALFF, ANJA RATTENHUBER, SVEN VOGEL** *STUDENT PROJECT*

FORUM FINAL
FRÅN ABF-KURS
TILL KONSTHÖG
SKOLA 17.6-16.8
1995 SKISSERNAS
MUSEUM FINN
GATAN 2 LUND
TIS-LÖR 12-16
SÖNDAG 13-17

201 202

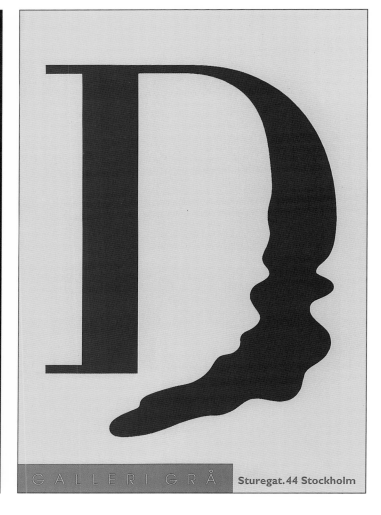

GALLERI GRÅ   **Sturegat. 44 Stockholm**

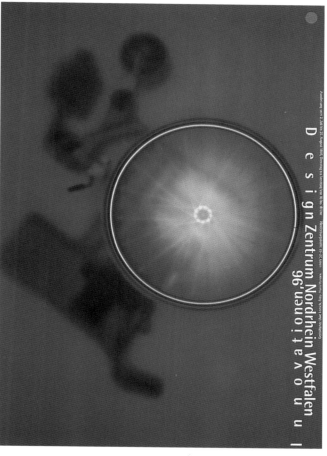

203 **UWE LOESCH** *MESSE DÜSSELDORF* □ 204 **UWE LOESCH** *DESIGN ZENTRUM NORDRHEIN* □ 205 **VIHERJUUREN ILME OY** *GRAFIA RY*
206 **RALPH SCHRAIVOGEL** *MUSEUM FÜR GESTALTUNG*

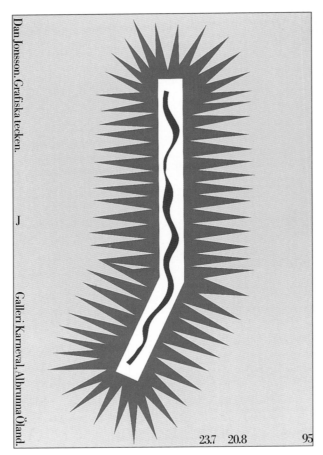

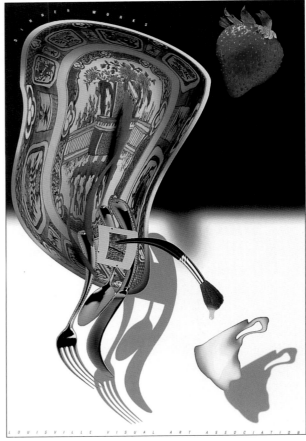

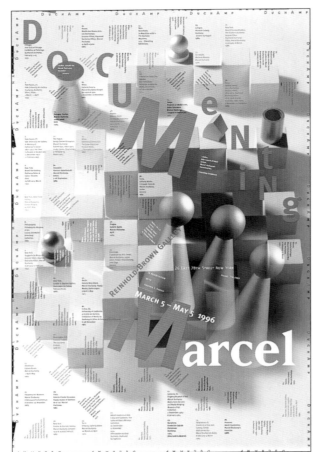

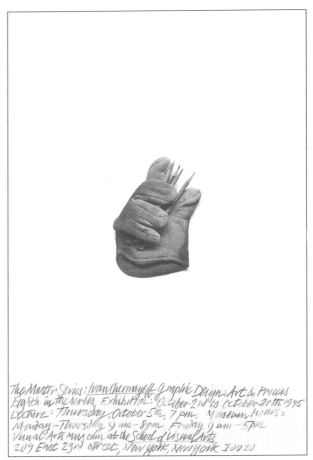

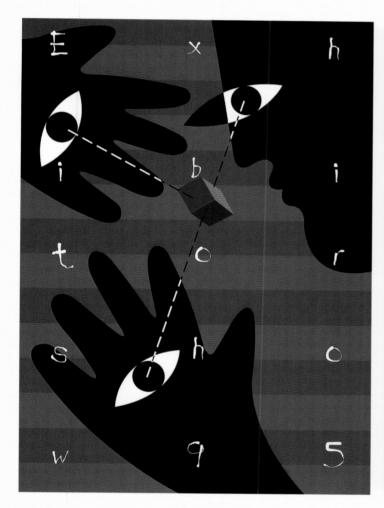

211 212

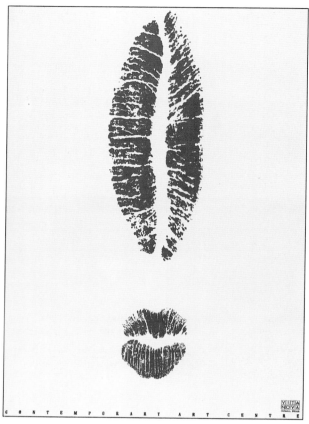

213 214

215 216

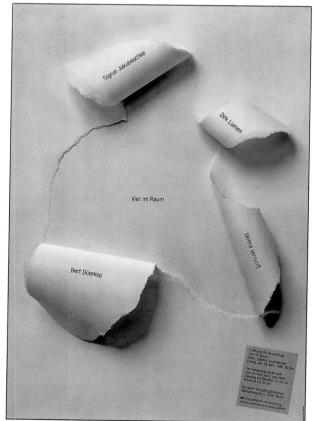

213 **PEPE GIMENO, S.L.** *GENERALITAT VALENCIA* □ 214 **ART STUDIO** *CONTEMPORARY ART CENTRE* □ 215 **FONS M. HICKMANN** *BAZON BROCK*
216 **ARMIN LINDAUER** *BERT DÜRKOP*

217

218

217 **LOGVIN DESIGN** *DESIGN ASSOCIATION of RUSSIA* □ 218 **VALERY VITER** *IN-HOUSE*

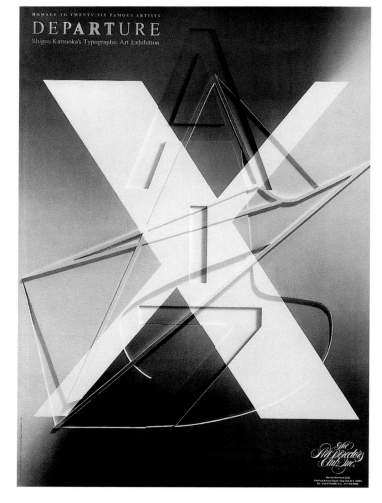

219 220

219, 220 **SHIGEO KATSUOKA DESIGN STUDIO** *IN-HOUSE*

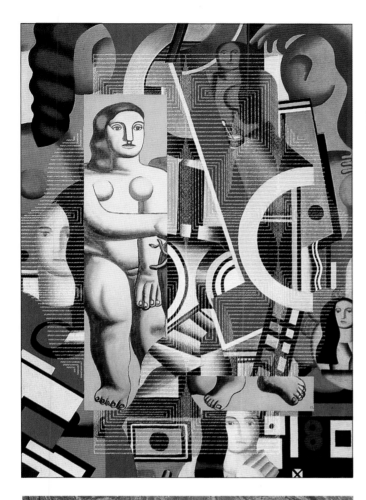

221 222

223 224

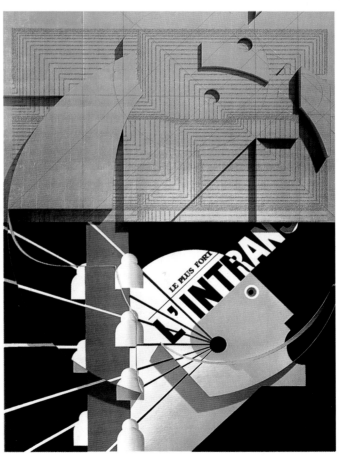

221-224 **SHIGEO KATSUOKA DESIGN STUDIO** *IN-HOUSE*

225
226
227

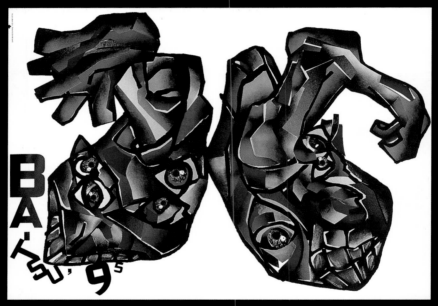

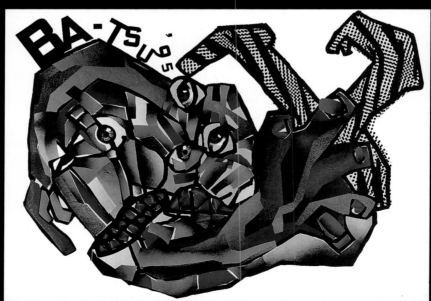

225-227 **MAKOTO SAITO DESIGN OFFICE INC.** BA-TSU COMPANY, LTD.

228 229

230

231

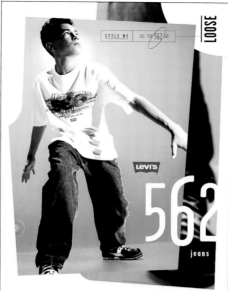

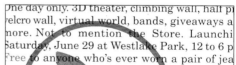

241 242

243 244

241 **MCCANN-ERICKSON INC.** *CASIO COMPUTER COMPANY, LTD.* □ 242 **KENZO IZUTANI OFFICE CORPORATION** *PARCO*
243, 244 **LEMON DESIGN** *SELF-PROMOTION*

245

246

245 **MAKOTO SAITO DESIGN OFFICE INC.** *Hawkins* □ 246 **URBAN OUTFITTERS** *In-house*

247 248 249

250 251 252

動機は、不純な方がうまくいく。

とりあえずだったら、欲しくない。

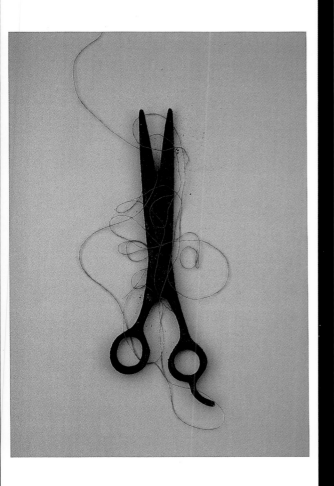

Nakayama co.,ltd.
#503, 3-6-24,
nishigotanda,
shinagawa-ku, Tokyo,
ZIP:141, Tel.03-3491-2590 Fax.03-3490-9307
Japan.

Nakayama co.,ltd.
#503, 3-6-24,
nishigotanda,
shinagawa-ku, Tokyo,
ZIP:141, Tel.03-3491-2590 Fax.03-3490-9307
Japan.

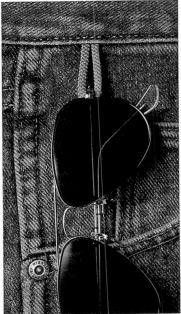

It's like a trailer hitch for your jeans.

If you're looking for a great pair of jeans, look for the loop. It's there to tell you that you've found the only jeans built specifically for the great outdoors.

Wrangler RUGGED WEAR

Geared For The Outdoors

All those in favor of Wrangler shirts, raise your hand.

Champion bull riders Ty Murray, Adam Carrillo, Ted Nuce, Charles Sampson and Jim Sharp know where to find the West's best shirts. Now you do, too.

The Western Original

In the military you are required to dress like the guy next to you. What's your excuse?

If you want to look like everyone around you, join a marching band.

An oxford shirt and chinos are fine. If you're into camouflage.

256-258 **R&D THE RICHARDS GROUP** *WEARABOUT*

IODICE BLUE JEANS

IODICE

ALPARGATAS SANTISTA

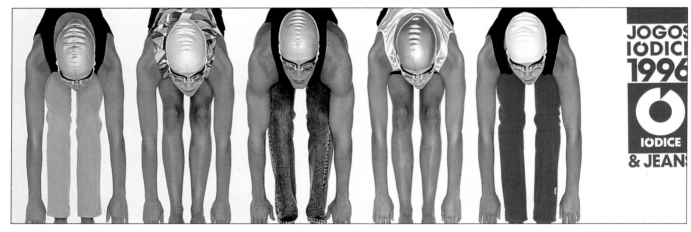

JOGOS IODICE 1996

IODICE & JEANS

IODICE BLUE JEANS

IODICE

ALPARGATAS SANTISTA

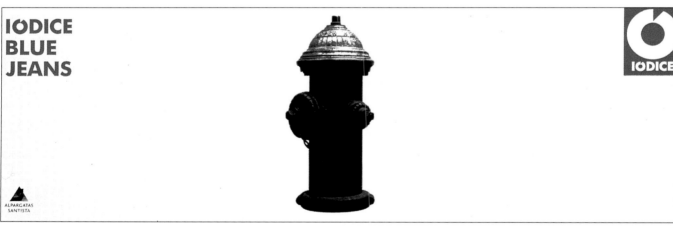

IODICE BLUE JEANS

IODICE

ALPARGATAS SANTISTA

259-262 **DDB NEEDHAM BRAZIL** *Valdemar Iódice*

IL TENNIS NON E' UNA .

Air Max' SPA.

SE SONO PESANTI SICURAMENTE HAI PESTATO QUALCOSA.

Air Max Uptempo.

UN ALTRO DONO DI MADRE NATURA.

Air Deschütz IV.

LE BUONE NOTIZIE CORRONO VELOCI.

Air Max Structure.

263 264

265 266

263-266 **MATITE GIOVANOTTE** *NIKE ITALY*

67 268

69 270

267 **SOMMESE DESIGN** *CENTRAL PENNSYLVANIA FESTIVAL OF THE ARTS* □ 268 **TRINITY DESIGN** *FESTIVAL INTERNATIONAL DE LOUISIANE*
269 **EMERY VINCENT DESIGN** *MELBOURNE INTERNATIONAL FESTIVAL OF THE ARTS* □ 270 **RADUF KARRAY** *CHAMBRE DE COMMERCE DE SFAX*

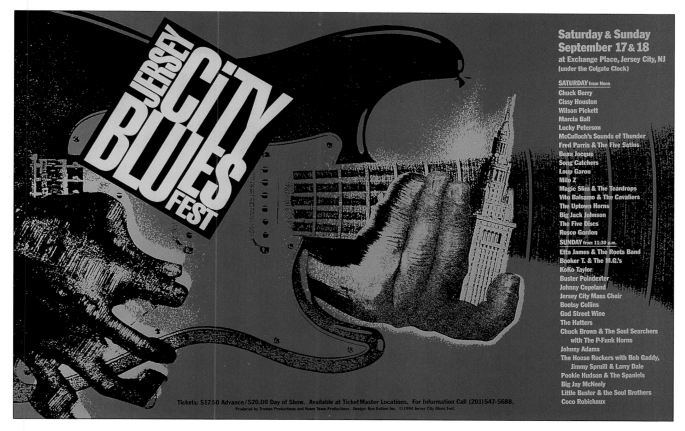

271 **S. TEAM BATES SAATCHI & SAATCHI ADVERTISING BALKANS** *Skopje Jazz Festival*
272 **RON KELLUM INC.** *Tramps Productions*

273 274

275 276

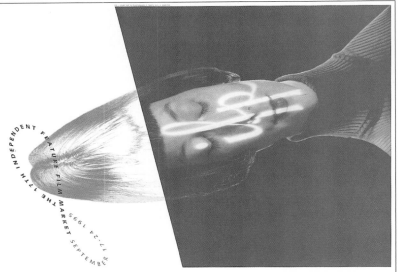

273 **BURT KLEEGER INC.** *MIRAMAX FILMS* ▫ 274 **SCHAUER & KOSCH GMBH** *TRANSIT FILM GMBH*
275 **FAHRENHEIT DESIGN PARTNERSHIP** *SHED FILMS* ▫ 276 **STUDIO XL** *IFP*

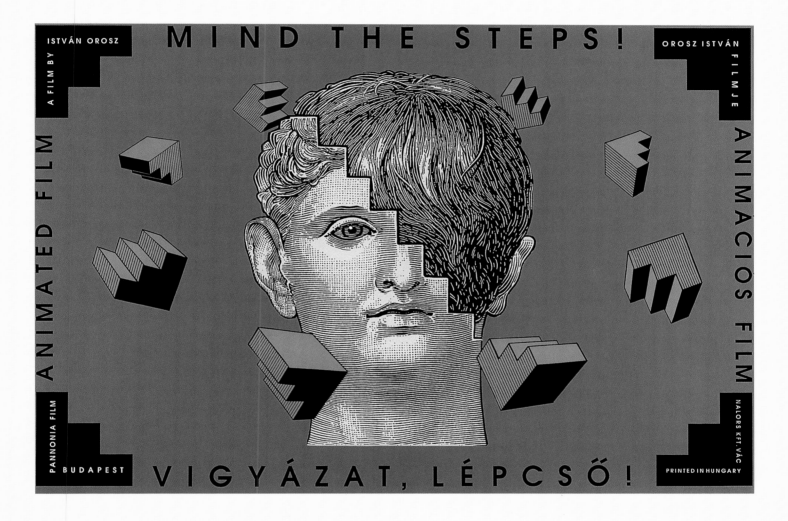

THE REELS OF
INDUSTRY

Rolling into action!

INDUSTRY PICTURES
641 WEST LAKE STREET, SUITE 100, CHICAGO
ILLINOIS 60661 312-648-0505 FAX 312-648-4220

SUSAN KINAST, DIRECTOR
BRIAN CLARE, DIRECTOR
CLIFF GRANT, EXECUTIVE PRODUCER
CANDACE GELMAN, REPRESENTATIVE

POTLATCH PRESENTS A FILM ABOUT THE WORLD'S GREATEST DESIGNER
A RIGHTEOUS PRODUCTION WRITTEN AND DIRECTED BY DANA ARNETT AND BOB RICE
STARRING KYLE COLERIDER-KRUGH PRODUCED BY KATHLEEN URSULA ROONEY MUSIC BY EVAN CHEN CASTING BY JANE BRODY
DIRECTOR OF PHOTOGRAPHY GARY KATZ EDITED BY SEAN BERRINGER POST PRODUCTION SUPERIOR STREET
Potlatch

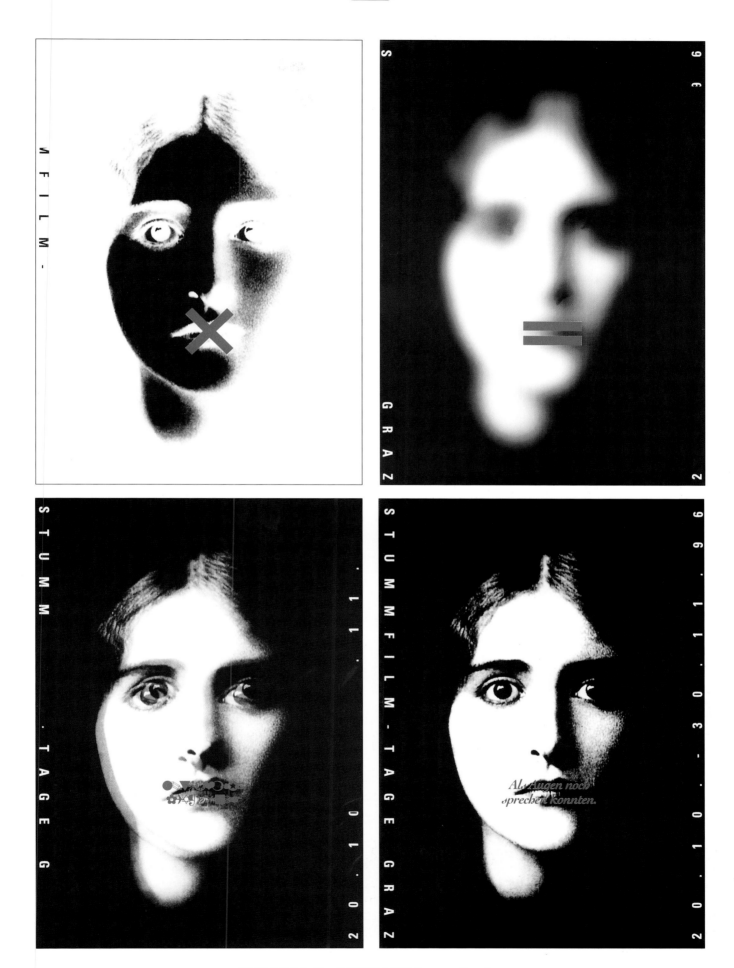

280-283 **FONS M. HICKMANN** *STUMMFILM-TAGE GRAZ*

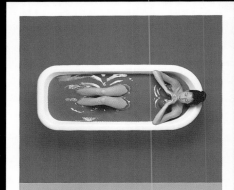

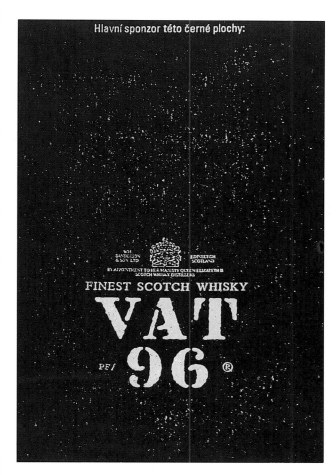

288 289

290 291

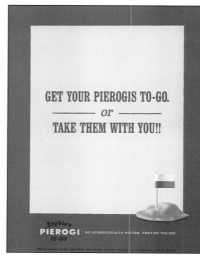

292 293 294

295 296 297

298 299 300

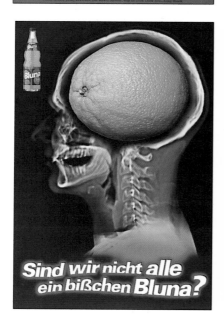

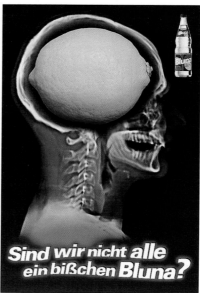

292-294 **HORNALL ANDERSON DESIGN WORKS, INC.** *Jamba Juice*
295-297 **MCCONNAUGHY STEIN SCHMIDT BROWN** *Sophie's Perogis To-Go*
298 **JUNG VON MATT WERBEAGENTUR** *Mineralbrunnen AG* □ 299 **TURNER DUCKWORTH** *McKenzie River Corporation*
300 **JUNG VON MATT WERBEAGENTUR** *Mineralbrunnen AG*

Fresh Herbs CULINARY

Herbs provided by *HerbThyme Farms* · 415.952.4372   ✂   Poster published by *Celestial Arts*, P.O. Box 7123, Berkeley, California 94707 · 510.559.1600   ✂   Photographed & composed by *Larry Kunkel*, San Francisco

301 **LARRY KUNKEL** *Celestial Arts*

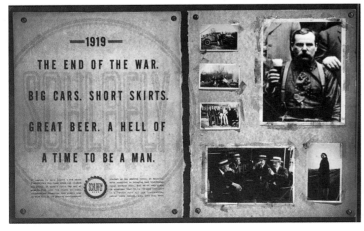

302-304 **CORE/R&D/THE RICHARDS GROUP** *Schlafly* □ 305-307 **DPZ PROPAGANDA** *Palace Brands*

308 309

310 311

312 313

314-316 **HEYE & PARTNER** *BAD BRAMBACHER MINERALQUELLEN* □ 317 **ALMAP/BBDO** *MILLER CO.* □ 318 **ALMAP/BBDO** *PEPSICO & CO.*
319 **ALMAP/BBDO** *MILLER CO.*

320 321

322 323

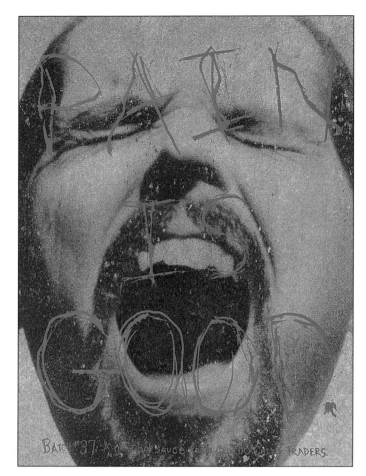

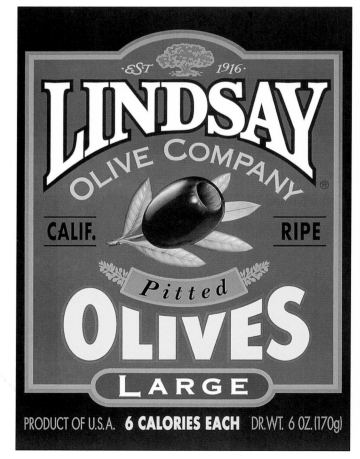

320, 321 **CORE / R & D / THE RICHARDS GROUP** *Calido Chili Traders*
322 **MONNENS-ADDIS DESIGN** *Bell-Carter Foods Inc.* □ 323 **PULSAR ADVERTISING** *Lulu's Dessert Factory*

French wine that doesn't cost a bomb.

326

327

328

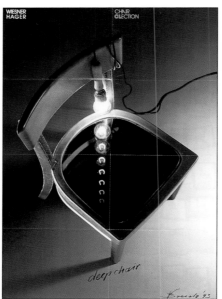

326 **BANG BANG BANG** *Table Lamp & Chair* ▢ 327-328 **PILGER HARDEN** *Wiesner Hager Möbel Gmbh*

FURNITURE

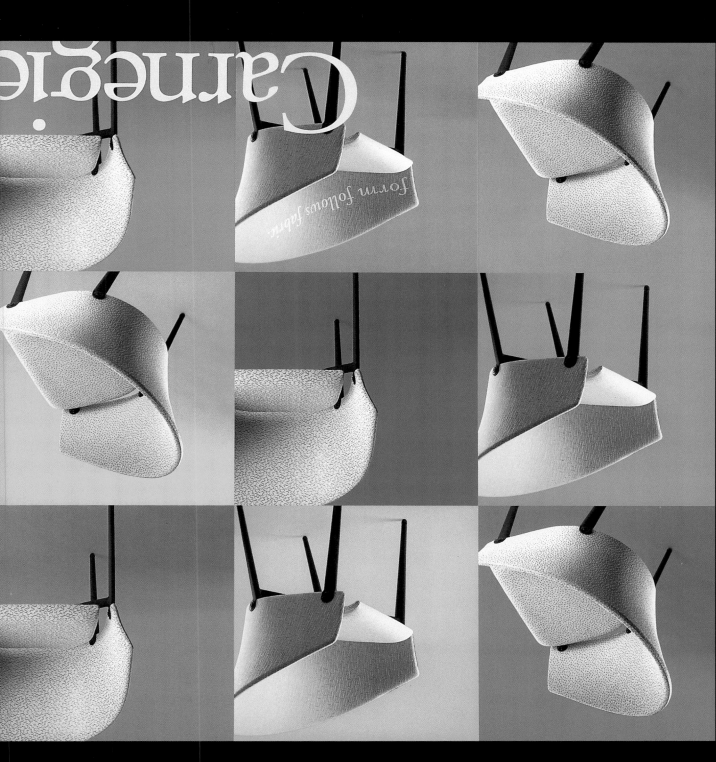

Carnegie

Form follows fabric.

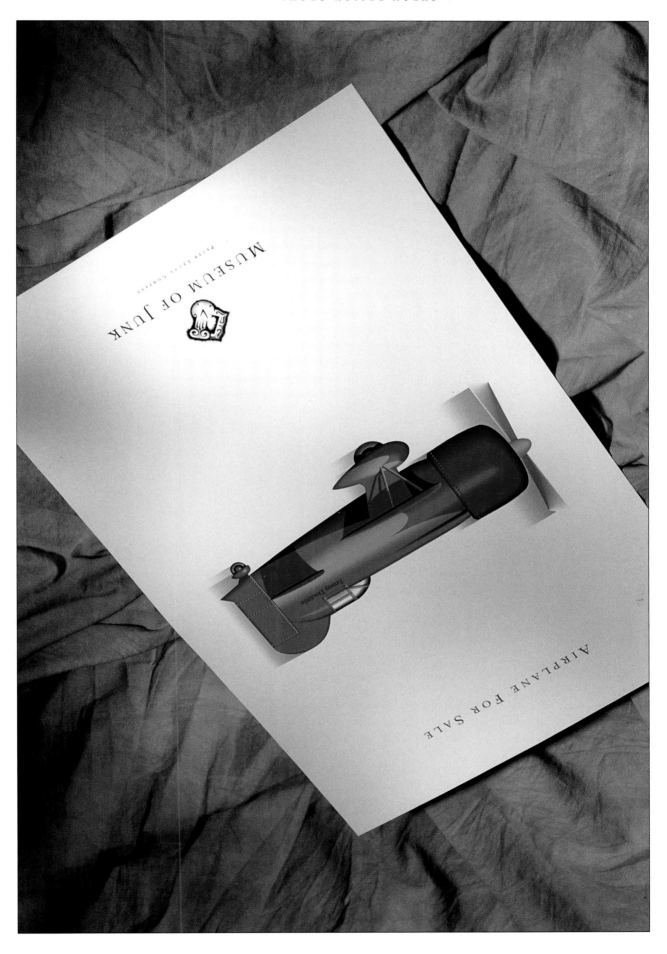

Ernst Leitz, Wetzlar · Leica IIf · 1951–56

335 336

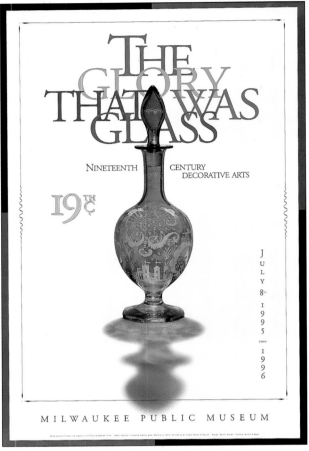

337 338

339 340

337 **MORLA DESIGN, INC.** *BACCUS PRESS* □ 338 **BECKER DESIGN** *MILWAUKEE PUBLIC MUSEUM* □
339 **CDT DESIGN LIMITED** *DESIGN MUSEUM* □ 340 **STAWICKI** *KÜNSTLER FUR ARTENSCHUTZ*

341

341 **UWE LOESCH** *RUHRLANDMUSEUM ESSEN*

342 **ART STUDIO** *Liniagrafic* □ 343 **BRUCE HALE DESIGN** *Seattle Symphony*

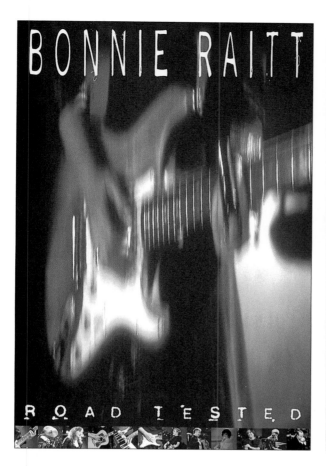

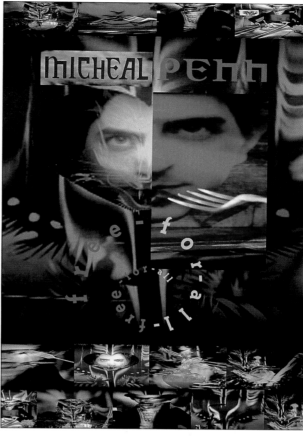

344 345

346 347

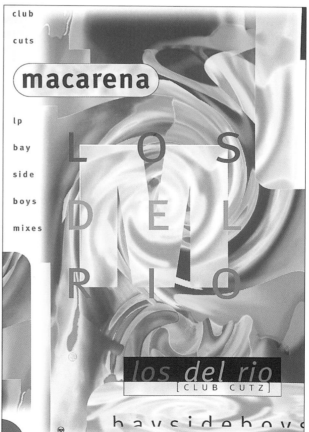

344 **DESIGN/ART, INC.** CAPITOL RECORDS □ 345 **DESIGN/ART, INC.** RCA RECORDS □ 346 **DESIGN/ART, INC.** A&M RECORDS
347 **DESIGN/ART, INC.** RCA RECORDS

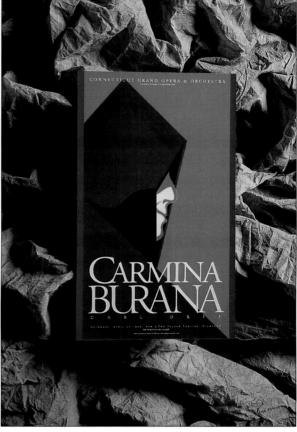

348 349

350 351

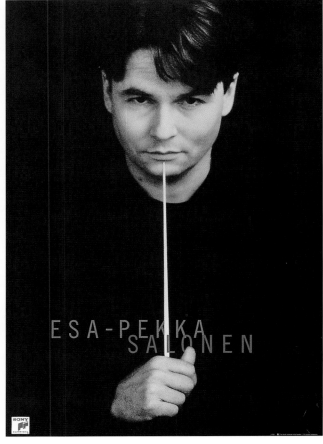

354 355

356 357

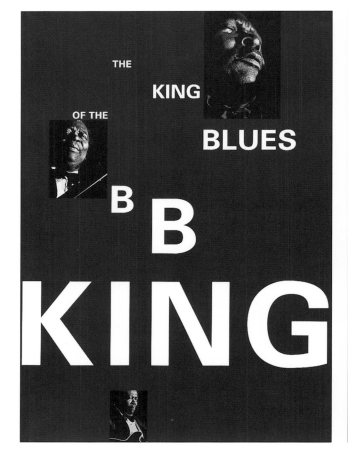

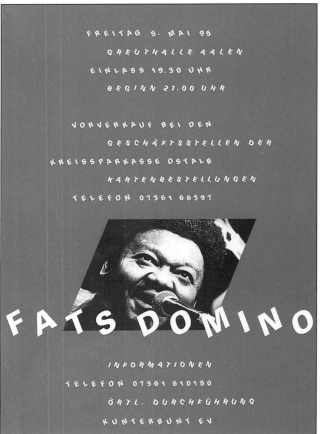

354 **MIRKO ILIC CORP.** *HELIDON* □ 355 **SONY MUSIC** *IN-HOUSE* □ 356 **CAPITOL RECORDS** *IN-HOUSE*
357 **BÜRO FÜR GESTALTUNG, KOMMUNIKATION UND KULTUR** *GKP*

358

359

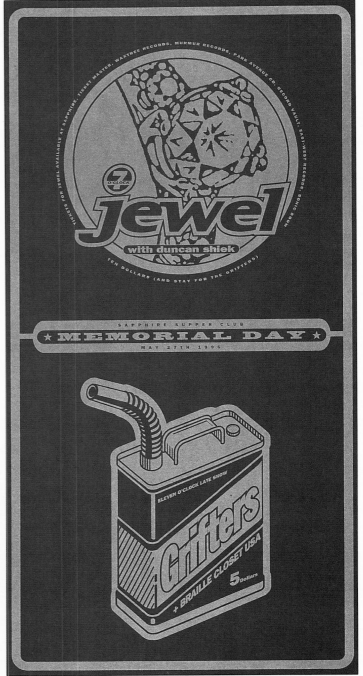

360 361

360 **JEFF & MIKE** *SELF-PROMOTION* □ 361 **LARKIN MEEDER & SCHWEIDEL** *FIGUREHEAD*

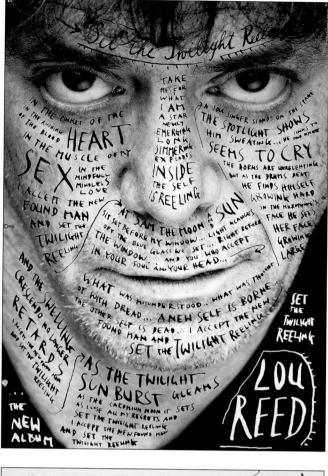

362 **KENZO IZUTANI OFFICE CORPORATION** *YOUGEY INC.* □ 363 **SAGMEISTER INC.** *LOU REED/WARNER BROTHERS*
364 **BESSER JOSEPH PARTNERS** *NATIONAL RESOPHONIC GUITARS* □ 365 **SANDSTROM DESIGN** *KINK RADIO*

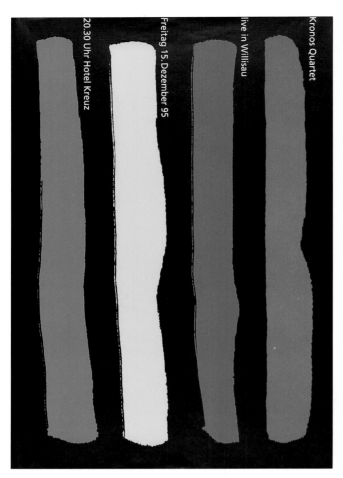

366, 367 **NIKLAUS TROXLER GRAFIK STUDIO** *Jazz in Willisau* □ 368 **ST. HIERONYMUS PRESS INC.** *Napa Valley Wine Auction*
369 **ST. HIERONYMUS PRESS, INC.** *Berkeley Symphony Orchestra*

370

371

372
373
374

372 **GAUGER & SILVA** *COMMERCIAL BANK OF SAN FRANCISCO* □ 373, 374 **MITHOFF ADVERTISING INC.** *HANLEY PAINT MANUFACTURING CO., INC.*

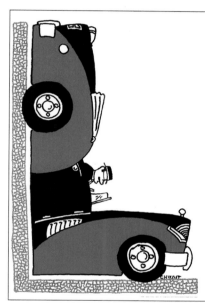

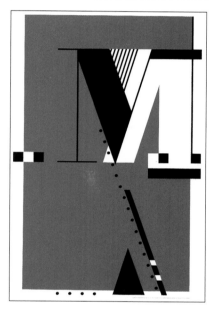

375 376 377

378 379 380

381 382 383

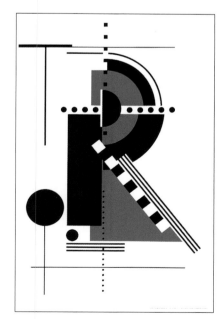

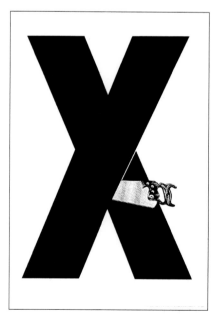

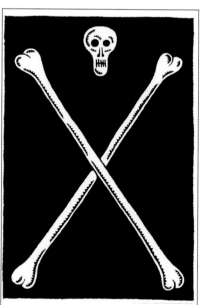

375-383 **PENTAGRAM DESIGN INC.** *Ambassador Arts Inc./Champion*

384 385

386 387

384 **PACKAGING CREATE INC.** *Musa Co., Ltd.* □ 385 **PACKAGING CREATE INC.** *Oji Paper Co., Ltd.*
386 **CHARLES S. ANDERSON DESIGN COMPANY** *French Paper Company* □ 387 **EXECUTIVE ARTS** *Potlatch Corp.*

388 389

390 391

388-391 **IWAO MATSUURA DESIGN OFFICE CO., LTD.** *Takeo Co., Ltd.*

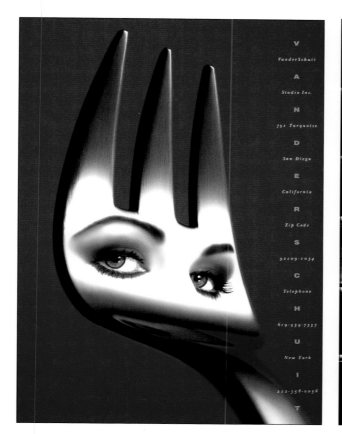

V
A
N
D
E
R
S
C
H
U
I
T

VanderSchuit
Studio Inc.

751 Turquoise

San Diego

California

Zip Code

92109-1034

Telephone

619-539-7337

New York

212-358-0056

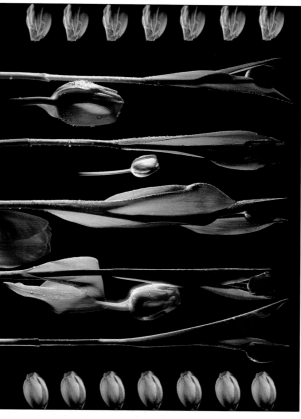

394 395

396 397

394 **MIRES DESIGN** *Vanderschuit Studio* □ 395 **FOTOSTUDIO ZIMMERMANN** *In-house*
396, 397 **GOULD DESIGN** *Wace USA / The Etheridge Company*

[SUNFLOWERS IN AUTUMN] PHOTOGRAPHED BY ALAN R. EPSTEIN
PRINTED BY MAGNANI & McCORMICK, INC. ON A WATERLESS PRESS
DESIGNED BY HANS TEENSMA / IMPRESS, INC. [ ]

[TULIPS IN WINTER] PHOTOGRAPHED BY ALAN R. EPSTEIN
PRINTED BY MAGNANI & McCORMICK, INC. ON A WATERLESS PRESS
DESIGNED BY HANS TEENSMA / IMPRESS, INC. [ ]

[ANEMONES IN SPRING] PHOTOGRAPHED BY ALAN R. EPSTEIN
PRINTED BY MAGNANI & McCORMICK, INC. ON A WATERLESS PRESS
DESIGNED BY HANS TEENSMA / IMPRESS, INC. [ ]

398 399 400

401 402 403

398-400 **IMPRESS INC.** *MAGNANI & McCORMICK* □ 401-403 **TBWA** *NIKON/DFA*

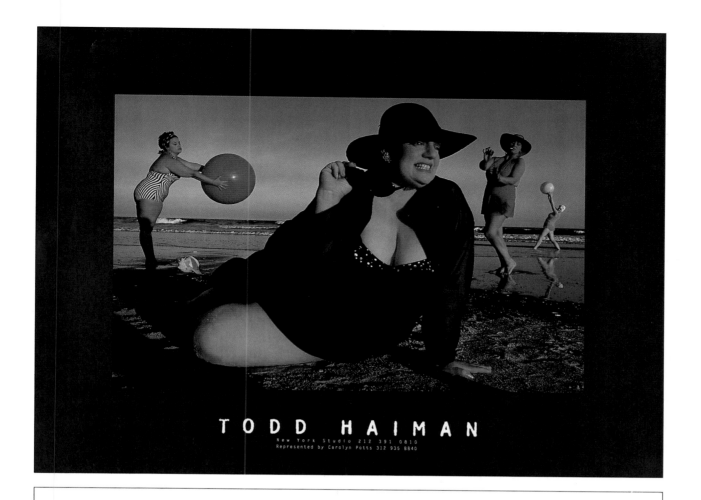

404 **TODD HAIMAN STUDIO** *SELF-PROMOTION* □ 405 **RIKKI CONRAD** *WILLIAM THOMPSON*

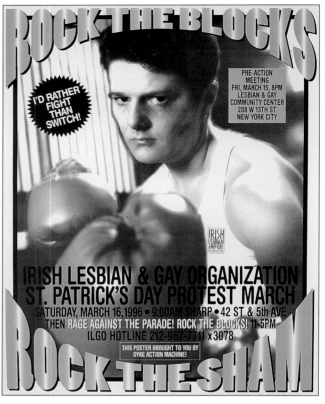

406 407

408 409

I'M HERE 1995
HIROSHIMA NAGASAKI 50

410

410 **CID LAB** *JAPAN GRAPHIC DESIGNERS ASSOCIATION*

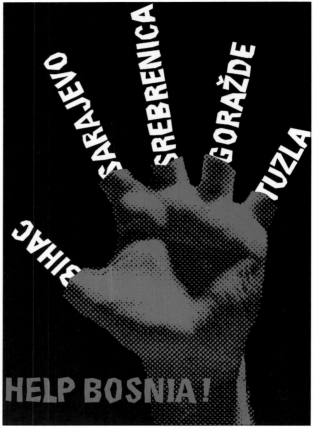

411 412

413 414

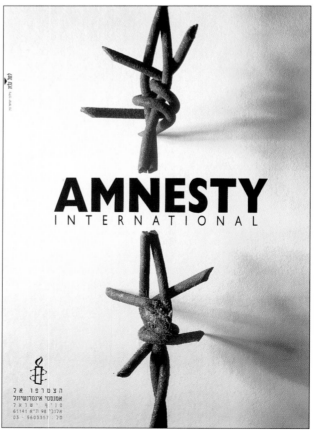

411 **LAURIE ANN MEGHAN MURPHY** □ 412 **FONS M. HICKMANN** *In-house* □ 413 **LEMEL GLAZER** *In-house*
414 **LEMEL GLAZER** *Amnesty International*

WE ARE THE AIDS CRISIS GENERATION

.Happy NEW Fear.

PROGRESS HAITI

Nouvelles perspectives pour l'éducation   Annou vance pou pi devan
Un pas vers l'avenir

415

416

417

415 **NAGAISHI OFFICE** *FM FUKUOKA* □ 416 **TARTAKOVER DESIGN** *SELF-PROMOTION*
417 **EMERSON WAJDOWICZ STUDIOS** *UNITED NATIONS OFFICE FOR PROJECT SERVICES*

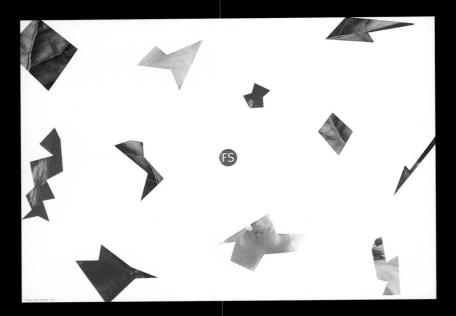

418

419

420

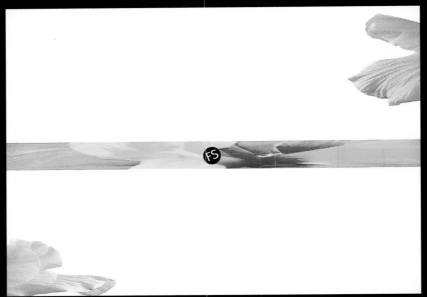

418-420 **FINN NYGAARD GRAPHIC DESIGN** *FS-Tryk*

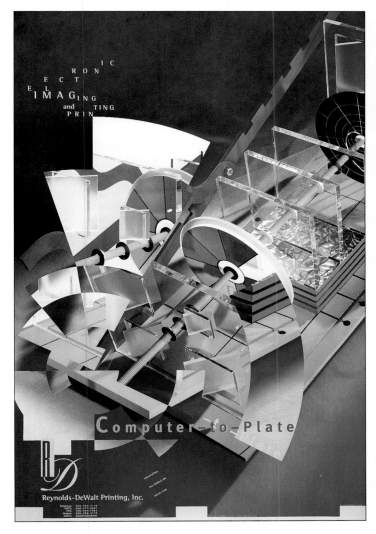

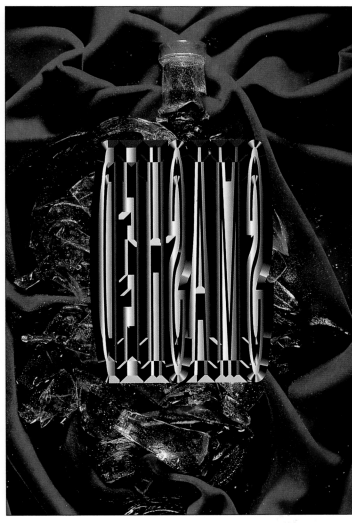

421 422

BLACK is Beautiful

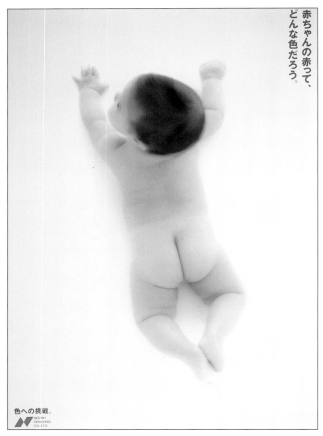

赤ちゃんの赤って、
どんな色だろう。

色への挑戦。

423 424

425 426

If the annual's late, the relationship's expired. We get it. Williamson Printing.

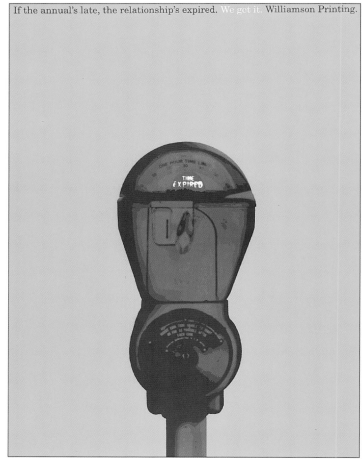

LiniaGrafic!

БЕЗ ЭТИКЕТКИ
ГРУСТНО!

423, 424 **MAGNA INC. ADVERTISING** *Nishiki Printing Co., Ltd.*
425 **THE RICHARDS GROUP** *Williamson Printing* □ 426 **LOGVIN DESIGN** *Liniagrafik Print Company*

429

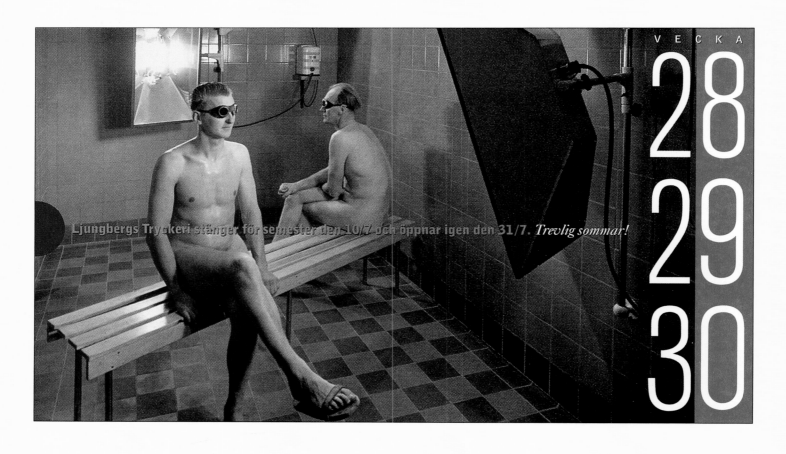

Ljungbergs Tryckeri stänger för semester den 10/7 och öppnar igen den 31/7. *Trevlig sommar!*

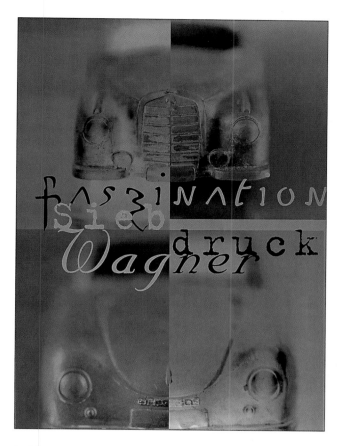

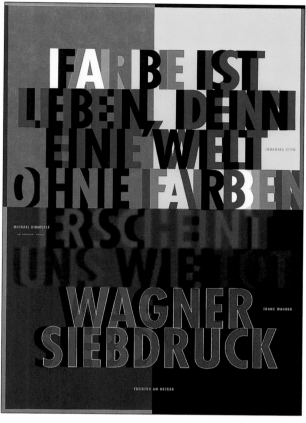

430 431

432 433

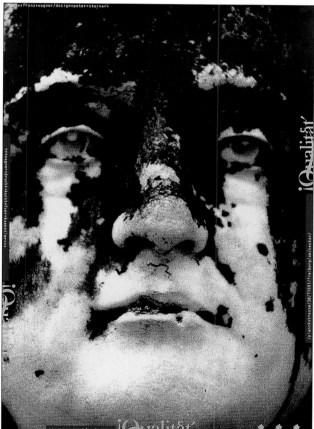

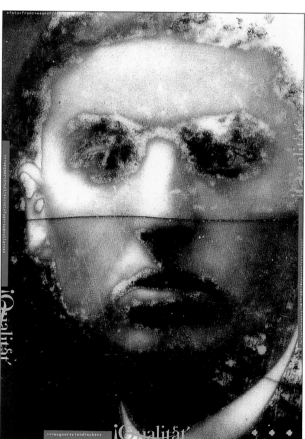

430-433 **WAGNER SIEBDRUCK GMBH** *In-house*

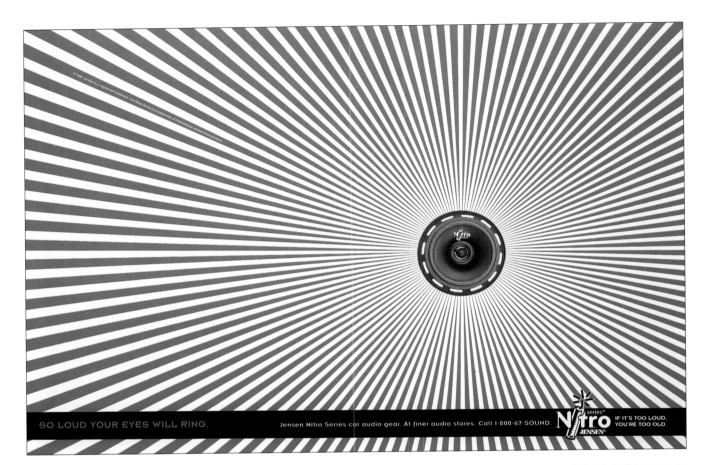

 434

435

434, 435 **HOFFMAN YORK & COMPTON** *JENSEN*

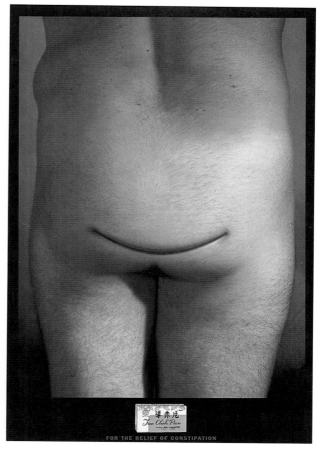

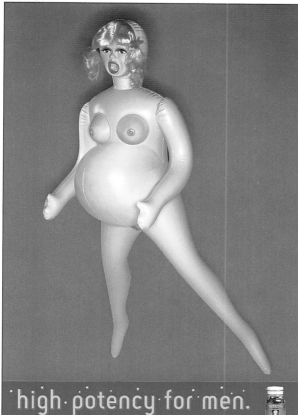

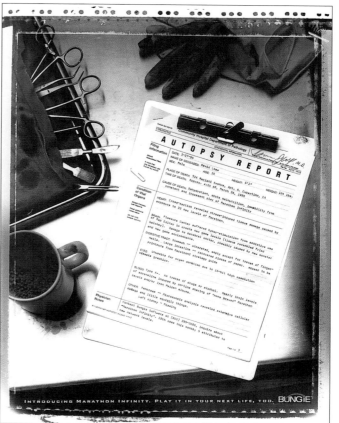

436 437

438 439

436 **CRISPIN & PORTER ADVERTISING** *Shimano American* □ 437 **BATEY ADS SINGAPORE** *Fei Fah Drug Store*
438 **BATEY ADS SINGAPORE** *The Jamu Centre* □ 439 **McCONNAUGHY STEIN SCHMIDT BROWN** *Bungie Software*

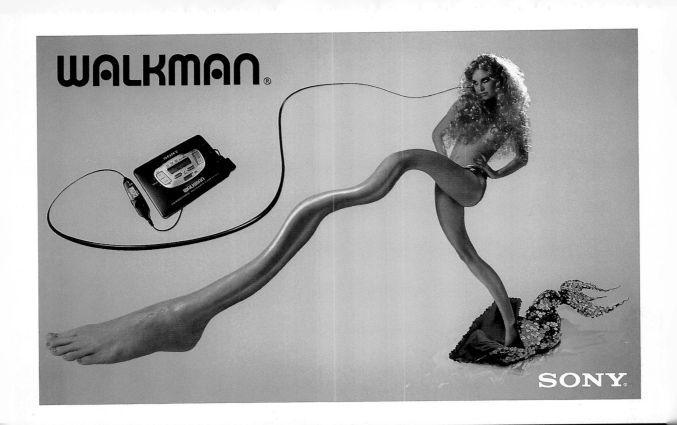

446 447

446 **VICTORE DESIGN WORKS** *Earth Day* □ 447 **STUDIO GIANNI BORTOLOTTI & C. SAS** *ANEP*

448

Most animal shelters really are humane. They put the animals to sleep before they incinerate them.

SOCIETY OF ST. FRANCIS ● NO-KILL ANIMAL SHELTER

Sadly, other shelters are forced to dispose of more than 70% of their cats and dogs. But with your help, we can provide an alternative. To adopt a pet or make a donation, call 414-657-7280. And remember to spay or neuter your pets.

Only 3 out of 10 animals from most shelters are placed in homes. The rest are placed here.

SOCIETY OF ST. FRANCIS ● NO-KILL ANIMAL SHELTER

More than 70% of the cats and dogs that enter shelters are killed. At ours, the figure is 0%. If you'd like to adopt a pet or make a donation, please call 414-657-7280. And remember to spay or neuter your pets.

Our shelter operates a little differently than others. For starters, we don't kill animals and toss them in incinerators.

SOCIETY OF ST. FRANCIS ● NO-KILL ANIMAL SHELTER

Seven out of ten cats and dogs that enter most shelters are killed. But not ours. If you'd like to help put an end to the mass slaughter, call us to adopt a pet or make a donation. 414-657-7280. And remember to spay or neuter your pets.

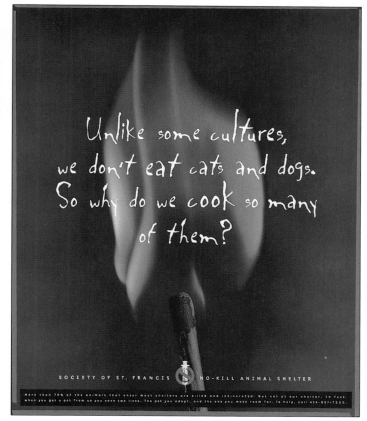

Unlike some cultures, we don't eat cats and dogs. So why do we cook so many of them?

SOCIETY OF ST. FRANCIS ● NO-KILL ANIMAL SHELTER

More than 70% of the animals that enter most shelters are killed and incinerated. But not at our shelter. In fact, when you get a pet from us you save two lives. The pet you adopt, and the one you make room for. To help, call 414-657-7280.

449 450

451 452

449-452 **CRAMER KRASSELT** *Society of St. Francis*

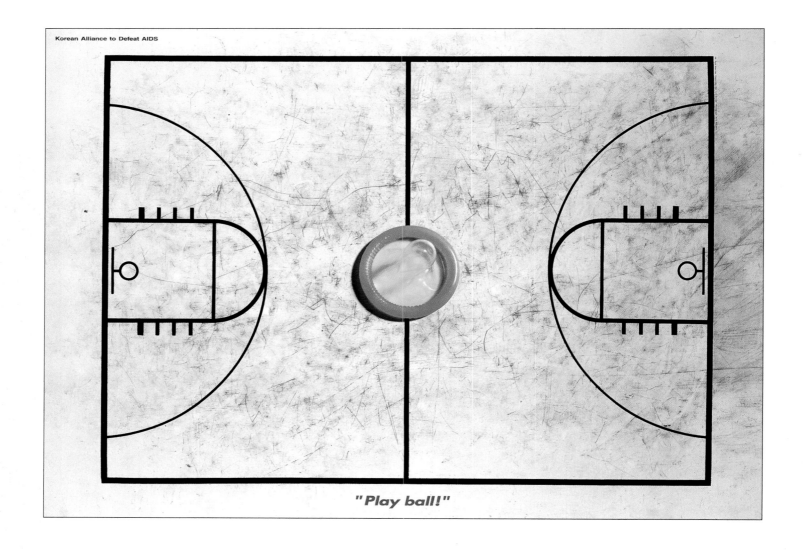

Korean Alliance to Defeat AIDS

"Play ball!"

453

453 **CHEIL COMMUNICATIONS INC.** *KOREAN ALLIANCE to DEFEAT AIDS*
(OPPOSITE) 454-457 **AFTER HOURS CREATIVE** *GAY MEN'S SEX PROJECT*

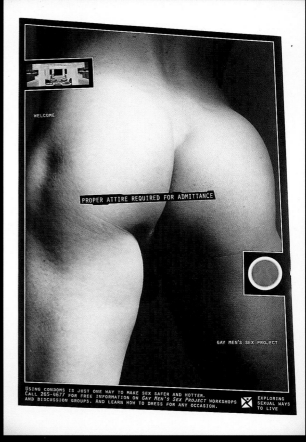

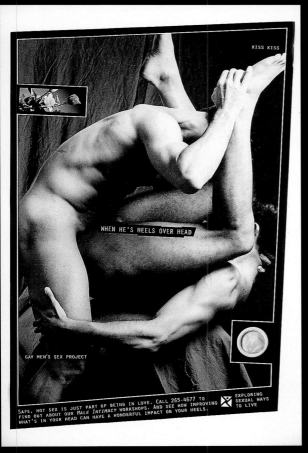

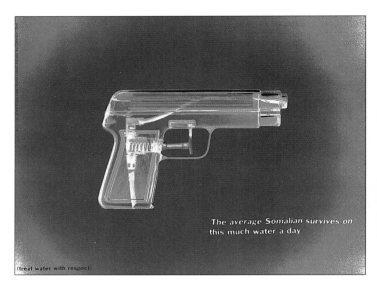

The average Somalian survives on
this much water a day

(treat water with respect)

In the next 30 years,
our available water supply
will run out.

(treat water with respect)

458 459

460 461

THIS IS HOW MANY SAFETY
REGULATIONS OUR GOVERNMENT
IMPOSES ON THE PRODUCT
THAT KILLS OVER 5,000
AMERICAN CHILDREN A YEAR.

There's not a single federal standard governing the safety of one of the most dangerous products made. It's time for our laws to start protecting children, instead of protecting guns.

CEASE FIRE
Children's Defense Fund and Friends

FOR MORE INFORMATION CALL 1-800-CDF-1200.

BY YOUR CHILD'S
FIRST YEAR, SHE
CAN SQUEEZE
YOUR FINGER WITH
SEVEN POUNDS
OF PRESSURE.
APPROXIMATELY THE
SAME AMOUNT NEEDED
TO SQUEEZE THE
TRIGGER OF A GUN.

Every year, hundreds of children accidentally shoot themselves or someone else. So if you get a gun to protect your child, what's going to protect your child from the gun?

CEASE FIRE
Children's Defense Fund and Friends

FOR MORE INFORMATION CALL 1-800-CDF-1200.

458, 459 **BATEY ADS SINGAPORE** *ASIAN PALS OF THE PLANET* ☐ 460, 461 **FALLON MCELLIGOTT** *CEASE FIRE*

CONGRATULATIONS. YOU'VE JUST
BROUGHT MORE VIOLENCE INTO YOUR HOME
THAN ABC, CBS, AND NBC COMBINED.

Bringing a gun into your home increases the chance of a gun death almost 300%. Which means instead of watching the evening news, you could be on it.   **CEASE FIRE**
Children's Defense Fund   and Friends

FOR MORE INFORMATION CALL 1-800-CDF-1200.

462 **BATEY ADS SINGAPORE** *ASIAN PALS OF THE PLANET*   □   463 **FALLON MCELLIGOTT** *CHILDREN'S DEFENSE FUND*

464 *465*

464 **KEILER & CO** *CONNECTICUT ART DIRECTORS CLUB* □ 465 **ANNE-METTE HANSEN** *RADET FÜR STÜRRE FAERDSELSSIKKERHED*

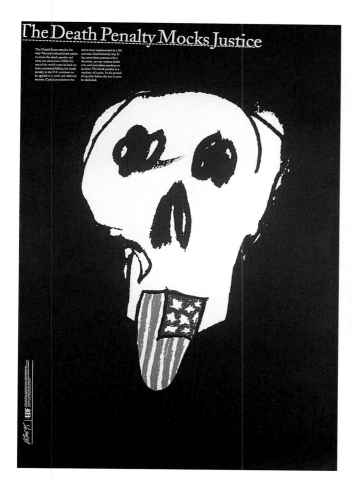

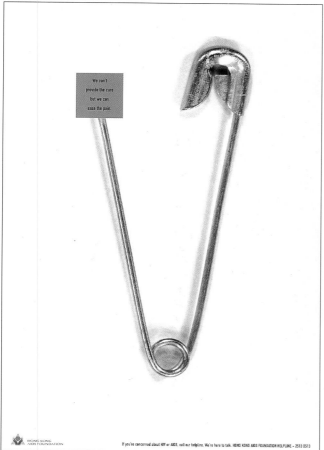

466   VICTORE DESIGN WORKS *NAACP/LDF* □ 467 HOMAYOUN MAHMOUDI
468 BBDO HONG KONG LTD. *Hong Kong AIDS Foundation* □ 469 TADANORI YOKOO *Jagda*

FOREST ≠ FOREVER

NO EVERLASTING STORY. NO EXCEPTIONS. FOR THE FOREST OR FOR US HUMAN BEINGS.

Creature of the War.

470 471

472 473

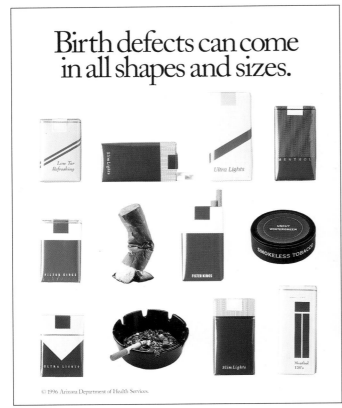

Birth defects can come in all shapes and sizes.

© 1996 Arizona Department of Health Services.

© 1996 Arizona Department of Health Services.

470, 471 **DENTSU Y&R** □ 472, 473 **RIESTER CORP.** *ARIZONA DEPARTMENT OF HEALTH SERVICES*

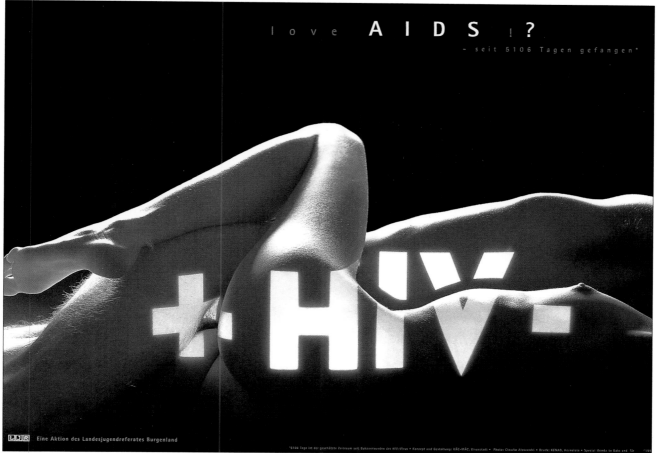

474, 475 **CLAUDIO ALESSANDRI GMBH** *AIDS HILFE AUSTRIA*

474
475

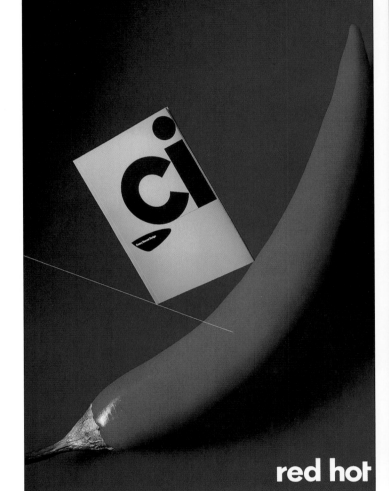

red hot

476 **EMERY VINCENT DESIGN** *SELF-PROMOTION* □ 477 **MAELSTROM STUDIOS** *MARVEL COMICS*

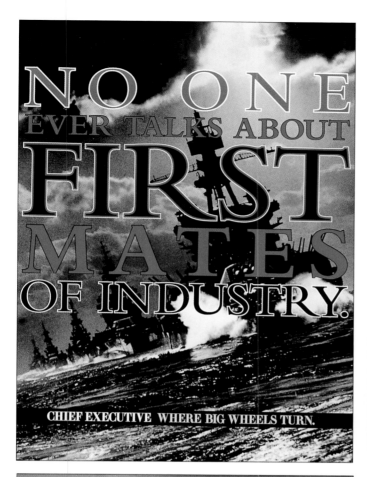

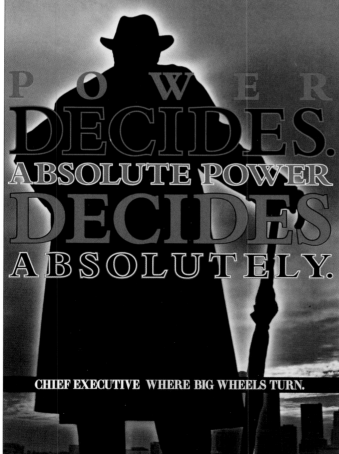

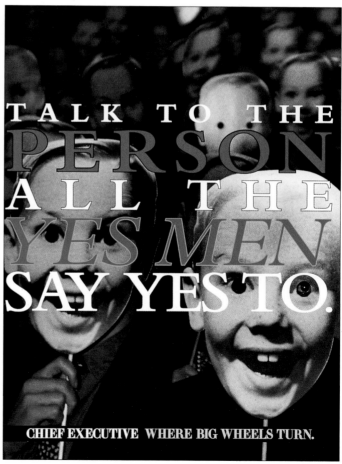

478-481 **MCCANN AMSTER YARD** *CHIEF EXECUTIVE MAGAZINE*

482

483 484

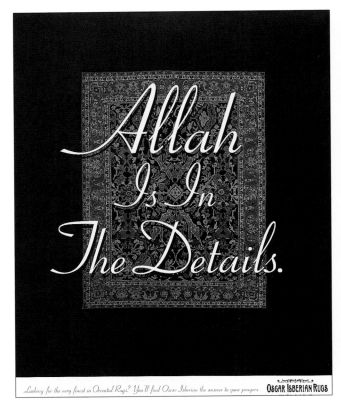

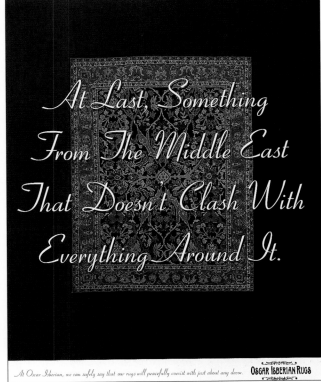

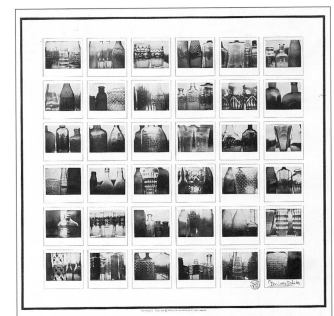

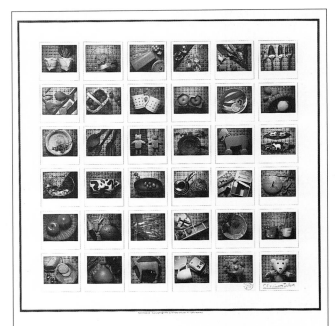

489
490
491

489-491 **CREATEAM WERBEAGENTUR GMBH & CO. KG** *PlusCity Betriebs Gmbh*

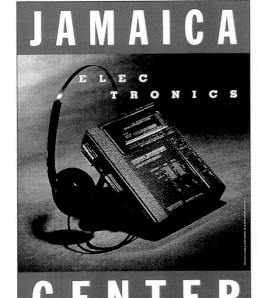

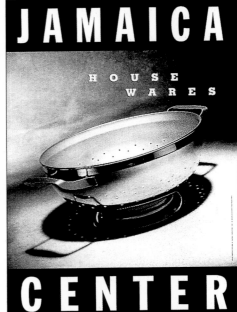

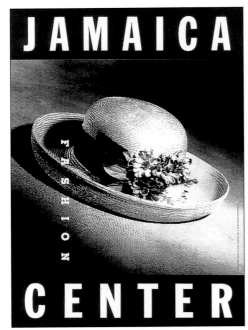

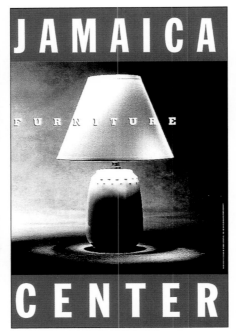

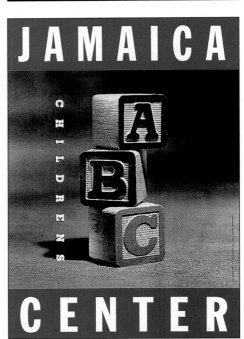

492 493 494

495 496 497

492-497 **ADAM GREISS DESIGN** *JAMAICA CENTER IMPROVEMENT ASSOCIATION*

THIS IS THE BOWL THAT WAITS ON THE CHEST
that LIES BY the COUCH that RESTS ON the FLOOR
OF OUR NEW DESIGN STORE
that OPENS MARCH 2ND IN BURLINGAME.

POTTERYBARN

THIS IS THE FAN THAT STIRS THE DRAPE
that COOLS THE SHEET that BRUSHES THE FLOOR
OF OUR NEW DESIGN STORE
that OPENS ON JUNE 1ST IN SHORT HILLS.

POTTERYBARN

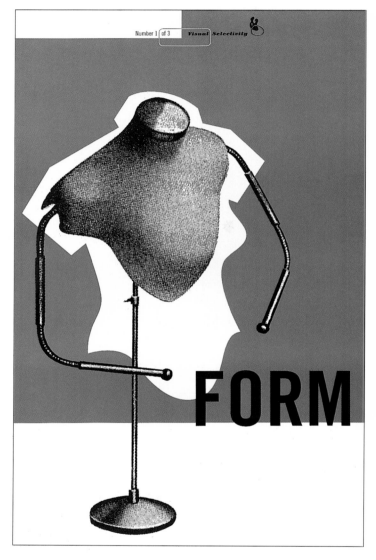

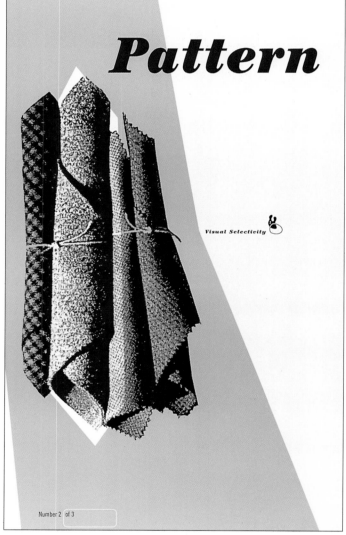

500 501

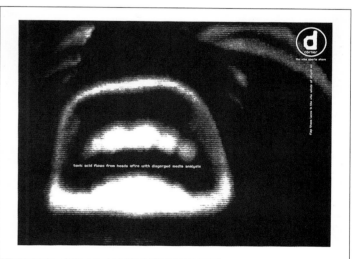

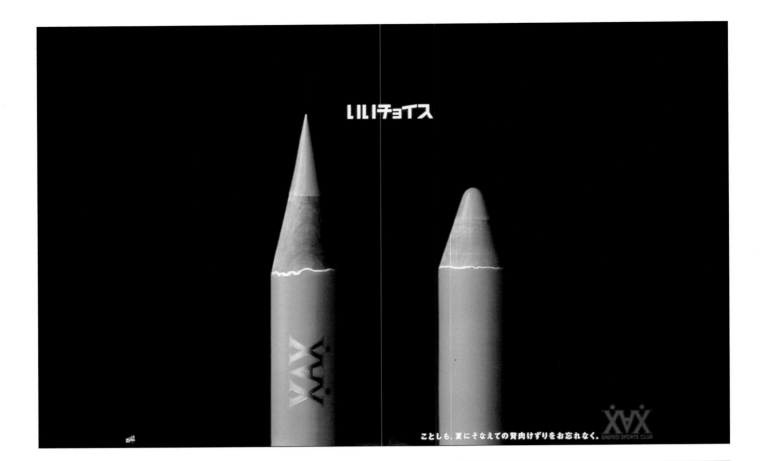

508
509

508, 509 **MCCANN-ERICKSON INC.** PEOPLE CO., LTD.

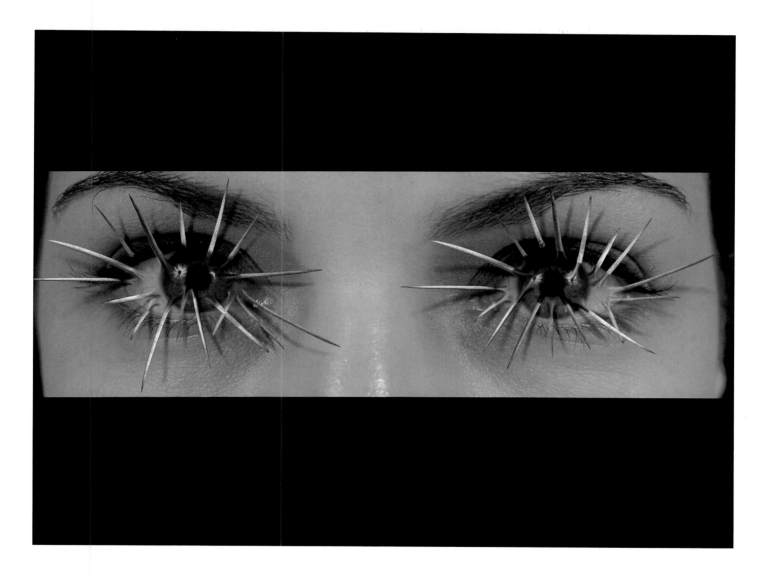

510

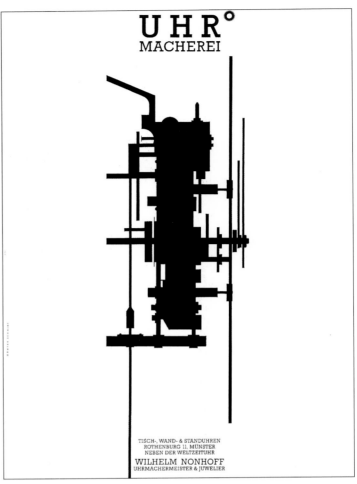

511 512

513 514

511, 512 **GÜNTER SCHMIDT** *Wilhelm Nonhoff* □ 513, 514 **BATEY ADS SINGAPORE** *Dotty's*

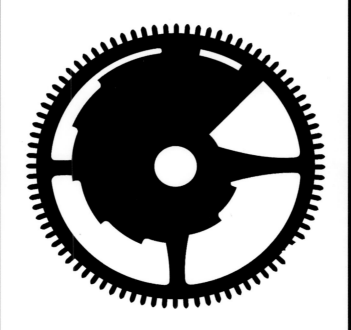

517

Service With A Smile.   Harris Design, Inc.; Integrated Marketing Communications, Graphic Design, Interactive Multimedia • 302-234-5700

517 **HARRIS DESIGN, INC.** *IN-HOUSE*

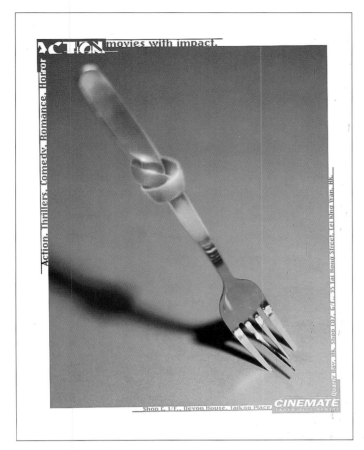

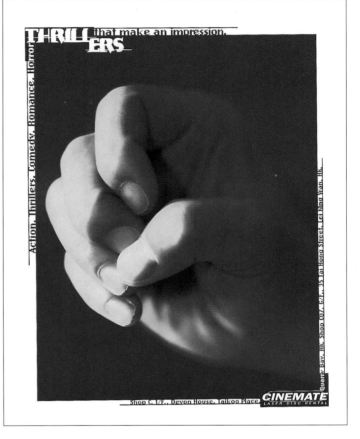

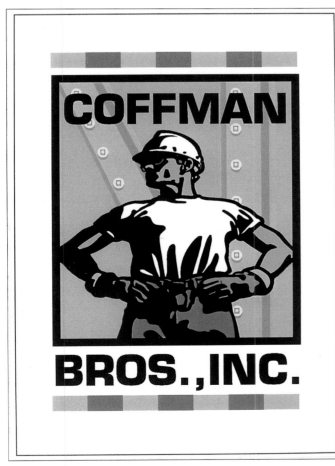

518, 519 **EURO RSCG BALL PARTNERSHIP** *Cinemate* □ 520 **SOLOMON TURNER ADVERTISING** *Coffman Brothers Inc.*
521 **BARKLEY & EVERGREEN** *Le Petite Academy*

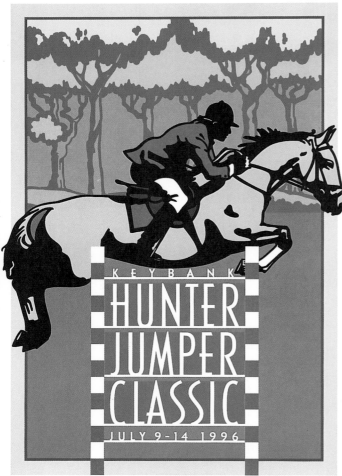

KEYBANK
HUNTER
JUMPER
CLASSIC
JULY 9-14 1996

Featuring the $30,000 KeyBank Cleveland Grand Prix, July 14, 2:00 pm
Chagrin Metropark Polo Field, Route 87 & Chagrin River Road, Moreland Hills, Ohio   216.834.1117

PERKINS SHEARER
11TH ANNUAL
POLO CUP

HIGHLANDS RANCH

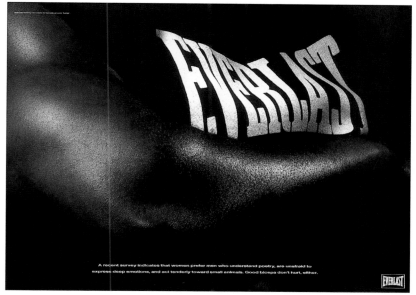

524

525

526

524-526 **GOLDSMITH/JEFFREY** *EVERLAST*

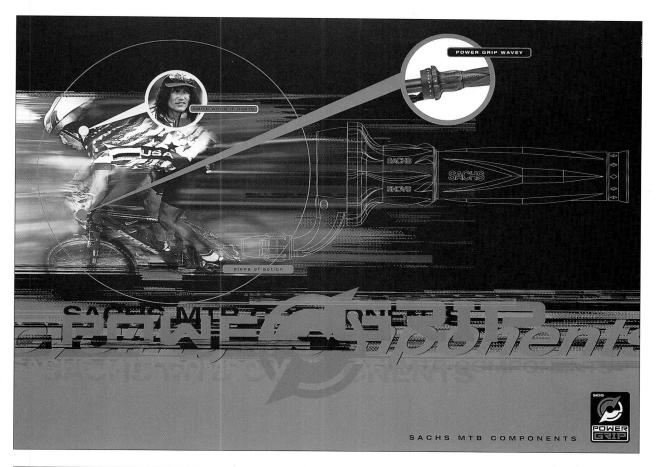

SACHS MTB COMPONENTS

Life's little pleasures.

529 **STUBENRAUCH & SIMON** *FICHTEL & SACHS* □ 530 **CARMICHAEL LYNCH** *SCHWINN*

531 532

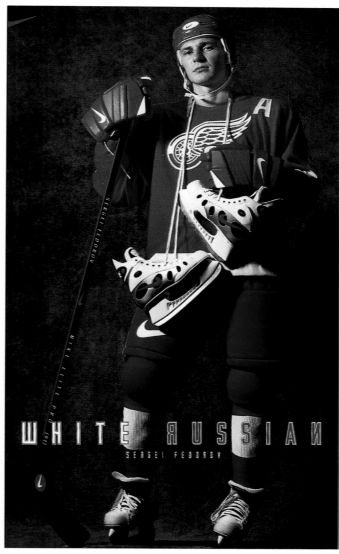

533 534

L'éthique du tennis selon Mary Pierce:
Si le public ne hurle pas,
frapper encore plus fort

L'éthique du tennis selon Pete Sampras:
Entendre les coups droits
et ne jamais les voir

L'éthique du tennis selon Andre Agassi:
Frapper la balle fort
Et encore plus fort l'ego
des adversaires

L'éthique du tennis selon Sjeng Schalken:
Vénérer ses héros
Puis les abattre

535 536

537 538

539

"Your kicks are so old, WHEN YOU STEP ON GUM you know the flavor."

NYC

535-539 **WIEDEN & KENNEDY** NIKE INC.

541 542

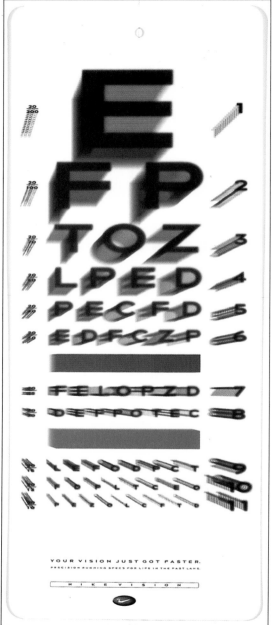

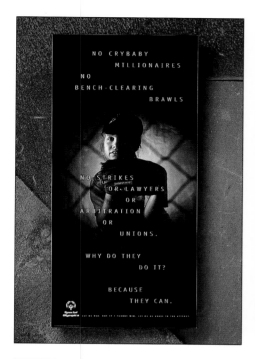

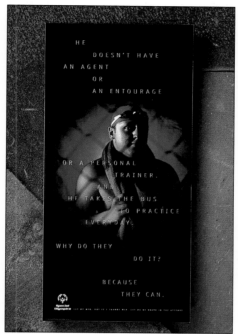

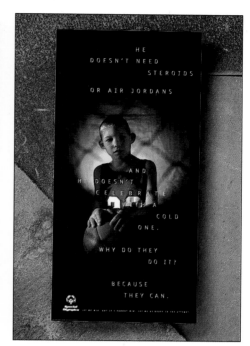

543 544 545

546 547 548

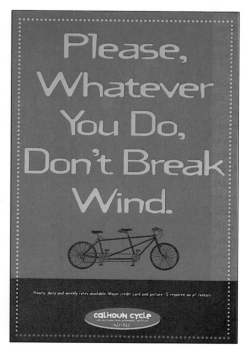

543-545 **THE MARLIN COMPANY** *SOUTHWEST AREA SPECIAL OLYMPICS* □ 546-548 **SIETSEMA ENGEL** *CALHOUN CYCLE*

Until your body develops a heat-retentive mesh coated with titanium, there is an alternative.

NEILPRYDE WETSUITS

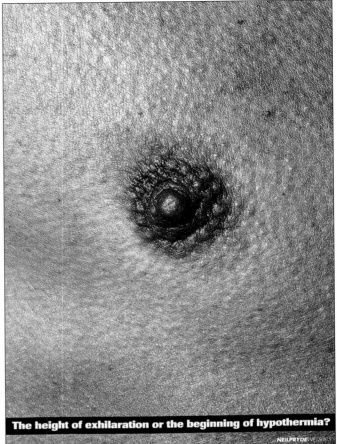

The height of exhilaration or the beginning of hypothermia?

NEILPRYDE WETSUITS

549 550

551 552

ORION CUP

ORION=OPTIMA FORMA

50 år
i 1 division
Håndbold

549-550 **OGILVY & MATHER** *NEIL PRYDE* □ 551 **IMA-PRESS PUBLISHERS** *ORION CUP*
552 **FINN NYGAARD GRAPHIC DESIGN** *IN-HOUSE*

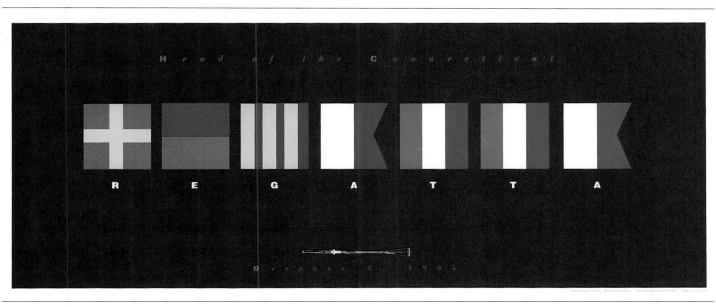

553 **TED BERTZ GRAPHIC DESIGN, INC.** *MIDDLESEX COUNTY CHAMBER OF COMMERCE*
554 **TED WRIGHT DESIGN/ILLUSTRATION** *US OLYMPIC COMMITTEE*

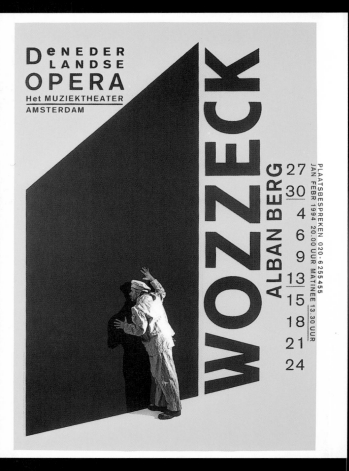

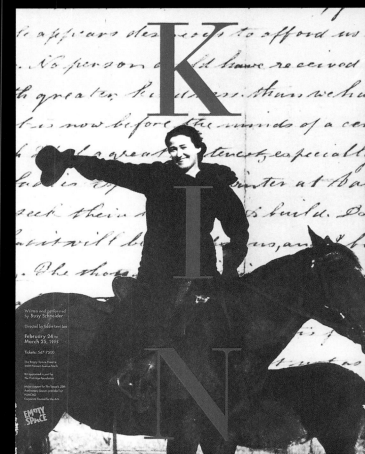

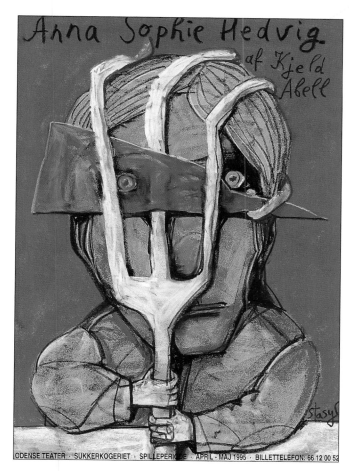

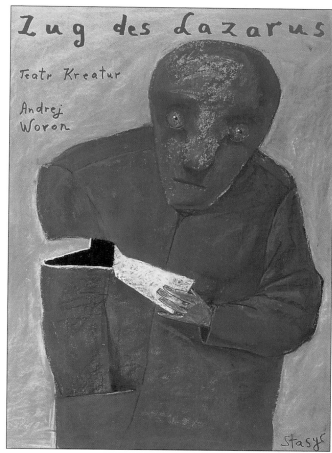

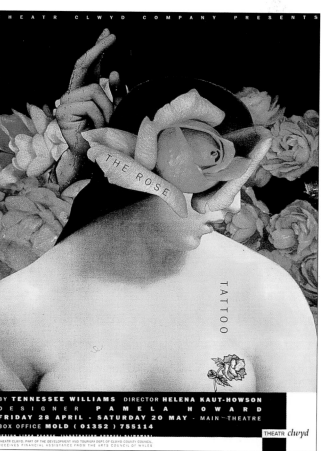

557 558

559 560

557 **STASYS EIDRIGEVICIUS** *Teatre Odense* □ 558 **STASYS EIDRIGEVICIUS** *Teatre Amufer*
559, 560 **LIPPA PEARCE** *Theater Clwyd*

RENT book, music and lyrics by
JONATHAN LARSON
NEDERLANDER THEATRE   NYC   directed by MICHAEL GREIF

THE PUBLIC THEATER/NEW YORK SHAKESPEARE FESTIVAL PRESENTS

BRING IN 'DA **NOISE** BRING IN 'DA **FUNK**

DESIGN: PENTAGRAM. PHOTO: RICHARD AVEDON

562

"VISUALLY STUNNING!
AT TIMES THE DANCING SEEMS LIKE AN ASSAULT ON THE FEET- THEY DANCE ON THEIR TOES, THEIR HEELS, SEEMINGLY ON THEIR ANKLES, INVARIABLY WITH RELENTLESS ABANDON."
Howard Kissel, Daily News

"THIS EPIC POEM OPENS THE DOOR THROUGH WHICH TAP CAN ENTER THE 21ST CENTURY. IT SLAMS RAW RHYTHMS INTO YOUR HEART!"
Sally Sommer, The Village Voice

"A MEDITATION ON TAP,

" WHAT IS 'NOISE/FUNK'? IT IS DANCE THEATER. IT IS MUSICAL THEATER. IT IS EPIC THEATER. AS DANCE, AS MUSICAL, AS THEATER, AS ART, HISTORY AND ENTERTAINMENT, THERE'S NOTHING IT CANNOT AND SHOULD NOT DO."
Margo Jefferson, The New York Times

"SAVION GLOVER IS A HUMAN DIVINING ROD OF RHYTHM. 'NOISE/FUNK' IS SO FRESH, PURE, AND ALIVE, IT VIBRATES!"
Sydney Weinberg, Time Out New York

"A JOYOUS CELEBRATION! THE CAST IS SUPERB!"
Clive Barnes, New York Post

"A JOYOUS

GEORGE C. WOLFE AND SAVION GLOVER HAVE CONCOCTED A SHORT-HAND VERSION OF AMERICAN HISTORY, IN WHICH THE BEAT OF DANCE IS EQUATED WITH SOMETHING LIKE AN UNSTOPPABLE LIFE FORCE. THE MOST ORIGINAL MUSICAL PRODUCTION OF THE SEASON."
Vincent Canby, WQXR-FM

"STUNNING!
GLOVER'S DANCING IS A REVELATION OF VIRTUOSITY AND EXPRESSIVENESS. THIS MUSICAL HAS BROUGHT BACK 'DA BEAT."
Aileen Jacobson, NY Newsday

"TO GET ONE SHOWSTOPPING MOMENT IN A SHOW IS LUCKY; TO GET TWO IS EXCEPTIONAL; BUT TO GET SEVEN—WHICH IS WHAT WOLFE AND GLOVER DO IN THEIR FABULOUS 'NOISE/FUNK'—IS HEROIC! THE GENIUS OF GLOVER'S CHORE-OGRAPHY AND THE EXHILARATION OF THE EXPERIENCE DISTRACT THE PUBLIC AND THE PERFORMERS FROM THE REALM OF PAIN OUT OF WHICH THE DANCE COMES. BY STAGING TAP IN THIS NARRATIVE WAY, WOLFE HAS CREATED SOMETHING AT ONCE ARTICULATE, TERRI-FYING AND VERY BEAUTIFUL."
John Lahr, The New Yorker

"GEORGE WOLFE AND SAVION GLOVER ARE THE INSPIRED CREATORS OF THIS BREATH-TAKING AND REVELATORY SHOW WHICH RESTORES EMOTIONAL CONTENT TO SHOW-BIZ CHOREOGRAPHY IN WAYS CURRENTLY UNMATCHED ON BROADWAY STAGES. ITS RHYTHMS WILL PULSE IN YOUR BLOODSTREAM LONG AFTER IT'S OVER!"
John Heilpern, NY Observer

"'NOISE' ROCKETS THE AMERICAN MUSICAL INTO THE MODERN AGE!"
Ben Brantley, The New York Times

CALL **TELE-CHARGE®** THE AMBASSADOR THEATRE
IN NY 212-239-6200 219 WEST 49TH STREET
NJ/CT OUTSIDE NY METRO AREA 800-432-7250 BEGINS APRIL 9TH

563 564

565 566

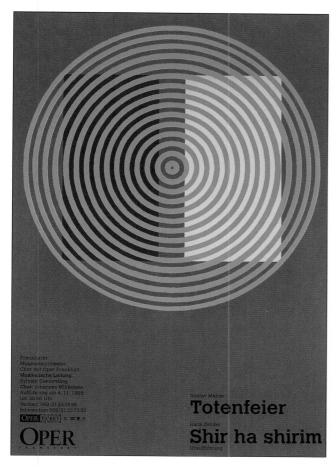

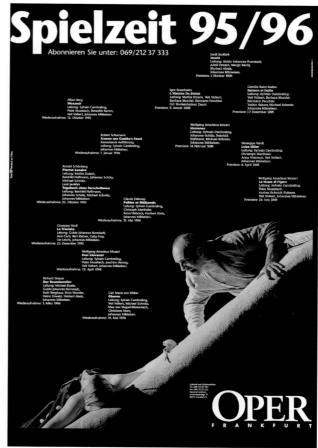

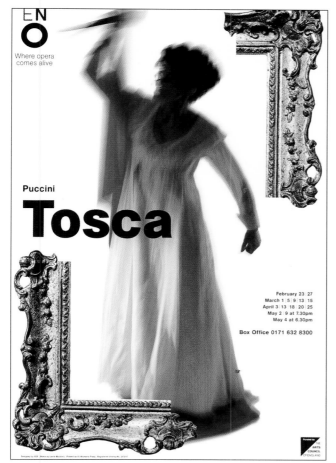

569, 570 **BÜRO WALTER VORJOHANN** *OPER FRANKFURT*
571, 572 **CDT DESIGN LIMITED** *ENGLISH NATIONAL OPERA*

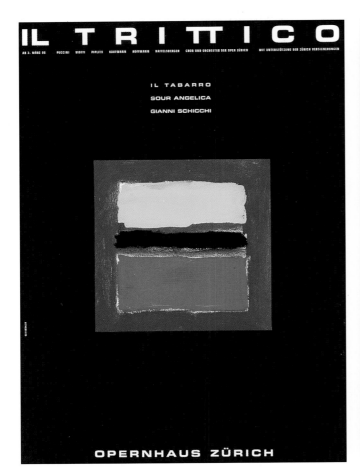

573 574

575 576

573-576 **K.D. GEISSBÜHLER** *Opernhaus Zürich*

577

JETZT BLOSS KEINEN FEHLER MACHEN.

BENSON & HEDGES SIMPLY GOLD

Die EG-Gesundheitsminister: Rauchen gefährdet die Gesundheit. Der Rauch einer Zigarette dieser Marke enthält 1,0 mg Nikotin und 13 mg Kondensat (Teer). (Durchschnittswerte nach ISO.)

FÜR EINE WIRKLICH GUTE ZIGARETTE KANN MAN MIT FAST ALLEM WERBEN.

BENSON & HEDGES SIMPLY GOLD

Die EG-Gesundheitsminister: Rauchen gefährdet die Gesundheit. Der Rauch einer Zigarette dieser Marke enthält 1,0 mg Nikotin und 13 mg Kondensat (Teer). (Durchschnittswerte nach ISO.)

MUTTER ERDE RAUCHT DOCH AUCH.

BENSON & HEDGES SIMPLY GOLD

Die EG-Gesundheitsminister: Rauchen gefährdet die Gesundheit. Der Rauch einer Zigarette dieser Marke enthält 1,0 mg Nikotin und 13 mg Kondensat (Teer). (Durchschnittswerte nach ISO.)

SIE SIND NICHT IRGENDWER. RAUCHEN SIE NICHT IRGENDWAS.

BENSON & HEDGES SIMPLY GOLD

Die EG-Gesundheitsminister: Rauchen gefährdet die Gesundheit. Der Rauch einer Zigarette dieser Marke enthält 1,0 mg Nikotin und 13 mg Kondensat (Teer). (Durchschnittswerte nach ISO.)

ER KOMMT MIT, ER KOMMT OHNE, ER KOMMT MIT...

BENSON & HEDGES SIMPLY GOLD

Die EG-Gesundheitsminister: Rauchen gefährdet die Gesundheit. Der Rauch einer Zigarette dieser Marke enthält 1,0 mg Nikotin und 13 mg Kondensat (Teer). (Durchschnittswerte nach ISO.)

SEIEN SIE TOLERANT. AUSSER BEI IHRER ZIGARETTE.

BENSON & HEDGES SIMPLY GOLD

Die EG-Gesundheitsminister: Rauchen gefährdet die Gesundheit. Der Rauch einer Zigarette dieser Marke enthält 1,0 mg Nikotin und 13 mg Kondensat (Teer). (Durchschnittswerte nach ISO.)

One of 21 parks. 116 square miles, without a single insipid theme park. Yet. To keep it that way, call 415 65 PARKS.

One of 21 parks. 116 square miles, without a single moronic water slide. Yet. To keep it that way, call 415 65 PARKS.

THE GOLDEN GATE
NATIONAL
PARKS

(ABOVE AND OPPOSITE) 585-590 **GOODBY, SILVERSTEIN & PARTNERS** *GOLDEN GATE NATIONAL PARK ASSOCIATION*

587 588

589 590

591 **JON WARREN LENTZ** *THE PORT OF SAN FRANCISCO*

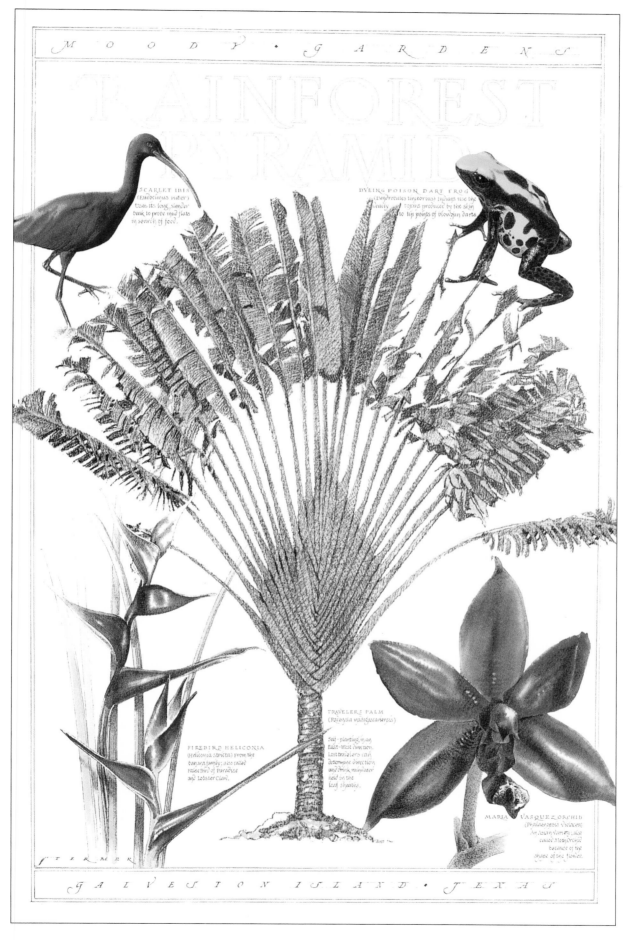

MOODY · GARDENS

RAINFOREST PYRAMID

SCARLET IBIS
(Eudocimus ruber)
Uses its long, slender
beak to probe mud flats
in search of food.

DYEING POISON DART FROG
(Dendrobates tinctorius) Indians use the
deadly toxins produced by the skin
to tip points of blowgun darts.

TRAVELERS PALM
(Ravenala madagascariensis)

Self-planting in an
East-West direction.
Lost travelers can
determine direction
and drink rainwater
held in the
leaf sheaths.

FIREBIRD HELICONIA
(Heliconia stricta) From the
banana family; also called
false bird of Paradise
and Lobster Claw.

MARIA VASQUEZ ORCHID
(Phalaenopsis violacea)
An Asian variety; also
called Moth Orchid
because of the
shape of the flower.

GALVESTON ISLAND · TEXAS

592

593

593 **TIROL WERBUNG** *IN-HOUSE*

594 595 596

597

594-596 **CRISPIN PORTER & BOGUSKY DESIGN** *TRAVEL CHANNEL LATIN AMERICA* □ 597 **MINKO IMAGES** *IN-HOUSE*

A ist der
erste
Buchstabe
des
Alphabets
Wir haben
noch
25 andere
typeshop gmbh
Wrangelstr. 19
D-20255
Hamburg
Fon
040-4204875
Fax.
040-4204870

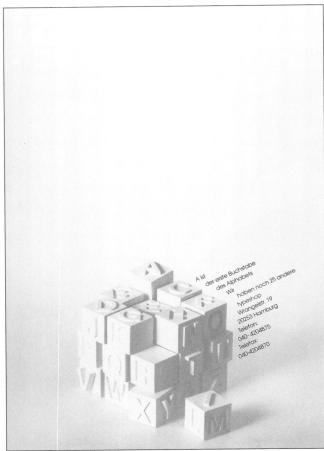

A ist
der erste Buchstabe
des Alphabets
Wir
haben noch 25 andere
typeshop
Wrangelstr. 19
20253 Hamburg
Telefon:
040- 4204875
Telefax:
040-4204870

598 599

600 601

Typographie
kann
unter Umständen
Kunst sein
Typeshop
Wrangelstr. 19
20253 Hamburg
Telefon:
040-4204875
Telefax:
040-4204870

598-600 **JIAYANG LIN** *HOCHSCHULE DER KÜNSTE BERLIN* □ 601 **KAN TAI-KEUNG**

What, Blanche?   Well,   Stella—you're going to reproach me, I know that you're bound to reproach me—but before you do—take into consideration —*you* left! I stayed and struggled! You came to New Orleans and looked out for yourself. I *stayed* at Belle Reve and tried to hold it together! I'm not meaning this in any reproachful way, but **all the burden descended on my shoulders.** The best I could do was make my own living, Blanche. I know, I know. But *you* are the one that abandoned

STOP this

Belle Reve, not I! **I stayed and fought for it, bled for it, almost died for it!**

hysterical outburst

and tell me what's *happened?* What do you mean **fought** and bled?

What kind of—? *I knew you would, Stella. I knew you would take this attitude about it!* About—what?—*please!*

The *loss*—the *loss*...No!

Belle Reve? Lost, *is it?*

Yes Stella.   But *how did it go?* What **happened?**

You're a fine one to ask me how it went!

B l a n c h e !

You're a fine one to sit there accusing me of it! Blanche!

I, I, I took the blows in *my face* and *my body!* All those deaths! The long parade to the graveyard! *Father, mother!* Margaret, that dreadful way! So *big* with it, it couldn't be put in a coffin! But had to be burned like rubbish! *You just came home in time for the funerals, Stella.* And funerals are pretty compared to deaths. Funerals are quiet, but deaths—not always. Sometimes *their breathing is hoarse,* and sometimes it *rattles,* and sometimes they even cry out to you, "Don't let me go!" Even the old, sometimes, say *"Don't let me go."* As if you were able to stop them! But funerals are quiet, with pretty flowers. And, *oh* what gorgeous boxes they pack them away in! Unless you were there at the bed when they cried out, "Hold me!" you'd never suspect there was the **struggle** for breath and bleeding. You didn't dream, *but I saw!* Saw! Saw! And now you sit there telling me with your eyes that I let the place go! *How in hell do you think all that sickness and dying was paid for?* Death is expensive, *Miss Stella!* And old Cousin Jessie's right after Margaret's hers! Why, the Grim Reaper had put up his tent on our doorstep!...Stella. Belle Reve was his headquarters! *Honey—that's how it slipped through my fingers* Which of them *left us a fortune!* Which of them left a cent of insurance even? Only poor Jessie—one hundred to pay for her coffin. **That was all, Stella!** And I with my pitiful salary at the school. Y e s ,   a c c u s e   m e ! *Sit there and stare at me, thinking I let the place go!* I let the place go? *Where were you!* In bed with your—**Polack!**

Where are you going?   I'm going to the bathroom to wash my face.

Blanche! You be still!   That's enough!

Oh, Stella, Stella, you're crying!

602

603 604

605 606

DAS ORIGINAL

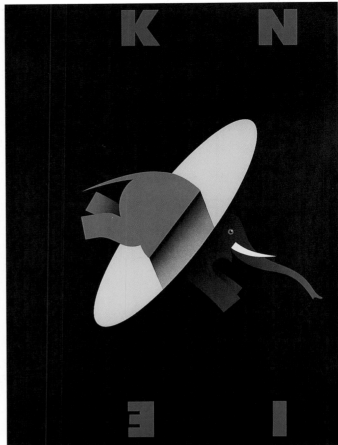

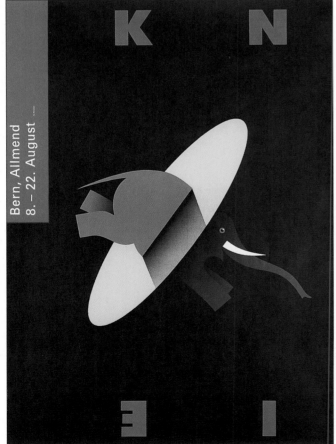

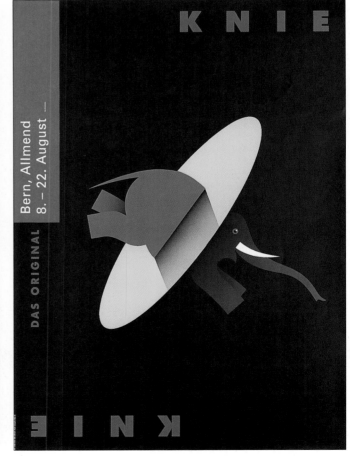

603-606 **CLAUDE KUHN GRAPHIK DESIGN** *ZIRKUS KNIE*

CAPTIONS AND INDICES

LEGENDEN UND KÜNSTLERANGABEN

LÉGENDES ET ARTISTES

PAGE 4 ART DIRECTOR: *Trace Hallowell* DESIGNER: *Mila Borden* AGENCY: *Thompson & Company* COPYWRITER: *Jimmy Hamiter, Rick Baptist* CLIENT: *Memphis College Of Art* ■ *"Your contribution goes here."* The directive was to encourage contributions for a fundraising campaign for the Memphis College of Art. ● «*Ihre Spende geht hierhin.*» Hier ging es darum, Leute zu Spenden für eine private Kunstschule zu ermuntern. ▲ «*Vos dons vont là.*» L'objectif était de récolter des dons pour une école d'arts privée.

PAGE 6 DESIGNER: *Géza Molnár* ■ Poster for exhibition of a glass artist, Agnes Smetana. ● Plakat für die Ausstellung einer Glas-Künstlerin. ▲ Affiche pour l'exposition d'une artiste travaillant le verre.

PAGE 24 #1, 2 ART DIRECTOR/ILLUSTRATOR: *Iwao Matsuura* DESIGNER: *Kamikura Atsushi* AGENCY: *Iwao Matsuura Design Office Co. Ltd.* CLIENT: *Steelcase Japan K K*

PAGE 24 #3 ART DIRECTOR/ DESIGNER: *Poul Allan* AGENCY: *Grafisk Design Studio* ■ Poster for an event on the subject of city planning and ecology, organized by an association of architects of Jutland, Denmark. ● Plakat für eine Tagung zum Thema Stadtplanung und Ökologie, veranstaltet von einem Architektenverband von Jutland, Dänemark. ▲ Affiche pour un congrès consacré à l'urbanisation et à l'écologie, organisé par une association d'architectes du Jutland, Danemark.

PAGE 24 #4 DESIGNER: *Dieter Marx* AGENCY: *Edition Lidiarte* ILLUSTRATOR: *Susanne Mocka* PUBLISHER: *Edition Lidiarte* ■ The Pantheon of Rome, one of the subjects of architectural posters published and sold by Edition Lidiarte. ● Das Pantheon in Rom als Thema eines der Architekturplakate, die von der Edition Lidiarte herausgegeben und verkauft werden. ▲ Le Panthéon à Rome, thème d'une des affiches consacrées à l'architecture et commercialisées par Edition Lidiarte.

PAGE 25 #5 ART DIRECTOR/ DESIGNER/ILLUSTRATOR/AGENCY: *Tadanori Yokoo* CLIENT: *JAGDA*

PAGE 26 #6 ART DIRECTOR: *Erik Hogrefe* AGENCY: *Barten & Barten Die Agentur GmbH* PHOTOGRAPHER/ILLUSTRATOR: *Fotografen Hejkal & Reichmann* COPYWRITER: *Martin Buhl* CLIENT: *Moto Witt GmbH, Harley Davidson*

PAGE 26 #7 ART DIRECTORS: *Mark Fuller* CREATIVE DIRECTOR: *Mike Hughes* PRINT PRODUCER: *Jenny Schoenherr* AGENCY: *The Martin Agency* PHOTOGRAPHER/ILLUSTRATOR: *Oli Tennet* COPYWRITER: *Joe Nagy* CLIENT: *Moto Europa* ■ *"So lust is one of the seven deadly sins. See you in Hell."* ● «*Lust ist also eine der sieben Todsünden. Auf Wiedersehen in der Hölle.*» s «*La luxure est l'un des sept péchés capitaux. On se reverra en enfer!*»

PAGE 26 #8 ART DIRECTOR/ DESIGNER: *Stephen Gray* AGENCY: *Ritta & Associates* PHOTOGRAPHER: *Greg Jarem* COPYWRITER: *Kay Ritta* DIGITAL COMPOSITION: *Carmine Corinella* CLIENT: *BMW of North America* ■ *"Street Legal."* To introduce BMW's M3 sedan, a four-door version of the M3 race car, the agency "morphed" the race car and the family sedan. ● Für die Einführung des BMW M3, einer viertürigen Version des M3-Rennwagens, wurde eine manipulierte Kombination von Rennauto und Limousine gezeigt. ▲ Affiche conçue pour le lancement de la BMW M3 sedan, une version quatre portes de la voiture de course M3. L'image montre une version hybride de la voiture de course et de la berline familiale.

PAGE 27 #9 ART DIRECTOR: *Mark Fuller* CREATIVE DIRECTOR: *Mike Hughes* PRINT PRODUCER: *Jenny Schoenherr* AGENCY: *The Martin Agency* PHOTOGRAPHER: *Oli Tennet* COPYWRITER: *Joe Nagy* CLIENT: *Moto Europa* ■ *"Tell her lawyer she can keep the damn house."* ● «*Sag' ihrem Anwalt, sie kann das verdammte Haus behalten.*» ▲ «*Dis à son avocat qu'elle peut garder cette foutue bicoque!*»

PAGE 27 #10 ART DIRECTORS *Mark Fuller* CREATIVE DIRECTOR: *Mike Hughes* PRINT PRODUCER: *Jenny Schoenherr* AGENCY: *The Martin Agency* PHOTOGRAPHER: *Dean Hawthorne* COPYWRITER: *Joe Nagy* CLIENT: *Moto Europa* ■ *"Then he said, 'my car didn't cost that much.' Pathetic Idiot."* ● «*Dann sagte er, 'mein Auto hat nicht soviel gekostet'. Was für ein Idiot.*» ▲ «*Puis il a dit 'ma voiture ne m'a pas coûté si cher'. Quel idiot!*»

PAGE 28 #11, 12 ART DIRECTOR/DESIGNER: *David Weinstein* AGENCY: *Vox Advertising & Design* CLIENT: *Harley-Davidson* ■ *"History, nostalgia, leather & chrome." "On June 23rd, expect thunder in the vicinity of Lexington Avenue and 57th Street."* The client needed to generate interest within and outside of the motorcycling community for the grand opening of its Manhattan store. Poster visuals utilized the famous bar and shield logo as well as the orange and black color scheme, while the headline played on the now famous Harley engine sound. ● «*Geschichte, Nostalgie, Leder und Chrom.*» «*Machen Sie sich am 23. Juni in der Nähe der Lexington Avenue und der 57. Strasse auf Donner gefasst.*» Die Eröffnung einer Harley-Davidson-Verkaufsstelle in Manhattan wird mit diesem Plakat, das nicht nur eingefleischte Harley-Fans erreichen sollte, gross angekündigt, wobei das bekannte Logo, das Farbsystem von Orange und Schwarz und das inzwischen berühmte Harley-Motorgeräusch die bestimmenden Elemente sind. ▲ «*Histoire, Nostalgie, Cuir et Chrome.*» «*Le 23 juin, attendez-vous à un spectacle du tonnerre du côté de Lexington Avenue et de la 57e!*» Affiche annonçant l'ouverture d'un point de vente Harley Davidson à Manhattan. Le célèbre logo de la marque, le code couleur orange et noir et la headline constituent les principaux éléments.

PAGE 28 #13 ART DIRECTORS: *Steve Wedeen, Dan Flynn* DESIGNERS: *Dan Flynn* AGENCY: *Vaughn/Wedeen Creative* PHOTOGRAPHER: *Dave Nufer* COMPUTER IMAGING: *Stan McCoy* CLIENT: *US West Communications* ■ This poster was part of an internal sales promotion for US West Communications. The grand prize for the salesperson selling the most additional telephone lines was a 1996 Corvette Coupe. ● Das Plakat war Teil einer internen Aktion für den Aussendienst von US West Communications, mit der die Verkaufsanstrengungen für zusätzliche Telephonanschlüsse belohnt werden sollen. Der erste Preis war ein 1996er Corvette Coupé. ▲ Affiche réalisée dans le cadre d'une campagne interne pour le service extérieur d'US West Communications dans le but de stimuler les ventes de lignes téléphoniques. Prix au meilleur vendeur: un coupé Corvette 1996.

PAGE 28 #14 CREATIVE DIRECTOR: *David Tanimoto* ART DIRECTOR: *Steve Davis* AGENCY: *The Designory, Inc.* PHOTOGRAPHER/ILLUSTRATOR: *Clint Clemens* COPYWRITER: *Tony Assenza* CLIENT: *Porsche Cars North America* ■ *"Porsche: There is no substitute."* The directive was to create a brand-oriented poster that would convey the excitement of driving a Porsche and build showroom traffic. The agency chose a dynamic, bold action image to create the emotion while clearly presenting the beauty of the automobile. ● «*Porsche. Es gibt keinen Ersatz.*» Bei diesem Plakat für Porsche-Ausstellungsräume ging es um das Fahrerlebnis mit einem Porsche, das hier durch dynamische Aktion zum Ausdruck kommt, wobei gleichzeitig die Schönheit des Wagens gezeigt wird. ▲ «*Porsche, toujours unique.*» Affiche pour les show-rooms Porsche. Il s'agissait de créer une image dynamique, évoquant par le mouvement les sensations uniques procurées par la conduite d'une Porsche et de mettre en valeur les lignes racées du véhicule.

PAGE 29 #15 ART DIRECTOR: *Barry Shepard* DESIGNER: *Michael Barton* AGENCY: *SHR Perceptual Management* PHOTOGRAPHER: *Rodney Rascone* CLIENT: *Mercruiser* ■ The agency wanted to change perceptions in the competitive water-ski market in which brand loyalty is fierce. The agency sought to visually communicate ideas of precision and performance along with power and aggression and to make the product stand out from the competition. ● Mit diesem Plakat für eine Wasser-Ski-Marke sollte eine Käufergruppe gewonnen werden, die für ihre Markenloyalität bekannt ist. Dabei ging es um Darstellung von Präzision und Leistung, kombiniert mit dem Ausdruck von Kraft und Aggression, um die Aufmerksamkeit der Verbraucher zu gewinnen. ▲ Affiche d'une marque de skis nautiques. Le but de l'agence était d'avoir une nouvelle approche sur un marché réputé difficile en raison de la fidélité des consommateurs à des marques bien précises. Pour atteindre cet objectif, elle communique sur le mode de la précision, de la performance, de la puissance et de l'agressivité de façon à ce que le produit se démarque de la concurrence.

PAGE 29 #16 ART DIRECTOR/ DESIGNER: *Todd Miller* AGENCY: *Rubin Postaer and Associates* PHOTOGRAPHER: *Harry Vamos* COPYWRITER: *Jon Pearce* CLIENT: *American Honda Motor Co., Inc.* ■ *"A threat to big screen TV."* The agency sought to portray the interior of the car while suggesting "empowerment"– the idea that the car can bestow a sense of freedom. The eight hour shoot for this campaign was conducted in sub-freezing alpine conditions. ● «*Eine Gefahr für den grossen TV-Bildschirm.*» Die Aufgabe war, das Innere des Autos zu zeigen und dabei zum Ausdruck zu bringen, dass das Auto dem Fahrer ein Gefühl von Freiheit vermittelt und ihn an Orte bringt, die mit dem Auto unerreichbar sind. Die äusseren Bedingungen der Aufnahmen waren eine weitere Herausforderung: Aufnahmen, die bei eisigen Temperaturen acht Stunden dauerten. ▲ «*Une menace pour les TV à écran panoramique.*» L'objectif était de montrer l'habitacle et la sensation de liberté éprouvée par le conducteur d'un tel véhicule. Les prises de vues ont constitué un défi de taille en raison des conditions extérieures extrêmes: huit heures de travail par des températures polaires!

PAGE 30 #17 ART DIRECTORS: *Terence Reynolds* AGENCY: *R&D/The Richards Group* PHOTOGRAPHER: *Richard Reens* COPYWRITER: *Todd Tilford* CLIENT: *A M General Corp*

PAGE 30 #18 ART DIRECTORS: *Terence Reynolds, Todd Tilford, Christian Wojciechowski* AGENCY: *R&D/The Richards Group* PHOTOGRAPHER/ILLUSTRATOR: *Richard Reens*

COPYWRITER: *Todd Tilford* CLIENT: *A M General Corp.* ■ *A poster designed for dealers to reinforce the Hummer's off-road capabilities.* ● *Ein für Händler bestimmtes Plakat.* ▲ *Affiche pour les concessionnaires.*

PAGE 30 #19 ART DIRECTORS: *Terence Reynolds* AGENCY: *R&D/The Richards Group* PHOTOGRAPHER: *Richard Reens* COPYWRITER: *Todd Tilford* CLIENT: *A M General Corp*

PAGE 31 #20-23 ART DIRECTOR: *Marcello Serpa* AGENCY: *Almap/BBDO* PHOTOGRAPHER: *Maricio Nahas* COPYWRITER: *Alexandre Gama* CLIENT: *Senna Import*

PAGE 31 #24, 25 CREATIVE DIRECTOR: *Sam Ajluni* ART DIRECTOR: *Tom Helland* DESIGNER: *Scott Markel* AGENCY: *The Hot Shop Design Group/Bozell Worldwide, Inc.* PHOTOGRAPHER: *Madison Ford* COPYWRITER: *Fred Beal* CLIENT: *Chrysler* ■ *"There's nothing like living off campus." "Arrival of the Fittest." The overall design objective was to produce striking posters that would enhance awareness of Jeep vehicles in the college market. By featuring a dramatic product angle and a unique brushstroke border technique, the agency showcased the automobiles in an exciting and aggressive manner meant to appeal to college students.* ● *«Es gibt nichts Schöneres, als ausserhalb des Campus zu leben.» «Ankunft des Fittesten.» Das Ziel war, mit eindrucksvollen Plakaten College-Studenten für Jeeps zu interessieren. Die Dramatik der Produktdarstellung und der in einer speziellen Technik gemalte Rahmen sind deshalb ganz auf das junge Publikum ausgerichtet.* ▲ *«Rien n'est plus beau que de vivre en-dehors du campus.» «Arrivée du plus fort.» Affiches Jeep visant les étudiants. La présentation dramatique du produit et la technique utilisée pour les bords confèrent un côté jeune et dynamique.*

PAGE 32 #26 ART DIRECTOR/ DESIGNER: *Michael Vanderbyl* AGENCY: *Vanderbyl Design* PHOTOGRAPHER/ILLUSTRATOR: *Gaby Brink* CLIENT: *Type Directors Club* ■ *This competition announcement discusses the concept of good and bad typography.* ● *Ankündigung eines Wettbewerbs zum Thema guter und schlechter Typographie.* ▲ *Annonce d'un concours sur le thème de la bonne et de la mauvaise typographie.*

PAGE 32 #27 ART DIRECTOR: *Randy Hughes* AGENCY: *Martin/Williams* PHOTOGRAPHER: *Shawn Michienzi* PHOTO ENHANCEMENT: *Brad Palm* COPYWRITER: *Charlie Callahan* CLIENT: *NAMA* ■ *"You've spent all year working on farm advertising and what do you have to show for it?" The objective was to generate enthusiasm for agricultural advertising. It had been a long year for farmers and creatives, all working in their respective fields.* ● *«Sie haben das ganze Jahr damit verbracht, Werbung für die Landwirtschaft zu machen - und was ist dabei herausgekommen?» Mit diesem Plakat soll Werbung für die Landwirtschaft gefördert werden. Es war ein langes Jahr für alle gewesen, und Bauern wie Werber hatten ihre Felder bestellen müssen.* ▲ *«Vous avez passé l'année à faire de la publicité pour l'agriculture et quels sont les résultats?» Affiche visant à encourager la publicité pour l'agriculture. L'année avait été longue tant pour les agriculteurs que pour les créatifs, chacun travaillant dans ses champs respectifs.*

PAGE 33 #28 ART DIRECTOR: *Keisuke Kimura* DESIGNERS: *Keisuke Kimura, Maki Yanagishima* AGENCY: *Magna Inc. Advertising* PHOTOGRAPHER: *Kyoko Harada* CLIENT: *Toyo Information Systems Co., Ltd.*

PAGE 34 #29 ART DIRECTOR/ DESIGNER: *Matthew Chun* CLIENT: *Association of Graphic Communications* ■ *This poster was the designer's first printed piece and was created during his second year in design school. The magnet is an embodiment of the client's organization and draws upon the flowing entities of technology and printing.* ● *Dieses Plakat war das erste gedruckte Ergebnis der Anstrengungen eines Studenten im zweiten Jahr an der Design-Schule. Der Magnet verkörpert den Auftraggeber, einen Graphikerverband, und ist gleichzeitig eine Anspielung auf die Verbindung von Technologie und Druck.* ▲ *Première affiche d'un étudiant réalisée au cours de sa deuxième année d'études de design. L'aimant symbolise le client, une association de graphistes, et fait également allusion à la combinaison technologie et impression.*

PAGE 34 #30 ART DIRECTORS: *Nancy Skolos, Thomas Wedell* DESIGNER: *Nancy Skolos* AGENCY: *Skolos/Wedell* PHOTOGRAPHER: *Thomas Wedell* COPYWRITER: *Jon McKee* CLIENT: *Lyceum Fellowship Committee* ■ *This poster was to announce the 11th annual Lyceum Fellowship Competition, a traveling fellowship for undergraduate students of architecture from invited schools. The 1996 program challenged participating students to think about their role as architects to create a "home" as opposed to a "house".* ● *Thema dieses Plakates ist ein Reisestipendium, das an Architekturstudenten der unteren Semester von verschiedenen Schulen vergeben wird. Das Programm 1996 war darauf ausgerichtet, die teilnehmenden Studenten dazu anzuregen, bei ihren Entwürfen an ein Zuhause und nicht nur an ein Haus zu denken.* ▲ *Affiche d'un concours doté d'une bourse*

d'études pour les étudiants en architecture et ouvert à plusieurs écoles. Le programme 1996 devait encourager les futurs architectes à construire un véritable «chez-soi» plutôt qu'une simple maison.

PAGE 35 #31 ART DIRECTOR/DESIGNER: *Kazumasa Nagai* AGENCY: *Nippon Design Center, Inc.* CLIENT: *Nakagawa Chemical Inc.*

PAGE 35 #32 ART DIRECTOR/ DESIGNER/PHOTOGRAPHER: *João Machado* CLIENT: *Centro Artes S. João da Madeira* ■ *Poster for a national footwear design contest.* ● *Ankündigung eines nationalen Wettbewerbs, bei dem es um die Kreation von Schuhen geht.* ▲ *Affiche d'un concours national consacré à la création de chaussures.*

PAGE 35 #33 ART DIRECTOR: *Scott Bremner* DESIGNERS: *Allison Uchiyama, Scott Bremner* AGENCY: *Team One Advertising* PHOTOGRAPHER: *John Mattos* COPYWRITER: *Rebecca Rivera* CLIENT: *Lexus*

PAGE 35 #34 ART DIRECTOR/ DESIGNER: *Peter Wong* AGENCY: *Atlanta College of Art, Communication Design Department* ILLUSTRATOR *Doug Evans* COPYWRITER: *Susan Laitas* CLIENT: *American Center for Design* ■ *This poster was designed to attract student and faculty attendance of a student design conference. At the same time it functioned as an informative document for attendees. Since the guest speakers at the conference were drawn from a team of designers who worked on design for the summer Olympics, the symbol of the solitary runner at the final stage of his race was used.* ● *Studenten und Lehrkörper werden mit diesem Plakat zu einer Tagung über Studenten-Design eingeladen. Gleichzeitig diente es als Information für die Teilnehmer. Da die Gastreferenten zu einem Design-Team gehörten, die das Design für die Sommer-Olympiade entwickelt hatten, wurde ein einzelner Läufer kurz vor dem Ziel als Symbolfigur gewählt.* ▲ *Invitation à un congrès sur le design destiné aux étudiants et aux professeurs. L'affiche comprend aussi des informations pour les participants. Les conférenciers invités ayant fait partie d'une équipe de designers chargée du graphisme des Jeux olympiques d'été, un coureur solitaire proche de la ligne d'arrivée a été choisi comme symbole.*

PAGE 36 #35, 36 ART DIRECTORS: *Tom Kim, Dave Loew* DESIGNER: *Joe Stuart* AGENCY: *McConnaughy Stein Schmidt Brown* COPYWRITER: *Dave Loew* CLIENT: *Bungie Software* ■ *For an industry trade show, the agency wanted to give the client a gritty, "underground image" that would stand out from the slick material of many multimedia companies. These posters were also handed out as flyers by an actor posing as a "conspiracy theory nut."* ● *Für eine Multimedia-Fachmesse bestimmtes Plakat, mit dem der Kunde im Gegensatz zu den glatten, überproduzierten visuellen Auftritten vieler Multimedia-Firmen ein rauhes Untergrund-Image erhalten sollte. Die Plakate wurden von einem Schauspieler verteilt.* ▲ *Affiche réalisée pour un salon multimédia. Pour se démarquer des productions tape-à-l'œil propres aux sociétés multimédias, le client a choisi une affiche sous forme de flyer, inspirée de la culture underground. Un acteur a distribué les flyers.*

PAGE 36 #37 ART DIRECTOR: *Doug Mukai* AGENCY: *TBWA Chiat/Day* COPYWRITER: *Jay Cranford* CLIENT: *Sony*

PAGE 36 #38 ART DIRECTOR: *Victor Wang* DESIGNER: *Ed Pardo* AGENCY: *Xeno* PHOTOGRAPHER/ILLUSTRATOR: *Philip Harvey* CLIENT: *Macromedia* ■ *"Macromedia, it's brainware." This poster was used as a giveaway for college students. It was intended to establish and reinforce awareness of the client, a multimedia and design software company, on college campuses.* ● *Dieses Plakat für eine Multimedia- und Software-Firma wurde an College-Studenten verteilt, um sie als Kunden zu gewinnen.* ▲ *Affiche d'une société spécialisée dans le multimédia et les logiciels, distribuée à des étudiants dans le but de gagner de nouveaux clients.*

PAGE 37 #39 ART DIRECTORS: *Brian Burlison, Christian Wojciechowski* AGENCY: *R&D / The Richards Group* ILLUSTRATOR: *Philip Esparza* COPYWRITER: *Todd Tilford* CLIENT: *GT Interactive*

PAGE 37 #40, 41 ART DIRECTOR: *Mike Salisbury* DESIGNER: *Mary Evelyn McGough* AGENCY: *Mike Salisbury Communications* PHOTOGRAPHER/ILLUSTRATOR: *Maurice Tabard* CLIENT: *Stathouse* ■ *To introduce the electronic capabilities of Los Angeles' oldest service bureau, the agency used fine art photography in which dots are the major design element.* ● *Hier ging es um die elektronischen Kapazitäten eines Kopier- und Druckbetriebes, dem ältesten von Los Angeles. Punkte dienten als wichtiges Gestaltungselement der verwendeten künstlerischen Aufnahme.* ▲ *Affiche réalisée pour une société spécialisée dans la reprographie et l'impression, la plus ancienne de Los Angeles. Les points de la photo d'art représentent le principal élément graphique.*

PAGE 38 #42 ART DIRECTOR: *Margaret Johnson* AGENCY: *R&D / The Richards Group* PHOTOGRAPHER: *Eric Dinyer* COPYWRITERS: *Chad Rea, Todd Tilford* CLIENT: *GT Interactive* ■ *Instead of using digitized screen shots, the agency chose to use more realistic images to promote this PC game.* ● *Hier wurden realistische statt digitaler Bilder eingesetzt, um zu vermitteln, wie realistisch und furchterregend das PC-Spiel «Hexen» ist.* ▲ *Pour évoquer le climat angoissant du jeu vidéo «Hexen» (sorcières), l'agence a choisi des images réalistes plutôt que numériques.*

PAGE 38 #43 CREATIVE DIRECTOR: *Todd Tilford* ART DIRECTORS: *Margaret Johnson* AGENCY: *R&D / The Richards Group* PHOTOGRAPHER: *Richard Reens* COPYWRITER: *Todd Tilford* CLIENT: *G.T. Interactive* ■ *A poster to promote a PC game.* ● *Werbung für das letzte Kapitel eines PC-Spiels.* ▲ *Publicité pour le dernier chapitre d'un jeu vidéo.*

PAGE 38 #44 ART DIRECTOR: *Brian Burlison* AGENCY: *R&D / The Richards Group* PHOTOGRAPHER: *Hans Neleman* CLIENT: *G.T. Interactive Software*

PAGE 38 #45 ART DIRECTORS: *Margaret Johnson, Christian Wojciechowski* AGENCY: *R&D / The Richards Group* PHOTOGRAPHER: *Richard Reens* CLIENT: *G.T. Interactive Software*

PAGE 39 #46, 47 ART DIRECTOR/DESIGNER: *Kum-Jun Park* AGENCY: *Cheil Communications Inc.* PHOTOGRAPHER: *Hoo-Man Park* ILLUSTRATOR: *Wan-Gue Lee* COPYWRITER: *Joon-Young Bae* CLIENT: *Samsung Electronics* ■ *"Any desire..." "any dream..."* ● *«Jeglicher Wunsch...» «Jeglicher Traum...»* ▲ *«N'importe quel désir...» «N'importe quel rêve...»*

PAGE 40 #48 ART DIRECTOR/DESIGNER/AGENCY: *Bagby & Company* PHOTOGRAPHER: *Rodney Oman* COPYWRITER: *Rick Shaughnessy* CLIENT: *Zenith Electronics/Inteq Product Line*

PAGE 40 #49 ART DIRECTOR: *Denise Davis* DESIGNER: *Lisa DeMaio* AGENCY: *Metropolis Corporation* PHOTOGRAPHER: *Michael Sundra* METAL SCULPTOR: *Karen Rossi* CLIENT: *Booz Allen & Hamilton, Inc.* ■ *The client wanted to effectively portray its intricate strategy-driven system of operation. The agency used a mobile, made of intricate, delicately balanced pieces of sculpture to represent the interactivity of independent units.* ● *Um darzustellen, wie die Interaktivität von unabhängigen Einheiten zu einem soliden Ganzen führt, wurde ein Mobile mit raffiniert ausbalancierten kleinen Skulpturen als Bildgegenstand gewählt. Damit werden die Struktur und die stragegisch kluge Operationsweise des Auftraggebers, einer Firma für Unternehmensberatung, verdeutlicht.* ▲ *Pour illustrer la complexité de la stratégie du client, l'agence a opté pour un mobile. Les petites sculptures représentent les diverses unités indépendantes qui, en interaction, forment une structure solide.*

PAGE 41 #50-52 ART DIRECTOR: *Arthur Eisenberg* DESIGNER: *Lauren DiRusso* AGENCY: *Eisenberg And Associates/Rosenberg Advertising* CLIENT: *Pepsi Food Service* ■ *"You can't please all the people all the time." "The truck stops here." "Ask not what your customers can do for you. Ask what you can do for your customers." These posters were part of a nationwide employee campaign. They were distributed to announce the first annual award for outstanding achievement in customer service and company performance.* ● *«Man kann es nicht immer allen recht machen.» «Der Wagen hält hier.» «Fragen Sie nicht, was Ihre Kunden für Sie tun können. Fragen Sie, was Sie für Ihre Kunden tun können.» Die Plakate gehören zu einer nationalen Kampagne, die an die Angestellten der Firma gerichtet ist. Dabei geht es um einen Preis, der für hervorragende Leistungen im Dienst am Kunden und für die Firma vergeben wird.* ▲ *«On ne peut pas faire plaisir à tout le monde!» «Le camion s'arrête ici.» «Ne demandez pas à vos clients ce qu'ils peuvent faire pour vous. Demandez-leur ce que vous pouvez faire pour eux.» Affiches réalisées dans le cadre d'une campagne nationale destinée aux employés de la société. Elles ont été distribuées à l'occasion du premier prix annuel récompensant la meilleure performance dans le domaine du service à la clientèle.*

PAGE 41 #53 ART DIRECTOR: *John Ball* DESIGNER: *John Ball* AGENCY: *Mires Design, Inc.* PHOTOGRAPHER/ILLUSTRATOR: *Marshall Harrington* COPYWRITER: *Brian Woolsey* CLIENT: *Equifax* ■ *Because the client has a marketing research/information product that helps users make better decisions, the agency highlighted in a dramatic way the importance of making good decisions.* ● *Da der Auftraggeber Anbieter einer Marktforschungs-Software ist, die dem Benutzer als Entscheidungshilfe dienen soll, wurde die Bedeutung richtiger Entscheidungen zum Thema dieses Plakates.* ▲ *Affiche destinée à la promotion d'un logiciel conçu pour les études de marché. Thème de l'affiche: l'importance de prendre les bonnes décisions.*

PAGE 42 #54 ART DIRECTOR/ DESIGNER/PHOTOGRAPHER/ILLUSTRATOR: *Takahiro Shima* AGENCY: *Shima Design Office, Inc.* CLIENT: *Nitta Gelatin Inc.*

PAGE 42 #55 ART DIRECTORS: *Dave King, Kelly O'Keefe* DESIGNER: *Carolyn McGeorge* AGENCY: *Cadmus/O'Keefe* PHOTOGRAPHER: *Sonny Bowyer* PRODUCTION: *Daisey Sanders* CLIENT: *AI Network* ■ *AI Network is an insurance company for high-risk drivers. The agency made vanity plates by using names which describe high-risk drivers.* ● *AI Network ist eine Versicherung für Autofahrer, deren Fahrstil ein hohes Risiko bedeutet. Die Agentur stellte Nummernschilder her, deren Buchstabenkombination auf einen passenden Namen für den Fahrer schliessen lassen, z. B. Bd.Luck (Bad Luck = Pech). In den USA ist es möglich, ein Nummernschild mit einer bestimmten Kombination von Buchstaben und Zahlen zu erwerben.* ▲ *Affiche pour AI Network, une assurance destinée aux automobilistes à hauts risques. L'agence a créé des plaques minéralogiques dont les lettres donnent le profil du conducteur. Aux Etats-Unis, il est possible d'acheter une plaque minéralogique portant la combinaison de son choix.*

PAGE 43 #56 ART DIRECTOR: *Norio Kudo* DESIGNERS: *Norio Kudo, Yoshifumi Hioki* AGENCY: *Magna Inc. Advertising* ARTIST: *Masato Okamura* PHOTOGRAPHER: *Akio Tomari* COPYWRITER: *Chiaki Kasahara* CLIENT: *Tokyo University of Agriculture*

PAGE 44 #57 ART DIRECTOR/DESIGNER: *Mike Hicks* AGENCY: *Hixo, Inc.* ILLUSTRATORS: *Mike Hicks, Bill Geisler* COPYWRITERS: *Brian Sharples, Mike Hicks* CLIENT: *IntelliQuest* ■ *The directive was to create a distinct image to convey the future of technology and to thank participants in a worldwide study.* ● *Aufgabe dieses Plakates war es, die Zukunft der Technologie eindrucksvoll darzustellen und gleichzeitig den Teilnehmern einer weltweiten Untersuchung zu danken.* ▲ *Affiche visant à illustrer de façon marquante l'avenir de la technologie et à remercier les personnes ayant participé à une étude inernationale.*

PAGE 44 #58 ART DIRECTOR/DESIGNER: *William Chau* AGENCY: *Borders, Perrin & Norrander* PHOTOGRAPHER: *Cristiana Ceppas* COPYWRITER: *J. Michael Smith* CLIENT: *Western Wireless* ■ *The agency needed to convey that the client's cellular network provided better coverage than competitors. The poster was designed to make a quick visual impact.* ● *Bei diesem Plakat, das eindrucksvoll und leicht zugänglich sein sollte, ging es um die Darstellung der Überlegenheit des Kunden, was den Ausbau seines Netzes für Funktelephone angeht.* ▲ *Affiche promotionnelle illustrant la supériorité du réseau sans câble du client. Le visuel devait être fort et accrocheur.*

PAGE 44 #59 ART DIRECTOR/DESIGNER/PHOTOGRAPHER/ILLUSTRATOR: *Kathy Stanton* AGENCY: *Herman Miller, Inc.* *Kathy Stanton* COPYWRITERS: *Ellen Shapiro, Nancy Nordstrom* CLIENT: *Herman Miller, Inc.* ■ *This poster was created for the agency's annual picnic for employees/owners. The directive was to reflect the spirit of the picnic and the company.* ● *Plakat zum jährlichen Picknick der Möbelfirma Herman Miller. Dabei sollten die Stimmung des Picknicks und der Geist des Unternehmens zum Ausdruck kommen.* ▲ *Affiche pour le pique-nique annuel d'un fabricant de meubles, illustrant l'esprit de l'événement et la philosophie d'entreprise.*

PAGE 44 #60 ART DIRECTOR: *Andy Dreyfus* DESIGNER: *Michael Schwab* AGENCY: *CKS Partners* DESIGN FIRM: *Michael Schwab Studio* CLIENT: *American Presidents Line* ■ *Image used as the cover image for a 1996 calendar. The client is a worldwide container shipping line. The agency wanted to convey the visual drama and immensity of the company.* ● *Bild für den Umschlag eines Kalenders für 1996. Der Auftraggeber ist eine Reederei, deren Containerschiffe in alle Welt fahren.* ▲ *Image utilisée pour le calendrier 1996 d'une compagnie maritime internationale. Elle illustre l'importance de la société.*

PAGE 44 #61 ART DIRECTOR: *Dave Dickey* AGENCY: *Bozell* PHOTOGRAPHER: *Steve Umland* COPYWRITER: *Scott Jorgenson* CLIENT: *Bozell* ■ *This poster was placed in colleges to promote the agency's worldwide summer internship program. It was hung along with the "for sale" signs around campuses and employs the typical tear-off address and phone number found in such places.* ● *Mit diesem Plakat werden College-Studenten auf das Praktikumsangebot der Agentur aufmerksam gemacht. Es wurde in den Colleges an Orten ausgehängt, an denen auch die üblichen Zettel-Anzeigen zu finden sind. Wie diese benutzt das Plakat Abreissetiketten mit Namen und Telephonnummer.* ▲ *Placardée dans des universités au tableau des petites annonces, cette affiche proposait des stages dans l'agence du client. Les étudiants pouvaient détacher les étiquettes portant les coordonnées de l'agence.*

PAGE 44 #62 ART DIRECTOR/ DESIGNER: *Yang Kim* AGENCY: *Herman Miller, Inc.* COPYWRITERS: *Ellen Shapiro, Nancy Nordstrom* CLIENT: *Herman Miller, Inc.* ■ *Each year the agency sends out a poster to schools to promote its graphic design internship pro-*

gram. Its contents vary each year, and it has to grab attention on a low budget. Since the year-long program introduces young designers to the realities of professional practice, Ellen Shapiro's article "Reality Check: the market for design school graduates," was used. To make it convenient for students and so that the poster will not get stolen, there is a tear-off pad of application forms with all the information . ● Jedes Jahr verschickt Herman Millers interne Graphik-Abteilung ein Plakat an Schulen, um auf die Praktikumsmöglichkeiten aufmerksam zu machen. Es ist jedes Jahr anders, muss aber mit einem niedrigen Budget auskommen. Da es bei dem Jahresprogramm darum geht, die Studenten mit der Praxis und der Realität der Jobsuche vertraut zu machen, wurde ein Vortrag von Ellen Shapiro zu diesem Thema verwendet. Bewerbungsformulare mit den nötigen Informationen für die Studenten sind abreissbar, damit die Plakate nicht gestohlen werden. ▲ Chaque année, le service graphisme de l'agence envoie une affiche aux écoles pour les rendre attentives aux possibilités de stages. L'affiche, tous les ans différente, est réalisée à moindres frais. Le programme de l'année visant à familiariser les étudiants avec les réalités de la pratique et la recherche d'un emploi, une conférence sur ce thème a été donnée par Ellen Shapiro. Pour éviter le vol des affiches, celles-ci sont pourvues de formulaires d'inscription détachables comportant toutes les informations nécessaires.

PAGE 46 #63 ART DIRECTOR: *Charles Herbstreith* AGENCY: *Blum/Herbstreith, New York* PHOTOGRAPHER: *Craig Cutler* COPYWRITER: *Alan Blum* CLIENT: *Lalique, New York*

PAGE 46 #64 ART DIRECTOR/ DESIGNER: *Tom Antista* AGENCY: *Antista Fairclough Design* PHOTOGRAPHER: *Tom Antista* CLIENT: *Mont Source* ■ This poster was created as part of an identity for a men's skin care product line. Since the products use ingredients from around the world, the globe and fragmented shapes were used to convey this message. ● Das Plakat ist Teil einer Imagekampagne für eine Herren-Hautkosmetiklinie. Der Globus und die Formenfragmente sollten zum Ausdruck bringen, dass die Ingredienzen der Linie aus aller Welt stammen. ▲ Affiche faisant partie du programme d'identité visuelle d'une ligne de produits cosmétiques pour hommes. Le visuel illustre la provenance des composants des produits, sélectionnés dans le monde entier.

PAGE 46 #65 DESIGNER: *Susan Nye* AGENCY: *Susan Nye (Student Project)* CLIENT: *Clairol Hair*

PAGE 46 #66 DESIGNER: *Sarah Orchard (Student Project)* CLIENT: *Clairol Hair*

PAGE 47 #67-68 ART DIRECTOR: *Daisuke Nakatsuka* DESIGNER: *Kanna Numajiri* AGENCY: *Nakatsuka Daisuke Inc.* PHOTOGRAPHER/ILLUSTRATOR: *Shozo Nakamura* COPYWRITER: *Tom Nakatsuka* CLIENT: *Shu Uemura Cosmetics Inc.* ■ "Enjoy. Color's a personal experience." "Choose. Color's a personal matter." Poster series created for lipsticks. The posters present a color index and emphasize the lipsticks' unique colors, making it easier for customers to choose among the many varieties. ● Diese Plakate für Lippenstifte mit Farben-Index betonen die besonderen Farben der Lippenstiftmarke und erleichtern den Kundinnen die Entscheidung bei der grossen Auswahl. ▲ Affiche pour des rouges à lèvres comportant un index des couleurs afin de faciliter le choix des clientes parmi la vaste gamme proposée.

PAGE 48 #69 ART DIRECTOR/ DESIGNER: *Pierre David* AGENCY: *Pierre David Design* PHOTOGRAPHER: *Normand Gregoire* CLIENT: *Les Ballets Jazz de Montreal* ■ Announcement of dance performances by the Compagnie les Ballets Jazz de Montréal. ● Ankündigung von Jazz-Ballettaufführungen einer Balletttruppe. ▲ Affiche annonçant un spectacle de la compagnie Les Ballets Jazz de Montréal.

PAGE 48 #70 ART DIRECTOR/ DESIGNER: *Armin Lindauer* CLIENT: *Deutsche Oper Berlin* ■ Poster for a guest performance of the Tokyo Ballet at the Deutsche Oper Berlin. The objective was to find a symbol for "Tokyo/Japan" and another for "ballet" without showing preference to any particular performance. ● Plakat für eine Gastaufführung des Balletts von Tokio an der Deutschen Oper Berlin. Es ging darum, ein Symbol für Tokio/Japan und ein weiteres für Ballett zu finden, ohne sich auf eine bestimmte Aufführung zu beziehen. ▲ Affiche annonçant un spectacle du ballet de Tokyo à l'opéra de Berlin. L'objectif était de trouver un symbole pour Tokyo et le Japon, et un autre pour le ballet, toutefois sans faire référence à une représentation particulière.

PAGE 48 #71 ART DIRECTOR: *Julius Friedman* DESIGNERS: *Julius Friedman, Mike Slone* AGENCY: *Images* PHOTOGRAPHER/ILLUSTRATOR: *Dan Kremer* CLIENT: *The Louisville Ballet* ■ The agency utilized the symbols of the nutcracker dolls in a fantasy setting to depict the classic "Nutcracker" ballet. ● Nussknackerfiguren für die Ankündigung einer Aufführung des «Nussknacker»-Balletts. ▲ Personnages fantaisistes utilisés pour annoncer une représentation de Casse-Noisette.

PAGE 48 #72 ART DIRECTOR: *Robert Achten* DESIGNERS: *Robert Achten, Katherine Taylor* AGENCY: *Origin Design Company Ltd.* ILLUSTRATOR: *Ian Robertson* CLIENT: *The Royal New Zealand Ballet* ■ The client wanted an eye-catching image that would give a contemporary interpretation of one of the most well-known classical ballets. The agency kept the poster design very simple by using a stunning image with very elegant type. ● Gefragt war eine attraktive, zeitgenössische visuelle Interpretation der bekanntesten klassischen Ballette. Schlichtes Design und eine elegante Schrift unterstützen die Wirkung des ausdrucksvollen Bildes. ▲ Affiche au visuel moderne et accrocheur, présentant les grands ballets classiques. Le design épuré et la typographie élégante renforcent encore l'impact de l'affiche.

PAGE 49 #73 ART DIRECTOR/ DESIGNER/ILLUSTRATOR: *Kari Piippo* AGENCY: *Kari Piippo Oy* CLIENT: *Savcor*

PAGE 50 #74 ART DIRECTOR/ DESIGNER: *Candace Morgan* AGENCY: *The Leonhardt Group* PHOTOGRAPHER: *Ben Kerns* CLIENT: *Pacific Northwest Ballet* ■ The agency wanted to create a provocative poster that captured the essence of Swan Lake. Dramatic photography and hand lettering created a fluid and classic mood. Limited color assured a comfortable budget and striking contrast. ● Das Ballett «Schwanensee,» interpretiert durch dramatische Photographie, die zusammen mit der Handschrift eine klassische Note schuf. Der sparsame Einsatz von Farben sorgte für starke Kontraste - und dabei für niedrige Kosten. ▲ Affiche pour le Lac des cygnes, jouant avec une mise en scène dramatique et une écriture calligraphiée. L'emploi limité des couleurs renforce les contrastes et permit d'exploiter le budget au mieux.

PAGE 50 #75 ART DIRECTOR/DESIGNER: *Jean Benoît Levy* AGENCY: *7M.R.S. Communication* ILLUSTRATOR: *Philippe Pache* CLIENT: *Prix De Lausanne* ■ Poster for an internationally recognized classical dance competition. The graphics try to express the movement of dance. ● Plakat für einen international anerkannten Tanzwettbewerb. Hier ging es um die Darstellung tänzerischer Bewegungen. ▲ Affiche pour un célèbre concours de danse international, évoquant le mouvement des danseurs.

PAGE 50 #76 ART DIRECTOR/DESIGNER: *Jon Simonsen* AGENCY: *Muller & Company* PHOTOGRAPHER: *Kenny Johnson* ILLUSTRATOR: *Jon Simonsen* CLIENT: *Westport Ballet Theater* ■ Poster created for an urban dance event located in the historical Westport section of Kansas City. The agency wanted to create an image that would match the event's setting and mood. ● Plakat für eine städtische Tanzveranstaltung im historischen Westport-Viertel von Kansas City. Ort und Stimmung der Veranstaltung lieferten das Thema. ▲ Affiche pour un spectacle de danse donné dans le quartier historique de Westport à Kansas City. Thème de l'affiche: le lieu et la nature du spectacle.

PAGE 50 #77 ART DIRECTOR: *Larry Vignon* DESIGNER: *Brian Jackson* AGENCY: *Vigon / Ellis* PHOTOGRAPHER: *Taek* CLIENT: *University of California, Los Angeles Center For The Performing Arts* ■ This poster seeks to capture the spirit of the UCLA Performing Arts '95-'96 season. It is meant to be a high-profile piece which can be merchandised. ● Plakat für die Saison 95/96 des Zentrums für die darstellenden Künste an der University of California. Es sollte den Geist des Theaters wiedergeben und sich auch für den Verkauf eignen. ▲ Affiche visant à illustrer l'esprit du programme 95-96 de la section Arts du temps de l'Université de Californie. Cette affiche haut de gamme est destinée à la vente.

PAGE 52 #78, 79 ART DIRECTOR: *Dennis McKnew* DESIGNER: *Brian Sasville* AGENCY: *MWA Creative* PHOTOGRAPHER: *Alan Rosenberg* CLIENT: *In-house* ■ The agency wanted to emphasize that choosing a new ad agency–or firing one–is not a casual endeavor. This poster targets an audience that is fed up with its current agency's performance. ● Die Slogans dieser Plakate basieren auf Wortspielen. Die Moral von der Geschichte: Eine neue Agentur zu engagieren oder sich gar von einer alten zu trennen ist keine leichte Sache. Dieses Plakat richtete sich an Firmen, die mit der Leistung ihrer Werbeagentur unzufrieden sind. ▲ Affiche jouant sur des jeux de mots. Le message: engager une nouvelle agence ou se séparer de l'ancienne n'est pas une décision qui se prend à la légère. Cette affiche s'adressait aux sociétés qui n'étaient pas satisfaites de leur agence de publicité.

PAGE 52 #80 ART DIRECTOR/ DESIGNER: *David Brier* AGENCY: *DBD International Ltd.* ILLUSTRATORS: *David Brier, Michael Perna* CLIENT: *In-house* ■ This poster is part of a series of quarterly calendars inspired by the 1930s era of design. The agency wanted to achieve the kind of timeless charm the old posters achieved without being contrived. The illustration was designed to look like WPA relief sculpture using Illustrator and Photoshop. The custom typography at the top was developed to complement this time period. ● Das Plakat gehört zu einer Reihe von Vierteljahreskalendern, deren Design vom Stil der 30er Jahre in den USA inspiriert ist. Es wurde versucht, den Charme alter

Plakate einzufangen, ohne gekünstelt zu wirken. Die Illustration entstand mit Hilfe von Illustrator und Photoshop, wobei die Schrift oben speziell entwickelt wurde, um dem Stil der Zeit gerecht zu werden. ▲Affiche faisant partie d'une série de calendriers trimestriels, dont le graphisme s'inspire des années 30. L'objectif était de lui conférer un côté rétro et authentique. L'illustration a été réalisée avec Illustrator et Photoshop, et une typo spéciale a été créée pour refléter l'esprit de l'époque.

PAGE 52 #81 ART DIRECTORS: *Steve Wedeen, Dan Flynn* DESIGNERS: *Dan Flynn* COMPUTER IMAGING: *Stan McCoy* AGENCY: *Vaughn/Wedeen Creative* PHOTOGRAPHER/ILLUSTRATOR: *Vivian Harder* CLIENT: *US West Communications*

PAGE 53 #82 ART DIRECTOR: *Bi Xuefeng* DESIGNERS: *Bi Xuefeng, Yike Chen* AGENCY/CLIENT: *Yike Chen Design Co. Ltd* PHOTOGRAPHER/ILLUSTRATOR: *Gao Zhimin* COPYWRITER: *Fortune DTP Compugraphic Ltd.*

PAGE 54 #83, 84 ART DIRECTOR/DESIGNER: *Leslie Chan Wing Kei* AGENCY: *Leslie Chan Design Co. Ltd.* CLIENT: *Taiwan Image Poster Design Association* ■*Series of posters on the theme of consumer products depicting the traditional folk culture of Taiwan. Modern design techniques were used to bring out the rich and vivid colors of Taiwan. ●Die traditionelle Kultur von Taiwan ist Gegenstand einer Plakatserie, die sich mit Gebrauchsgegenständen befasst. Moderne Design-Techniken wurden eingesetzt, um die kräftigen, lebendigen Farben Taiwans wiederzugeben. ▲Série d'affiches consacrée à la culture traditionnelle de Taïwan et illustrant des produits de consommation. Des techniques de design modernes ont été utilisées pour rendre les couleurs franches et vives de Taïwan.*

PAGE 55 #85, 86 ART DIRECTORS: *Lanny Sommese, Kristin Sommese* DESIGNER: *Kristin Sommese* AGENCY: *Sommese Design* ILLUSTRATOR: *Lanny Sommese* CLIENT: *In-house* ■ *These posters are part of a series sent out by the design studio to friends, clients, and prospective clients. The line images are "tongue in cheek" representations of the fact that the partners of the firm are a husband and wife/wife and husband team (depending on the way you look at the posters). ●Die Plakate gehören zu einer Serie, die von einem Design Studio an Freunde sowie an verhandene und potentielle Kunden verschickt wird. Dabei wird auf humorvolle Art verdeutlicht, dass es sich um ein Ehepaar handelt – je nach Betrachtungsweise um ein Mann-und-Frau- oder ein Frau-und-Mann-Team. ▲ Série d'affiches réalisée par une agence de design graphique et envoyée aux amis et aux clients potentiels. Le visuel représente de manière humoristique l'équipe de l'agence, un couple mari-femme ou femme-mari suivant comment on regarde l'affiche.*

PAGE 55 #87, 88 ART DIRECTOR: *Keisuke Kimura* DESIGNERS: *Keisuke Kimura, Maki Yanagishima* AGENCY: *Magna Inc. Advertising* PHOTOGRAPHER/ILLUSTRATOR: *Naohiro Isshiki* COPYWRITER: *Keisuke Kimura* CLIENT: *Rakuten Design Room*

PAGE 56 #89 DESIGNER: *Rob Latimer* AGENCY: *Hallmark Cards Inc.* CLIENT: *In-house* ■ *This assignment dealt with two requests: to create a poster exploring new techniques utilizing Adobe Photoshop and to incorporate a quote on design that would be the main emphasis of the piece. Photoshop filters were used to give a soft textured feel to the artwork. An Art Deco font was designed and then artwork was built around the typeface. ●Hier ging es um zwei Aufgaben: Das Plakat sollte ein Beispiel für den Einsatz neuer Techniken mit Adobe Photoshop sein und ausserdem ein Zitat über Design enthalten, das auch zum Thema des Plakates werden sollte. Photoshop-Filter wurden benutzt, um die sanfte, stoffliche Wirkung des Plakates zu erzielen. Das Design-Studio entwarf eine Art-Déco-Schrift, um die herum dann die anderen Bildelemente aufgebaut wurden. ▲Cette affiche poursuivait deux objectifs: illustrer d'une part de nouvelles techniques avec Adobe Photoshop et intégrer d'autre part une citation sur le design, élément-clé de l'affiche. Des filtres Photoshop ont été utilisés pour conférer un effet de texture spécial. Une typo art déco a été créée, autour de laquelle s'articulent les autres éléments de l'image.*

PAGE 56 #90 DESIGNER: *Steve Mark* AGENCY: *Hallmark Cards Inc.* CLIENT: *In-house* ■ *This assignment dealt with two requests: to create a poster exploring new techniques utilizing Adobe Photoshop and to incorporate a quote on design that would be the main emphasis of the piece. This design focused on using various Photoshop plug-in filters to achieve an experimental effect and to emphasize using type as design elements. ●Hier ging es um zwei Aufgaben: Das Plakat sollte ein Beispiel für den Einsatz neuer Techniken mit Adobe Photoshop sein und ausserdem ein Zitat über Design enthalten, das auch zum Thema des Plakates werden sollte. Hier wurden verschiedene Photoshop Plug-in-Filter verwendet, um einen experimentellen Effekt zu erzielen, während Typographie das wichtigste Gestaltungselement ist. ▲Cette affiche poursuivait deux objectifs: illustrer d'une part de nouvelles techniques avec Adobe Photoshop et intégrer d'autre part une citation, élément-clé de l'affiche. Des filtres Photoshop ont été utilisés pour*

conférer un effet de texture spécial. Une typo art déco a été créée, autour de laquelle s'articulent les autres éléments de l'image.

PAGE 56 #91 DESIGNER: *Dave Bugay* AGENCY: *Hallmark Cards Inc.* CLIENT: *In-house* ■ *This assignment dealt with two requests: to create a poster exploring new techniques utilizing Adobe Photoshop and to incorporate a quote on design that would be the main emphasis of the piece. The quote was the Webster's dictionary's definition of design. The artwork and type were manipulated using various Photoshop plug-in filters to achieve an experimental effect. ●Hier ging es um zwei Aufgaben: Das Plakat sollte ein Beispiel für den Einsatz neuer Techniken mit Adobe Photoshop sein und ausserdem ein Zitat zum Thema Design enthalten, das auch Gegenstand des Plakates werden sollte. Das Zitat ist eine Definition des Begriffes Design aus dem Webster's-Lexikon. Bildelemente und Typographie wurden mit Hilfe verschiedener Photoshop-Plug-in-Filter manipuliert, um dem Plakat einen experimentellen Charakter zu verleihen. ▲Cette affiche poursuivait deux objectifs: illustrer d'une part de nouvelles techniques avec Adobe Photoshop et intégrer d'autre part une citation sur le design, élément-clé de l'affiche. La citation est une définition du terme «design» extraite du dictionnaire Webster. Les éléments de l'image et la typo ont été manipulés avec différents filtres Photoshop et confèrent un caractère expérimental au visuel.*

PAGE 56 #92 DESIGNER: *Jackson Wang* AGENCY: *Hallmark Cards Inc.* CLIENT: *In-house* ■ *This assignment dealt with two requests: to create a poster exploring new techniques utilizing Adobe Photoshop and to incorporate a quote on design that would be the main emphasis of the piece. Photoshop filters were used to create a dreamy and ominous look for the background. ●Hier ging es um zwei Aufgaben: Das Plakat sollte ein Beispiel für den Einsatz neuer Techniken mit Adobe Photoshop sein und ausserdem ein Zitat zum Thema Design enthalten, das auch Gegenstand des Plakates werden sollte. Photoshop-Filter wurden eingesetzt, um die traumartige, bedrohliche Wirkung des Hintergrunds zu erzeugen. ▲Cette affiche poursuivait deux objectifs: illustrer d'une part de nouvelles techniques avec Adobe Photoshop et intégrer d'autre part une citation sur le design, élément-clé de l'affiche. Des filtres Photoshop ont été utilisés pour créer l'effet menaçant du fond.*

PAGE 57 #93 ART DIRECTORS: *Stephen Starr, Robin Lazarus* DESIGNER: *Stephen Starr* AGENCY: *Shadow Design* PHOTOGRAPHER: *Stephen Starr* CLIENT: *Shadow Design/International Printing* ■ *The agency needed to take an ordinary subject and present it in an extraordinary way. To approximate the chrome values of the photograph, a chrome mylar stock was used; the image was proofed several times and adjusted. An extra press run was required for polishing. ●Hier sollte ein gewöhnliches Thema auf ungewöhnliche Art dargestellt werden. Um den Farbwerten der Aufnahme in etwa gerecht zu werden, wurde ein Spezialpapier (Chrome Mylar) verwendet; das Bild wurde mehrmals abgestimmt. Für den Glanz war ein extra Druckdurchgang nötig. ▲L'objectif était de présenter un thème commun de manière originale. Pour obtenir les couleurs du document original, un papier spécial (chrome mylar stock) a été utilisé, et l'image a été retravaillée plusieurs fois. Le brillant a requis une phase d'impression supplémentaire.*

PAGE 57 #94 ART DIRECTORS: *Willie Baronet, Steve Gibbs* DESIGNER: *Bronson Ma* AGENCY: *Gibbs Baronet* COPYWRITERS: *Bronson Ma, Willie Baronet* CLIENT: *In-house* ■ *Christmas design for a graphic design studio. ●Weihnachtsplakat eines Design-Studios. ▲Affiche de Noël d'une agence de design graphique.*

PAGE 58 #95 ART DIRECTOR/ DESIGNER: *Toyotsugu Itoh* AGENCY: *Toyotsugu Itoh Design Office* ILLUSTRATOR: *Fumihiko Mizutani* CLIENT: *International Design Center Nagoya, Inc.* ■ *This promotional poster was created for the International Design Center in Nagoya. The designer's focus was on "human beings: existence and thought" and what the future holds in store. ●Plakat für das International Design Center in Nagoya. Thema sind die Menschen, ihr Leben, ihre Gedanken und ihre Zukunft. ▲Affiche du Centre de design international de Nagoya. Thème de l'affiche: les gens, leur vie, leurs pensées et leur avenir.*

PAGE 58 #96 ART DIRECTOR/DESIGNER: *Yoshimaru Takahashi* AGENCY: *Koukokumaru Inc.* CLIENT: *Osaka Contemporary Art Center*

PAGE 59 #97 ART DIRECTOR: *Ken Slazyc* AGENCY: *Michael Schwab Studio* PHOTOGRAPHER/ILLUSTRATOR: *Michael Schwab* PRINTER: *Stevenson Photocolor/Signco* CLIENT: *Art Directors Club Of Cincinnati* ■ *This screen-printed poster was used as an announcement for a guest lecture by the artist in Cincinnati. The image was created from a previously rejected sketch from a past project. The model for this poster was Mark Fox, president of AIGA, San Francisco. The printer's mark appears in the lower left corner. ●Das Siebdruckplakat diente als Einladung und Information über eine Gastvorlesung* *des Künstlers Michael Schwab in Cincinnati. Das Modell für dieses Plakat ist Mark Fox, Präsident des AIGA San Francisco. Das Zeichen des Druckers ist unten links angebracht.* ▲ *Sérigraphie tenant lieu d'invitation et d'information pour une conférence de l'artiste Michael Schwab à Cincinnati. Mark Fox, président de l'AIGA San Francisco, pose sur l'affiche. Le logo de l'imprimerie figure en bas à gauche.*

PAGE 59 #98 ART DIRECTOR/DESIGNER/PHOTOGRAPHER/ILLUSTRATOR: *Popov Kamen* AGENCY: *Studio Radar* CLIENT: *Biensfeld Conseil*

PAGE 59 #99 ART DIRECTOR/ DESIGNER: *Wang Yue Fei* AGENCY: *Graficom Co. Ltd.* PHOTOGRAPHER/ILLUSTRATOR: *Wang Wen Liang* COPYWRITER: *Fortune Dip Compugraphic Ltd.* CLIENT: *Shenzhen Graphic Design Association* ■ *The designer used a pair of scissors from Europe and a hammer from China to form a letter "A."* ● *Eine Schere aus Europa und ein Hammer aus China bilden hier den Buchstaben «A».* ▲ *Des ciseaux européens et un marteau chinois forment la lettre «A».*

PAGE 59 #100 ART DIRECTOR: *Bi Xuefeng* DESIGNERS: *Bi Xuefeng, Yike Chen* AGENCY: *Yike Chen Design Co. Ltd.* PHOTOGRAPHER: *Gao Zhimin* ILLUSTRATOR: *Bi Xuefeng* COPYWRITER: *Fortune DTP Compugraphic Ltd.* CLIENT: *Yike Chen Design Co. Ltd.*

PAGE 60 #101-103 ART DIRECTOR: *John Muller* DESIGNER: *Jennifer Brosnahan* AGENCY: *Muller & Company* COPYWRITER: *David Marks* CLIENT: *In-house* ■ *Self-promotion for design firm/ad agency created to grab attention and position the firm as a creative shop available to clients across the US.* ● *Eigenwerbung eines Design- und Werbestudios, das Kunden aus allen Regionen der USA gewinnen möchte.* ▲ *Publicité autopromotionnelle d'une agence de design et de publicité s'adressant aux clients de toutes les régions des Etats-Unis.*

PAGE 61 #104 ART DIRECTOR/DESIGNER/PHOTOGRAPHER/ILLUSTRATOR: *Ray Redding* CLIENT: *Annie Watkins Redding*

PAGE 61 #105 ART DIRECTORS: *Louis Brunelle, Marie Couture* DESIGNERS: *Louis Brunelle, Denis St. Pierre* AGENCY: *Parallele Communication-Design* PHOTOGRAPHER: *François Brunelle* CLIENT: *In-house* ■ *The agency was seeking to communicate to its clients in a striking visual way the creative force resulting from the merger of two firms reputed for their excellence in graphic design. This was portrayed with two pencils joined together, offering a simple and highly effective solution.* ● *Hier ging es darum, potentielle Kunden auf den Zusammenschluss zweier Graphikstudios aufmerksam zu machen, die beide einen ausgezeichneten Ruf geniessen und zusammen ein enormes Potential an Kreativität bieten.* ▲ *Affiche annonçant la fusion de deux agences de graphisme réputées pour leur créativité.*

PAGE 62 #106 ART DIRECTORS: *Sergey Ilyin, Sergey Shanovich* AGENCY: *Grade Group* PHOTOGRAPHER/ILLUSTRATOR: *V. Teplov* COPYWRITER: *Ilyin Sergey* CLIENT: *In-house* ■ *Poster created as a Self-promotional piece.* ● *Eigenwerbung eines Graphikstudios aus der Ukraine.* ▲ *Publicité autopromotionnelle d'une agence de graphisme urkrainienne.*

PAGE 62 #107 AGENCY: *Alligator Design Associates* Client: *(In-house)*

PAGE 62 #108 ART DIRECTOR/ DESIGNER: *Makoto Saito* AGENCY: *Makoto Saito Design Office Inc.* CLIENT: *International Design Center Nagoya Inc.*

PAGE 62 #109 ART DIRECTOR/ DESIGNER: *Wang Xu* AGENCY: *Wang Xu & Associates* CLIENT: *Shenzhen Graphic Design Association*

PAGE 63 #110 ART DIRECTOR/ DESIGNER: *Timotei Nadasan* AGENCY: *Idea Design & Print* COPYWRITER/CLIENT: *Idea Design & Print*

PAGE 64 #111, 112 ART DIRECTOR/DESIGNER: *Ariel Pintos* ASSISTANT DESIGNER: *Gabriela Fontanillas* AGENCY/CLIENT: *Prodiseño School of Visual Communication* ■ *Promotion for Prodiseño School of Visual Communication. Diverse emblematic images representing the school were recreated in posters and assembled into one poster. The opposite side of each poster contains the annual program and the requirements to apply to the school.* ● *Werbung für eine Schule für visuelle Kommunikation. Verschiedene Bilder, die emblematisch für die Schule sind, wurden zu Plakaten, die wiederum in einem grossen Plakat zusammengefasst sind. Zu jedem Plakat sind auch das Jahresprogramm und die Anmeldebedingungen vermerkt.* ▲ *Publicité d'une école de communication visuelle. Les affiches – différentes images emblématiques de l'école – forment ensemble une grande affiche. Au dos de chaque affiche figurent le programme annuel et les conditions d'inscription.*

PAGE 64 #113 ART DIRECTOR: *Peter Wong* DESIGNERS: *Peter Wong, Alexis Horlbeck* AGENCY: *Atlanta College of Art, Communication Design Department* PHOTOGRAPHER: *Kevin Sartain* CLIENT: *In-house*

PAGE 64 #114 DESIGNER: *Alan Fletcher* CLIENT: *Icograda Student Seminar*

PAGE 65 #115 DESIGNERS: *Hans-Heinrich Sures, Ingo Eulen (Student Project)* SCHOOL: *Fachhochschule Dortmund* ■ *This poster was created for a symposium on the scope and super 35 movie formats. The strategy was to show the location of the symposium in the scope movie-format. The black "letterbox" is well known from television when broadcasting scope movies.* ● *Auftritt für ein Symposium über Cinemascope und Super-35-Kinofilmformate. Es ging darum, den Ort des Symposiums und das Cinemascope-Format darzustellen. Die schwarzen Streifen sind typisch für TV-Ausstrahlungen solcher Filmformate.* ▲ *Identité visuelle créée pour un symposium consacré au cinémascope et aux films en super 35. L'idée fut de montrer l'endroit où a lieu le symposium en cinémascope. Les bandes noires s'affichent sur le téléviseur lors de la diffusion de films de ce format.*

PAGE 65 #116 ART DIRECTOR/ DESIGNER: *Woody Pirtle* AGENCY: *Pentagram Design, Inc.* PHOTOGRAPHER: *William Whitehurst* CLIENT: *University of California - Los Angeles* ■ *"I'd rather be at the beach!" is the likely response to the idea of summer school in southern California. This poster for UCLA's summer sessions of continuing education courses makes light of this by using a surfer riding the pages of a book.* ● *«Ich wäre lieber am Strand» – eine naheliegende Reaktion, wenn ein Sommersemester in Südkalifornien zur Debatte steht. Dieses Plakat für das Weiterbildungsprogramm der UCLA im Sommer nimmt den Gedanken auf.* ▲ *«Je préférerais être à la plage!», une réaction classique à l'idée de passer le semestre d'été dans une université de la Californie du sud. Affiche réalisée pour le programme de formation continue de l'UCLA.*

PAGE 66 #117 ART DIRECTOR/ DESIGNER: *Bülent Erkman* AGENCY: *BEK* CLIENT: *Bogazigi University* ■ *Poster for the VIIth International Congress for the study of "child language."* ● *Plakat für einen internationalen Kongress, der sich mit Untersuchungen der Sprache der Kinder befasst.* ▲ *Affiche d'un congrès international consacré à l'étude du langage des enfants.*

PAGE 66 #118 ART DIRECTOR/DESIGNER: *Peter Good* AGENCY: *Cummings & Good* PHOTOGRAPHER: *Sean Kernan* CLIENT: *Conneticut Impressionist Art Trail* ■ *To creatively announce a collective of museums that have American Impressionist paintings, each paint tube has the name of one of the museums as its label.* ● *Dieses Plakat ist das Ergebnis einer gemeinsamen Aktion verschiedener amerikanischer Museen, die Werke amerikanischer Impressionisten besitzen. Jede Farbtube präsentiert den Namen eines der beteiligten Museen.* ▲ *Affiche résultant de la collaboration de différents musées américains possédant des œuvres d'impressionnistes américains. Les tubes de couleur présentent les noms des musées.*

PAGE 67 #119 ART DIRECTOR: *Silas H. Rhodes* DESIGNER/ARTIST/ILLUSTRATOR: *George Tscherny* AGENCY: *Visual Arts Press, Ltd.* PHOTOGRAPHER: *Oskar Villegas* COPYWRITER: *Silas H. Rhodes* CLIENT: *School of Visual Arts* ■ *This poster introduces the School of Visual Arts' new symbol and commemorates its 50th anniversary.* ● *Plakat zum 50jährigen Bestehen der School of Visual Arts, das gleichzeitig das neue Symbol der Schule vorstellt.* ▲ *Affiche réalisée pour le 50e anniversaire de la School of Visual Arts, présentant par la même occasion le nouveau symbole de l'école.*

PAGE 67 #120 ART DIRECTOR/COPYWRITER: *Silas H. Rhodes* AGENCY: *Visual Arts Press, Ltd.* ARTIST/ILLUSTRATOR: *Marshall Arisman* CLIENT: *School of Visual Arts*

PAGE 67 #121 ART DIRECTOR/COPYWRITER: *Silas H. Rhodes* DESIGNER: *James Victore* AGENCY: *Visual Arts Press, Ltd.* ARTIST/ILLUSTRATOR: *James Victore* CLIENT: *School of Visual Arts*

PAGE 67 #122 ART DIRECTOR/COPYWRITER: *Silas H. Rhodes* DESIGNER: *Milton Glaser* AGENCY: *Visual Arts Press, Ltd.* PHOTOGRAPHER: *Matthew Klein* CLIENT: *School of Visual Arts*

PAGE 67 #123 ART DIRECTOR/COPYWRITER: *Silas H. Rhodes* DESIGNER/PHOTOGRAPHER/ILLUSTRATOR: *Tony Palladino* AGENCY: *Visual Arts Press, Ltd.* CLIENT: *School of Visual Arts*

PAGE 67 #124 ART DIRECTOR/COPYWRITER: *Silas H. Rhodes* AGENCY: *Visual Arts Press, Ltd.* ILLUSTRATOR: *Jerry Moriarty* CLIENT: *School of Visual Arts*

PAGE 67 #125 ART DIRECTOR/COPYWRITER: *Silas H. Rhodes* AGENCY: *Visual Arts Press, Ltd.* ARTIST/PHOTOGRAPHER/ILLUSTRATOR: *Eve Sonneman* CLIENT: *School of Visual Arts*

PAGE 67 #126 ART DIRECTOR/COPYWRITER: *Silas H. Rhodes* DESIGNER/PHOTOGRAPHER/ILLUSTRATOR: *Paul Davis* AGENCY: *Visual Arts Press, Ltd.* CLIENT: *School of Visual Arts*

PAGE 67 #127 ART DIRECTOR/COPYWRITER: *Silas H. Rhodes* DESIGNER/PHOTOGRAPHER/ILLUSTRATOR: *Jim McMullan* AGENCY: *Visual Arts Press, Ltd.* CLIENT: *School of Visual Arts*

PAGE 68 #128-131 ART DIRECTOR/ DESIGNER: *Kazumasa Nagai* AGENCY: *Nippon Design Center, Inc.* CLIENT: *Japan Design Committee* ■ *"Save nature"; "Life"* ● *Plakate zum Thema Umwelt: «Rettet die Natur»; «Leben».* ▲ *Affiches sur le thème de l'environnement: «Sauvons la nature!»; «La Vie».*

PAGE 69 #132-134 ART DIRECTOR/ DESIGNER: *Savas Cekic* AGENCY: *Valor Tasarim* ILLUSTRATOR: *Savas Cekic*

PAGE 70 #135 ART DIRECTOR/ DESIGNER: *Nina Ulmaja* AGENCY: *Nina Ulmaja Grafisk Form* PHOTOGRAPHERS/COPYWRITERS: *Eric Erfors, Nina Ulmaja* CLIENT: *Stockholm Vatten AB/Artgenda Exhibition 96* ■ *"Flushed." Seventy tons of trash have to be hauled away every week from a single sewage treatment plant in Stockholm. The designer wanted to make people see the connection between the use of their toilets and the damage it causes to the environment. The traditional method for this type of public campaign would be to show photos of nature in an idyllic environment–pictures impossible to associate with personal use of water. The designer opted for a witty and non-traditional campaign by showing what is being flushed.* ● *«Runtergespült.» Siebzig Tonnen Abfall müssen pro Woche aus einer einzigen Kläranlage in Stockholm abtransportiert werden. Hier ging es darum, die Leute auf die Schäden aufmerksam zu machen, die sie mit dem unbedachten Gebrauch ihrer Toilette der Umwelt zufügen. Indem sie zeigt, was alles so weggespült wird, schuf die Gestalterin eine witzige, ungewöhnliche Kampagne.* ▲ *«Et hop!» Soixante-dix tonnes de déchets par semaine doivent être transportées d'une seule station d'épuration à Stockholm. L'objectif était d'attirer l'attention des gens sur les dommages causés à l'environnement lorsque l'on jette tout et n'importe quoi dans les toilettes. En montrant tout ce qui passe dans les toilettes, la graphiste a réalisé une campagne humoristique et originale.*

PAGE 70 #136 ART DIRECTOR/ DESIGNER: *Derrick Seah* CREATIVE DIRECTOR: *Jim Aitchinson* AGENCY: *Batey Ads Singapore* PHOTOGRAPHER/ILLUSTRATOR: *Procolor Pte. Ltd.* COPYWRITER: *Antony Redman* CLIENT: *Asian Pals of The Planet* ■ *"Each car spews 3 times its weight in carbon monoxide into the atmosphere every year." To show that automobiles do much more damage than the public may think, the agency took an automobile cliché (the hood ornament) and twisted it.* ● *«Jedes Jahr lässt jedes Auto das Dreifache seines Gewichtes an Kohlenmonoxid in die Atmosphäre ab.» Hier ging es darum, der Öffentlichkeit klar zu machen, dass Autos mehr Schaden anrichten, als allgemein angenommen wird. Die Kühlerfigur symbolisiert das Auto.* ▲ *«Par an, chaque véhicule dégage dans l'atmosphère le triple de son poids en oxyde de carbone.» L'objectif était de rendre les gens attentifs au fait que les voitures polluent beaucoup plus qu'on ne l'imagine. La figure de proue symbolise le véhicule.*

PAGE 70 #137, 138 ART DIRECTOR/DESIGNER: *Yoshimaru Takahashi* AGENCY: *Koukokumaru Inc.* CLIENT: *The Cultural Festival for Nations*

PAGE 71 #139 ART DIRECTOR/ DESIGNER/COPYWRITER: *Yossi Lemel* ■ *"We don't need another Hiro." This poster was a personal reaction to the nuclear experiments that were conducted by the French government 50 years after the atomic bomb exploded over Hiroshima. The designer played on the lyrics of the famous Tina Turner song. The campaign included posters and postcards that were sent to France and Japan.* ● *"We don't need another Hiro." Der Text des Plakates bezieht sich auf den berühmten Song von Tina Turner. Es richtet sich gegen die Atomversuche Frankreichs – 50 Jahre nach dem Abwurf der Atombombe auf Hiroshima. Zur Kampagne gehören Plakate und Postkarten, die an die Regierungen Frankreichs und Japans geschickt wurden.* ▲ *«We don't need another Hiro.» Affiche critiquant les essais nucléaires français 50 ans après Hiroshima. La headline fait référence à la célèbre chanson de Tina Turner. Cette campagne incluait des affiches et des cartes postales qui ont été envoyées aux gouvernements français et japonais.*

PAGE 71 #140 ART DIRECTOR: *Lanny Sommese* DESIGNER: *Marina Garza* AGENCY: *Practicum*

PAGE 72 #141 ART DIRECTOR/DESIGNER: *D.C. Stipp* AGENCY: *RBMM* COPYWRITER: *Rich Flora* CLIENT: *CHS Class Of '76* ■ *Twenty-year reunion poster created for the class of 1976. The patriotism of the bicentennial year and the class itself is reflected in the 1776 flag design. Note: D.C. Stipp passed away on December 26, 1996. He is remembered by his two sons, his wife Jeanette, and his colleagues at RBMM.* ● *Thema dieses Plakates ist ein Klassentreffen zwanzig Jahre nach Schulabschluss im Jahre 1976, dem Jahr der Zweihundertjahrfeier der USA. Die Flagge aus dem Jahre 1779 sorgt für die patriotische Note. Anmerkung: D.C. Stipp verstarb am 26. Dezember 1996. Seine Frau Jeanette, seine beiden Söhne und seine Kollegen der Agentur RBMM trauern um ihn.* ▲ *Thème de l'affiche: une réunion d'anciens étudiants vingt ans après la remise des diplômes en 1976, l'année du bicentenaire des Etats-Unis. Le drapeau de 1779 confère une touche patriotique. Remarque: D.C. Stipp est décédé le 26 décembre 1996. Sa femme Jeanette, ses deux fils et les collaborateurs de l'agence RBMM sont unis dans la douleur.*

PAGE 72 #142 ART DIRECTOR/DESIGNER: *Michael Gericke* AGENCY: *Pentagram Design, Inc.* CLIENT: *AIA Heritage Ball* ■ *Poster commemorating Philip Johnson's receipt of the AIA Honor Award.* ● *Plakat anlässlich der Verleihung des AIA Honor Award an den Architekten Philip Johnson.* ▲ *Affiche commémorant la remise de l'AIA Honor Award à Philip Johnson.*

PAGE 73 #143 ART DIRECTOR: *Karl Madcharo* AGENCY: *Cleveland Clark Inc.* PHOTOGRAPHER/ILLUSTRATOR: *David Kiesgan* COPYWRITER: *Bob Cianfrone* CLIENT: *Creative Club of Atlanta* ■ *Poster promoting a creativity workshop.* ● *Plakat für einen kreativen Workshop.* ▲ *Affiche pour un workshop créatif.*

PAGE 73 #144 ART DIRECTOR: *Tim Larsen* DESIGNER/PHOTOGRAPHER/ILLUSTRATOR: *David Shultz* AGENCY: *Larsen Design Office, Inc.* CLIENT: *American Marketing Association, Minnesota Chapter* ■ *This poster format was developed to encourage public display, thereby informing and persuading additional audiences in the business environment to attend a digital marketing conference.* ● *Das Plakat, das auf eine Tagung zum Thema digitales Marketing aufmerksam macht, ist auch für den Aussenaushang konzipiert, um ein breiteres Publikum anzusprechen.* ▲ *Affiche annonçant une conférence consacrée au marketing numérique et destinée aux lieux d'affichage publics pour atteindre un plus large public, en particulier les hommes d'affaires.*

PAGE 74 #145 ART DIRECTOR/ DESIGNER: *Primo Angeli* AGENCY: *Primo Angeli Inc.* COMPUTER ILLUSTRATORS: *Marcelo De Freitas, Mark Jones* CLIENT: *Atlanta Committee for the Olympic Games* ■ *Poster created to represent the 1996 Olympic Games. The design places the athletic figure at the center of the composition and takes on a classic Greek sculptural significance through use of the symbolic star and flame across its torso, defining the human form.* ● *Plakat für die Olympischen Spiele 1996. Die Gestalt eines Athleten im Mittelpunkt der Komposition erinnert an eine klassische griechische Skulptur.* ▲ *Affiche pour les Jeux olympiques de 1996. L'athlète figurant au centre de la composition rappelle les sculptures grecques classiques.*

PAGE 74 #146 ART DIRECTOR/ DESIGNER: *Logvin Andrey* AGENCY: *Logvin Design* CLIENT: *Liniagrafic Print Company*

PAGE 75 #147, 148 ART DIRECTOR: *Lowell Williams* DESIGNERS: *Lowell Williams, Bill Carsen* AGENCY: *Pentagram Design Inc.* ILLUSTRATOR: *David Grimes* CLIENT: *In-house*

PAGE 76 #149, 150 ART DIRECTOR/ DESIGNER: *Peter Felder* AGENCY: *Felder Grafik Design* PHOTOGRAPHER: *Georg Alfare* COPYWRITER: *Pablo Neruda* CLIENT: *Trama Visual AG* ■ *Poster design for the fourth poster biennial held in Mexico.* ● *Plakat für die 4. Plakatbiennale in Mexiko 1996.* ▲ *Affiche pour la 4ᵉ édition de la Biennale de l'Affiche à Mexico en 1996.*

PAGE 76 #151 ART DIRECTOR/DESIGNER: *Pierre Mendell* AGENCY: *Mendell & Oberer* CLIENT: *Bayerische Staatsoper*

PAGE 76 #152 ART DIRECTORS/ DESIGNERS: *Jeff Lin, James Pettus* AGENCY: *Keiler & Company* ILLUSTRATOR: *Jim Coon* COPYWRITER: *Doretta Wildes* CLIENT: *Connecticut Art Directors Club* ■ *The main challenge was encouraging participation for a statewide student design contest despite scant reception in previous years due to the latent fears that prohibit many young designers from exposing themselves to unknown and potentially unforgiving critics. The agency also had to compete for attention on densely populated campus bulletin boards. A spark plug was used to symbolize the creative fire everyone has to build from scratch. The copy took all its cues from the visual; in essence, a plug for self-started creativity.* ● *Dieses Plakat sollte Studenten zur Teilnahme an einem*

Design-Wettbewerb motivieren. Keine leichte Aufgabe in Anbetracht der eher mageren Beteiligung im Vorjahr, die einerseits auf die schulischen Anforderungen, andererseits auf die Furcht der Studenten vor unerbittlichen Juries zurückzuführen ist. Ausserdem musste sich das Plakat im dichten Gedränge der Mitteilungen an den schwarzen Brettern der Schulen durchsetzen können. ▲ Affiche invitant les étudiants à participer à un concours de design national. Une tâche ardue au vu de la maigre participation au concours précédent, les exigences étant élevées et les étudiants craignant la sévérité notoire du jury. L'affiche devait se démarquer au milieu des nombreuses petites annonces et autres communications du tableau d'affichage.

PAGE 77 #153 ART DIRECTOR: *Steve Mignogna, Hans Neubert* DESIGNERS: *Hans Neubert, Michelle Marks* AGENCY: *Belk Mignogna Associates, Ltd.* CLIENT: *Mead Fine Papers*

PAGE 77 #154 ART DIRECTORS/DESIGNERS/COPYWRITERS: *Traci Daberko, Dennis Clouse* AGENCY: *Cyclone* CLIENT: *AIGA Seattle* ■ *The objective was to invite AIGA members to Seattle for the 6th annual AIGA National Design Conference, but, at the same time, dissuade them from moving there!* ● *«Es regnet 300 Tage im Jahr. Wir leben in der Nähe eines aktiven Vulkans. Wir erwarten ein Erdbeben von 9.5 auf der Richterskala. Cobain ist tot, und die Möwen machen uns auf den Kopf.» An AIGA-Mitglieder gerichtete Einladung zur Teilnahme an der jährlich stattfindenden AIGA National Design Conference. Es lädt zwar zum Kommen, aber nicht zum Bleiben ein - eine Vorsichtsmassnahme, die angesichts der Attraktivität der Stadt Seattle geboten schien. ▲ «Il pleut 300 jours par an. Nous vivons près d'un volcan en activité. On attend un tremblement de terre de 9,5 sur l'échelle de Richter. Cobain est mort, et les mouettes nous chient sur la tête!» Affiche invitant les membres de l'AIGA à participer à la 6e édition annuelle de l'AIGA National Design Conference à Seattle.*

PAGE 78 #155 ART DIRECTOR/ DESIGNER: *Anil Revri* AGENCY: *Anil Revri Studio*

PAGE 78 #156 ART DIRECTORS/ DESIGNERS: *Art Chantry, Jamie Sheehan* AGENCY: *Sheehan Design* CLIENT: *Seattle Peace Heathens* ■ *This poster was designed for a festival that had trouble procuring permits and dealing with city officials. Therefore, the design message evolved from all these situations: a policeman was used as the spokesperson. Because the event stirred up so much controversy, the agency chose the "Reefer Madness" feel. The pot leaf iconography shows attendees the event is true to its pro-hemp stance and isn't afraid to show it.* ● *Verhandlungen mit der Stadtverwaltung für die Genehmigung des hier angekündigten Festivals erwiesen sich als sehr schwierig. Angesichts der Kontroversen entschied sich die Agentur für einen Look, der allen, die diese Bewegung zur Legalisierung weicher Drogen kennen, vertraut ist. Das Hanfblatt ist ein eindeutiger Hinweis auf die Einstellung der Veranstalter. ▲ Affiche réalisée pour un festival très controversé et pour lequel les organisateurs eurent beaucoup de peine à obtenir les autorisations nécessaires. La feuille de chanvre indique clairement la position des organisateurs qui n'ont pas peur d'afficher leur opinion sur la question.*

PAGE 78 #157 DESIGNER: *Fred Troller* AGENCY: *Troller Associates* CLIENT: *Escola Panamericana de Arte* ■ *Because this poster was created for an international design congress, it had to capture the imagination of a sophisticated peer group. The designer coined a simple message: Design Brazil/USA. The equal number of letters was pure luck and made a typographic play possible. The fractured letter forms invite the viewer to look and discover.* ● *Plakat für die Ankündigung eines internationalen Design-Kongresses - das sich also an Profis richtete. Der Gestalter entschied sich für eine schlichte Botschaft, wobei die gleiche Anzahl von Buchstaben, die das Spiel mit der Typographie ermöglichte, reines Glück war. ▲ Affiche annonçant un congrès de design international s'adressant à un public de spécialistes. Le concepteur a opté pour un message simple. Le fait que les mots comportent le même nombre de lettres a permis de jouer avec la typographie.*

PAGE 78 #158 ART DIRECTOR/DESIGNER/PHOTOGRAPHER/ILLUSTRATOR: *Tom Antista* AGENCY: *Antista Fairclough Design (In-house)* ■ *This Self-promotional poster was created for a new design partnership. The martini and olive symbolizes two things that work well together.* ● *Eigenwerbung für eine neue Partnerschaft von Designern. Martini und Olive symbolisieren eine gelungene Verbindung. ▲ Affiche autopromotionnelle pour un nouveau partenariat de designers. Le Martini et l'olive symbolisent cette heureuse union.*

PAGE 79 #159 ART DIRECTOR/ DESIGNER: *Louise Fili* AGENCY: *Louise Fili Ltd.* PHOTOGRAPHER: *Ed Spiro* CLIENT: *Cincinnati Art Directors Club* ■ *To announce her speaking engagement at the ADC of Cincinnati, a city to which the designer had vowed not to return until cappuccino was available, she designed the poster as a cappuccino cup.* ● *Ankündigung eines Vortrags von Louise Fili beim ADC von Cincinnati. Da sie geschworen hatte, diese Stadt zu meiden, bis man dort Cappuccino bekommt, gestaltete sie*

ihr Plakat als Cappuccino-Tasse. ▲ Tasse à café. Affiche annonçant une conférence de la graphiste américaine Louise Fili à l'ADC de Cincinnati: l'artiste avait déclaré qu'elle ne remettrait plus les pieds dans cette ville tant que l'on ne pourrait y boire de cappuccino!

PAGE 79 #160 CREATIVE DIRECTOR: *Jim Spruell* ART DIRECTOR: *Lola Carlisle* AGENCY: *Austin Kelley Advertising* PHOTOGRAPHER/ILLUSTRATOR: *David Seijo* PHOTO RETOUCHING: *Joe Arenella Studios* COPYWRITER: *Cathy Lepik* CLIENT: *AAAA* ■ *This poster was sent to agencies throughout the Southeastern US. Digitally retouched photography was used.* ● *Das Plakat wurde an Agenturen im Südosten der USA verschickt. Das Photo wurde digital bearbeitet, um es realistisch erscheinen zu lassen. ▲ Affiche envoyée aux agences du Sud-Est des Etats-Unis. La photo a été travaillée sur ordinateur pour la rendre plus réelle.*

PAGE 80 #161 ART DIRECTOR/ DESIGNER: *Chris Noel* AGENCY: *Chris Noel Design* PHOTO ILLUSTRATION: *Chris Noel* COPYWRITER: *Zane Carter* CLIENT: *AIGA Washington DC* ■ *This poster created for a carnival-like AIGA event focused on attitude, not design.* ● *Plakat für eine karnevalsähnliche Veranstaltung des AIGA. ▲ Affiche créée sur le modèle des affiches de cirque pour une manifestation de l'AIGA aux accents de carnaval.*

PAGE 81 #162 ART DIRECTOR/ DESIGNER/PHOTOGRAPHER/ILLUSTRATOR/COPYWRITER: *David Duncan* AGENCY: *David Duncan, Inc.* CLIENT: *Le Cercle Concours* ■ *The designer used black and silver metallic inks to create a duotone effect that would capture the quality of chrome and shiny paint. The Art Deco pattern frame was created by scanning in a piece of old artwork. He then created a puzzle piece out of it that was repeated and pieced together to create the pattern. The poster was a pro bono job and a short run. There was no press proofing, therefore the makeready on the printing was critical and decisions of density and balance had to be made quickly.* ● *Um den Duo-Ton-Effekt zu erzielen, verwendete der Gestalter schwarze und Silbermetallic-Farben, die sich gut für die Darstellung von Chrom und glänzender Farbe eignen. Ein altes Bild wurde eingescannt, um das Art-Déco-Muster zu erhalten. Dann wurde daraus ein Puzzle gemacht, das so wiederholt und zusammengesetzt wurde, dass daraus ein Muster entstand. Das ganze Verfahren war sehr aufwendig und musste doch schnell und preisgünstig durchgezogen werden, weil es sich um einen unbezahlten Beitrag des Gestalters handelte. ▲ Pour obtenir un effet à deux tons, le designer a utilisé des encres métallisées noire et argent bien adaptées à la représentation du chrome et des peintures brillantes. Une image ancienne a été scannée pour créer le motif art déco utilisé pour former les pièces d'un puzzle qui, assemblées, forment à leur tour un nouveau motif. Cette opération délicate était soumise à des contraintes de temps et d'argent, le designer ayant travaillé à titre bénévole.*

PAGE 81 #163 ART DIRECTOR/ DESIGNER/PHOTOGRAPHER: *Frank Viva* AGENCY: *Viva Dolan Communications & Design* COPYWRITERS: *Frank Viva, Doug Dolan* CLIENT: *Advertising & Design Club Of Canada* ■ *This call-for-entries poster tries to capture the interest of a creative audience by blending hard information with ironic commentary on the nature of awards competitions. The litany of tongue-in-cheek "reasons for entering" taps into some of the commonly expressed reservations people in the industry have about ad and design awards. The agency's ultimate goal was to encourage entries by showing that the organizers share this sense of irony and ambivalence yet still believe that it is an enterprise worth supporting.* ● *Bei diesem Plakat für einen Design-Wettbewerb wird mit einem Gemisch von knapper Information und ironischem Kommentar zu Wettbewerben im allgemeinen gearbeitet, um die Aufmerksamkeit des anvisierten Publikums auf sich zu ziehen. Es galt, die Skeptiker davon zu überzeugen, dass die Veranstalter ihre Vorbehalte hinsichtlich der Wettbewerbe kennen und trotzdem überzeugt sind, dass es sich lohnt, sich an ihrem Wettbewerb zu beteiligen. ▲ Affiche pour un concours de design combinant informations lapidaires et commentaires ironiques sur les concours en général dans le but d'attirer le public cible visé. Il s'agissait de convaincre les sceptiques en déjouant leurs propres réserves à l'égard de tels concours et en leur prouvant qu'il valait bel et bien la peine de participer.*

PAGE 81 #164 ART DIRECTOR/DESIGNER/ILLUSTRATOR: *John Muller* AGENCY: *Muller & Company* CLIENT: *Kansas City Blues and Jazz Festival* ■ *This poster was designed as a commemorative piece used to tie the festival in with Kansas City's rich blues and jazz heritage.* ● *Thema dieses Plakates ist die reiche Blues- und Jazz-Tradition der Stadt Kansas City. ▲ Affiche consacrée à la riche tradition de la ville de Kansas City dans les domaines du blues et du jazz.*

PAGE 81 #165 ART DIRECTOR: *Joe Paprocki* AGENCY: *Fallon McElligott* PHOTOGRAPHER/ILLUSTRATOR: *Bob Blewett* COPYWRITER: *Dave Pullar* CLIENT: *Burnsville Pistol Range* ■ *"Tuesday night is ladies' night." This poster was created to make women aware of an opportunity to use a pistol range with only women and to* have fun while learning. ● «Dienstagabend ist Frauenabend.» Hier werden Frauen auf die Möglichkeit aufmerksam gemacht, zusammen mit anderen Frauen einen Schiessstand zu benutzen und so beim Lernen Spass zu haben. ▲ «Le mardi soir appartient aux femmes.» Affiche invitant les femmes à rejoindre d'autres femmes sur un stand de tir et à apprendre à tirer en s'amusant.

PAGE 82 #166 ART DIRECTOR: *Charlie Zimmermann* DESIGNER/PHOTOGRAPHER: *Andreas Eder* AGENCY: *Zimmermann, Grafik Design & Marketing Services* CLIENT: *Projektstelle Zeitkultur, Tiroler Landesregierung* ■ Poster created to encourage the dialogue between the partner cities of Innsbruck and Sarajevo, and to support Sarajevo's identity as as a multi-cultural city even though war has destroyed much of its cultural heritage. ● Dieses Plakat soll den Dialog zwischen den Partnerstädten Innsbruck und Sarajevo fördern, mit besonderer Betonung von Sarajevos Tradition als multikulturelle Stadt, die sie trotz Zerstörungen im Krieg immer noch ist. ▲ Affiche visant à encourager le dialogue entre les villes jumelées d'Innsbruck et de Sarajevo et présentant Sarajevo comme une ville ayant su rester multiculturelle malgré les ravages de la guerre.

PAGE 82 #167 ART DIRECTOR/ DESIGNER: *Kazumasa Nagai* AGENCY: *Nippon Design Center, Inc.* CLIENT: *Shaken*

PAGE 82 #168, 169 ART DIRECTOR/DESIGNER: *Jerry Ketel* AGENCY: *Leopold Ketel & Partners* ILLUSTRATOR: *William Claxton* COPYWRITER: *Meg Rogers* CLIENT: *Starbucks* ■ Posters promoting a jazz concert series for a coffee retailer. The designer combined the jazz spirit with that of the coffee culture. ● Plakate für eine Reihe von Jazzkonzerten, organisiert von einem Kaffeegeschäft. Der Gestalter verband hier den Geist des Jazz mit der Kaffeekultur. ▲ Affiches pour une série de concerts de jazz sponsorisés par une marque de café et mariant l'esprit du jazz à la tradition du café.

PAGE 83 #170 ART DIRECTOR/DESIGNER: *Michael Gericke* AGENCY: *Pentagram Design, Inc.* PHOTOGRAPHER/ILLUSTRATOR: *Michael Gericke, Cesar Pelli* CLIENT: *American Institute of Architects, New York Chapter* ■ Poster designed for Cesar Pelli's lecture titled "Building & Thoughts." The image whimsically portrays one of the architect's buildings envisioning itself as an urban landmark (within a skyline of Pelli's buildings). ● «Bauen und Gedanken» ist der Titel des angekündigten Vortrags des Architekten Cesar Pelli. Das Gebäude von Pelli, das hier innerhalb einer Skyline aus weiteren Bauten Pellis gezeigt wird, sieht sich offenbar bereits als Wahrzeichen einer Stadt. ▲ «Construire et réflexions», tel était le titre d'une conférence de l'architecte Cesar Pelli. Le bâtiment de Pelli présenté au milieu d'un paysage urbain composé d'autres constructions de l'architecte se profile comme l'emblème d'une ville.

PAGE 83 #171 ART DIRECTORS: *Todd Tilford, Eric Tilford* AGENCY: *Core / R&D / The Richards Group* PHOTOGRAPHER: *James Schwartz* COPYWRITER: *Todd Tilford* CLIENT: *St. Louis Heritage* ■ Promotional poster for St. Louis Blues Festival. ● Plakat für das St. Louis Blues Festival. ▲ Affiche du festival de blues de St-Louis.

PAGE 84 #172 ART DIRECTOR/DESIGNER: *Tadeusz Piechura* AGENCY: *Atelier Tadeusz Piechura* COPYWRITER: *Barbara Fibingier* CLIENT: *Wojewodzki Dom Kultury*

PAGE 85 #173, 174 ART DIRECTORS: *Dana Arnett, Ken Fox* DESIGNER: *Ken Fox* AGENCY: *VSA Partners* PHOTO ILLUSTRATION: *VSA Partners* CLIENT: *DIFFA* ■ This poster was mailed to supporters of DIFFA/Chicago (Design Industries Foundation Fighting AIDS), inviting members to a cabaret-style evening where ticket proceeds go the help fund AIDS research. The poster needed to capture the provocative nature, sensual qualities, and the sophisticated decor of a cabaret-style event. ● Das Plakat wurde an Leute verschickt, die die DIFFA/Chicago (Stiftung der Graphik-Branche zur Bekämpfung von AIDS) unterstützen. Es geht dabei um eine Kabarettaufführung, deren Erlös der AIDS-Forschung zugute kommt. Das Plakat musste die provokative, sinnliche Stimmung eines Kabaretts in einer anspruchsvollen Umgebung zum Ausdruck bringen. ▲ Affiche envoyée aux donateurs soutenant la DIFFA de Chicago (Design Industries Foundation Fighting AIDS) et annonçant un spectacle de cabaret dont la totalité des recettes a été reversée à un fonds pour la recherche sur le sida. L'affiche devait rendre l'esprit du cabaret: provocation, sensualité et décors sophisitiqués.

PAGE 85 #175 ART DIRECTOR/ DESIGNER: *Vittorio Costarella* AGENCY: *Modern Dog* CLIENT: *Moe Cafe*

PAGE 85 #176 DESIGNER: *Robynne Raye* AGENCY: *Modern Dog* CLIENT: *AIGA Wichita*

PAGE 86 #177 ART DIRECTOR: *Sharon Werner* DESIGNERS: *Sharon Werner, Sarah Nelson*

AGENCY: *Werner Design Werks, Inc.* PHOTOGRAPHER: *Darrell Eager* CLIENT: *AIGA Minnesota / Walker Art Center* ■ Poster created as a self-mailer for a lecture series. All of the hard information is printed on the back (speakers' biographies, registration information, etc.) while the front is an easy-access reference to who's speaking on what day. ● Für den Aussand bestimmtes Plakat für eine Vortragsreihe. Die reine Information über die Vortragenden und Teilnahmebedingungen befindet sich auf der Rückseite, während auf der Vorderseite in leicht verständlicher Form darüber informiert wird, wer an welchem Tag spricht. ▲ Affiche-mailing pour une série de conférences. Le programme des conférences figurait au recto tandis que les informations sur les conférenciers et les conditions de participation se trouvaient au verso.

PAGE 86 #178 DESIGNER: *Rik Zak* AGENCY: *Yuri Dojc Inc.* CLIENT: *In-house* ■ The directive was to show the photographer through the eyes of his model and make the viewer aware the photographer is there, similar to a typographic version of Jan van Eyck's painting "Giovanni Arnolfini and his Bride." ● Aufgabe war es, den Photographen durch die Augen seines Modells zu zeigen und den Betrachter merken zu lassen, dass der Photograph anwesend ist – in Anlehnung an Jan van Eycks «Arnolfini-Hochzeit». ▲ L'objecif était de montrer le photographe à travers le regard de son modèle tout en indiquant sa présence, à l'instar du tableau de Jan Van Eyck «Les Epoux Arnolfini».

PAGE 86 #179, 180 ART DIRECTOR: *H.J. Kristhan* DESIGNER: *Jiajang Lin* SCHOOL: *Hochschule der Künste Berlin* ■ This is a student project, a poster for the World Fair to take place in the year 2000 in Hanover, Germany. The students' theme was "Man, Technology, Ecology." ● Das Plakat entstand im Rahmen eines Studentenprojekts für die Weltausstellung 2000 in Hannover. Das Thema war: Mensch, Technologie, Ökologie. ▲ Affiche conçue dans le cadre d'un projet d'étudiants sur l'Exposition universelle de l'an 2000 à Hanovre. Thème de l'affiche: l'homme, la technologie, l'écologie.

PAGE 87 #181 ART DIRECTOR/ DESIGNER: *Stefan Sagmeister* AGENCY: *Sagmeister Inc.* PHOTOGRAPHER/ILLUSTRATOR: *Tom Schierlitz* CLIENT: *AIGA, New York* ■ The agency decided to use two tongues opposite each other as a symbol for an AIGA design lecture called "Fresh Dialogue." Since humans have short tongues, the photographer bought two fresh cow tongues from a meat market and shot them with a 4x5 camera. Somehow the image came out phallic, and although the agency didn't mind, some AIGA members did. ● Bei den beiden Zungen, die hier einen vom AIGA angekündigten Design-Vortrag mit dem Titel «Frischer Dialog» symbolisieren, handelt es sich um zwei auf dem Fleischmarkt gekaufte Kuhzungen, die mit einer 4x5 Kamera photographiert wurden. Irgendwie kam dabei ein eher phallisches Bild heraus, was zwar die Macher nicht störte, wohl aber einige AIGA-Mitglieder. ▲ Affiche annonçant une conférence de l'AIGA intitulée «Fresh Dialogue». Le photographe a acheté deux langues de bœuf fraîches aux halles qu'il a photographiées avec un appareil 4x5. Le résultat présente un côté phallique qui ne dérangea pas l'agence, mais qui froissa la sensibilité de quelques membres de l'AIGA.

PAGE 87 #182 ART DIRECTOR: *Orlagh Daly* AGENCY: *J. Walter Thompson* COPYWRITERS: *Caren Spigland, Kim Nguyen* CLIENT: *In-house* ■ "Only good clients allowed." ● «Nur gute Kunden sind zugelassen.» ▲ «Réservé aux bons clients.»

PAGE 88 #183, 184 ART DIRECTOR/ DESIGNER/ARTIST: *Shinnoske Sugisaki* AGENCY: *Shinnoske Inc.* PHOTOGRAPHER/ILLUSTRATOR: *Yoshiyuki Mori* CLIENT: *Close-Up of Japan* ■ "Nippon-jin (Where are the roots of the Japanese?)" This poster was created for an exhibition on the cultural roots of the Japanese. ● «Nippon-jin (Wo sind die Wurzeln der Japaner?)». Thema der Ausstellung sind kulturellen Quellen der Japaner. ▲ «Nippon-jin (Où sont les racines des Japonais?)» Affiche d'une exposition consacrée aux racines culturelles des Japonais.

PAGE 88 #185, 186 ART DIRECTOR/ DESIGNER/ILLUSTRATOR: *Taku Tashiro* AGENCY: *Taku Tashiro Office* CLIENT: *Ebisu Mitsukoshi* ■ Posters created for an illustration exhibition. ● Ankündigung einer Ausstellung von Illustrationen. ▲ Affiches annonçant une exposition d'illustrations.

PAGE 89 #187 ART DIRECTOR/ DESIGNER: *Tadanori Yokoo* AGENCY: *Tadanori Yokoo* PHOTOGRAPHER/ILLUSTRATOR: *David LaChapelle* CLIENT: *Callaway Editions Inc.*

PAGE 90 #188-190 ART DIRECTOR/COPYWRITER: *Yasumi Numajiri* DESIGNERS: *Megumi Kaneko, Chikako Hori, Yasumi Numajiri* AGENCY: *Yasumi Numajiri Design Office* ARTIST: *Kazuo Takiguchi* PHOTOGRAPHER: *Tamotsu Fujii* CLIENT: *Ohara School Of Ikebana*

PAGE 90 #191 ART DIRECTOR/ DESIGNER/AGENCY: *Tadanori Yokoo* CLIENT: *Asahi Shinbon* ■ "Japanese Culture, the Fifty Postwar Years." ● «Japanische Kultur, die fün-

fzig Nachkriegsjahre.» ▲ *«Culture japonaise, les cinquante ans d'après-guerre.»*

PAGE 90 #192 ART DIRECTOR/DESIGNER/AGENCY: *Tadanori Yokoo* CLIENT: *Laforet Harajuku* ■ *Poster for Tadanori Yokoo's exhibition "Once Upon a Time."* ● *«Es war einmal» - Ankündigung einer Ausstellung des Plakatkünstlers Tadanori Yokoo.* ▲ *«Il était une fois» – exposition de l'affichiste Tadanori Yokoo.*

PAGE 91 #193 ART DIRECTOR/ DESIGNER: *Koichi Sato* AGENCY: *Koichi Sato Design Studio* CLIENT: *Japan Design Committee*

PAGE 91 #194 ART DIRECTOR/ DESIGNER: *Anil Revri* AGENCY: *Anil Revri Studio* ■ *Poster completed as part of thesis project at Corcoran School of Art.* ● *Das Plakat ist Teil einer Diplomarbeit. Die Aufgabe bestand darin, ein Publikum, das sich nicht unbedingt aus Designern zusammensetzt, über einen bestimmten Designer und dessen Bedeutung zu informieren, ohne den Stil dieses Designers zu imitieren.* ▲ *Affiche réalisée dans le cadre d'un travail de diplôme. Le thème: présenter à un public de néophytes un designer connu et la signification de son travail sans imiter son style.*

PAGE 92 #195, 196 ART DIRECTOR/ DESIGNER/COPYWRITER: *André Grau* CLIENT: *Galerie der Hochschule für Grafik und Buchkunst Leipzig* ■ *Posters created as part of a series for a college gallery. The posters were part of an exhibition that introduced actual works of the professors of the Painting and Graphic Arts departments to the students.* ● *Beispiele aus einer Reihe von Plakaten für die Galerie einer Hochschule. Diese Plakate waren Teil einer Ausstellung von Arbeiten der Professoren für die Klassen Malerei und Graphik.* ▲ *Série d'affiches pour la galerie d'une école supérieure présentées dans le cadre d'une exposition consacrée aux travaux des professeurs chargés d'enseigner la peinture et le graphisme.*

PAGE 93 #197 ART DIRECTOR/ DESIGNER: *Claude Kuhn* AGENCY: *Graphik Design Claude Kuhn* CLIENT: *Naturhistorisches Museum der Bürgergemeinde Bern*

PAGE 93 #198 AGENCY: *Holger Matthies* CLIENT: *Hamburger Sommer-Theaterfestival* ■ *This poster serves two purposes: to announce a theater festival and an exhibition of the poster arts in a factory in Hamburg which is home to a wide variety of cultural events.* ● *Das Plakat dient zwei Zwecken: der Ankündigung eines Theaterfestivals und einer Ausstellung des Plakatkünstlers in einer Hamburger Kulturfabrik.* ▲ *Affiche poursuivant deux objectifs: annoncer un festival de théâtre et une exposition de l'affichiste dans un centre culturel de Hambourg.*

PAGE 93 #199 DESIGNER/AGENCY: *Bruno Monguzzi* CLIENT: *Museo Cantonale d'Arte* ■ *Announcement of a retrospective exhibition of Livio Bernasconi and Hans Knuchel.* ● *Ankündigung einer Retrospektive der Arbeiten von Livio Bernasconi und Hans Knuchel in Lugano.* ▲ *Affiche annonçant une rétrospective des travaux de Livio Bernasconi et de Hans Knuchel.*

PAGE 93 #200 DESIGNERS: *Caroline Halff, Anja Rattenhuber, Sven Vogel* ■ *Poster design by three students.* ● *Gemeinschaftsarbeit von Studenten für die eigene Diplom-Austellung.* ▲ *Affiche réalisée par trois étudiants pour leur propre exposition.*

PAGE 94 #201 ART DIRECTOR/ DESIGNER/AGENCY: *K. G. Olsson* CLIENT: *Skissernas Museum* ■ *Screenprint poster created for a retrospective exhibition on the Forum art school at the Skissernas Museum. The designer used minimal expression.* ● *Siebdruckplakat für eine Retrospektive, die das Skissernas Museum einer Kunstschule widmete.* ▲ *Sérigraphie pour une rétrospective que le Skissernas Museum a dédié à une école d'arts.*

PAGE 94 #202 DESIGNER: *Dan Jonsson* CLIENT: *Galleri Gri* ■ *This poster was created in connection with the designer's exhibition, where he often works with his initials "D" and "J."* ● *Das Plakat entstand für eine Ausstellung des Designers, der oft mit seinen Initialen «D» und «J» arbeitet.* ▲ *Affiche conçue pour une exposition du designer qui travaille souvent avec ses initiales, le «D» et le «J».*

PAGE 95 #203 ART DIRECTOR/ DESIGNER/COPYWRITER: *Uwe Loesch* AGENCY: *Prof. Uwe Loesch Arbeitsgemeinschaft für Visuelle und Verbale Kommunikation Düsseldorf* PHOTOGRAPHER/ILLUSTRATOR: *In-house* CLIENT: *Messe Düsseldorf* ■ *Poster campaign for an international shoe fair.* ● *Plakat aus einer Kampagne für die GDS, Internationale Schuhmesse Düsseldorf.* ▲ *Affiche réalisée dans le cadre d'une campagne pour GDS, un salon international de la chaussure à Düsseldorf.*

PAGE 95 #204 ART DIRECTOR/ DESIGNER/COPYWRITER: *Uwe Loesch* AGENCY: *Prof. Uwe Loesch Arbeitsgemeinschaft für Visuelle und Verbale Kommunikation Düsseldorf* PHOTOGRAPHER/ILLUSTRATOR: *Hans Hansen* CLIENT: *Design Zentrum Nordrhein-Westfalen, Essen* ■ *Poster for the exhibition of the winning works from the competition "Design Innovations", organized by the Design Zentrum Nordrhein-Westfalen in Essen, Germany.* ● *Ankündigung der Ausstellung der Wettbewerbsergebnisse «Design Innovationen» des Design Zentrums Nordrhein-Westfalen in Essen.* ▲ *Affiche créée pour l'exposition des travaux du concours «Design Innovationen» du Design Zentrum Nordrhein-Westfalen à Essen.*

PAGE 95 #205 ART DIRECTOR/ DESIGNER: *Juha Pohjola* AGENCY: *Viherjuuren Ilme Oy* PHOTOGRAPHER/ILLUSTRATOR: *Horst Neumann* CLIENT: *Grafia Ry*

PAGE 95 #206 DESIGNER: *Ralph Schraivogel* CLIENT: *Museum für Gestaltung Zürich* ■ *Poster for an exhibition at the Museum of Arts and Crafts in Zürich showing the work of a London group of architects from the years 1961-1974.* ● *Ankündigung einer Ausstellung der Londoner Architektengruppe Archigram im Zürcher Museum für Gestaltung.* ▲ *Affiche pour une exposition du groupe d'architectes londoniens Archigram présentée au Museum für Gestaltung de Zurich.*

PAGE 96 #207 ART DIRECTOR/DESIGNER: *Dan Jonsson* AGENCY: *Studio Dan Jonsson AB* CLIENT: *Galleri Karneval* ■ *This poster was created in connection with the designer's exhibition, where he often works with his initials "D" and "J." The "J" in this poster is meant to resemble one of the neon lights of the supermarket.* ● *Plakat für eine Ausstellung des Designers, der oft mit seinen Initialen «D» und «J» arbeitet. Das «J» in diesem Plakat ist eine Anspielung auf das Neonlicht eines Supermarkts.* ▲ *Affiche conçue pour une exposition du designer qui travaille souvent avec ses initiales, le «D» et le «J». Le «J» fait allusion aux néons d'un supermarché.*

PAGE 96 #208 ART DIRECTOR/PHOTOGRAPHER: *Julius Friedman* DESIGNERS: *Julius Friedman, Mike Slone* AGENCY: *Images* ARTIST/ILLUSTRATOR: *Mike Slone* CLIENT: *Louisville Visual Art Association* ■ *Poster created for a national ceramic show for dinner works and table settings.* ● *Ankündigung einer nationalen Keramikausstellung mit Tafelgeschirr und Tischdekorationen.* ▲ *Affiche d'une exposition nationale de céramique consacrée en particulier à la vaisselle et aux décorations de table.*

PAGE 96 #209 ART DIRECTORS/ DESIGNERS: *Nancy Skolos, Thomas Wedell* AGENCY: *Skolos/Wedell* PHOTOGRAPHER: *Thomas Wedell* CLIENT: *Reinhold Brown Gallery in association with Virginia L. Green*

PAGE 96 #210 ART DIRECTOR: *Silas H. Rhodes* DESIGNER/PHOTOGRAPHER/ILLUSTRATOR: *Ivan Chermayeff* AGENCY: *Visual Arts Press, Ltd.* CLIENT: *Visual Arts Museum* ■ *Poster announcing the "The Master Series: Ivan Chermayeff," eighth in a series of exhibitions by the Visual Arts Museum at the School of Visual Arts, honoring the great visual communicators of our time. The poster is a variation on the theme of the designer's hand (symbolized by the glove) meeting the designer's tools (symbolized by the colored pencils) in a single image. The message is written with the magic of a child's rainbow pencil.* ● *Ankündigung einer Ausstellung im Rahmen der Reihe «Master Series» des Visual Arts Museum an der School of Visual Arts, die den Meistern der visuellen Kommunikation gewidmet ist - hier dem New Yorker Ivan Chermayeff. Die Hand des Designers wird durch den Handschuh symbolisiert, sein Werkzeug durch die Farbstifte. Die Botschaft wurde mit einem Regenbogenstift geschrieben.* ▲ *Affiche pour une exposition organisée dans le cadre de la série «Master Series» par le Visual Arts Museum à la School of Visual Arts et consacrée aux grands maîtres de la communication visuelle – ici, le New-Yorkais Ivan Chermayeff. Un gant symbolise la main du designer, et les crayons de couleur représentent ses outils. Le message a été écrit avec un crayon arc-en-ciel.*

PAGE 97 #211, 212 DESIGNER: *Michael Vanderbyl* AGENCY: *Vanderbyl Design* CLIENT: *Exhibitor Magazine*

PAGE 98 #213 DESIGNER: *Pepe Gimeno* AGENCY: *Pepe Gimeno, S.L.* CLIENT: *Generalitat Valenciana*

PAGE 98 #214 DESIGNERS: *Vladimir Tsesler, Sergej Voitshenko* AGENCY: *Art Studio* CLIENT: *Contemporary Art Centre*

PAGE 98 #215 ART DIRECTOR/ DESIGNER: *Fons Hickmann* AGENCY: *Fons M. Hickmann* PHOTOGRAPHER/ILLUSTRATOR: *Frank Göldner* CLIENT: *Bazon Brock* ■ *Poster for an exhibition of Dr. Bazon Brock, artist and theorist at the German Historical Museum of*

Berlin, presenting souvenirs, teaching aids, theoretical objects, and devotional objects from museum shops from all over the world. The German headline plays on the words "Warenwunder" (marvellous objects) and "wahren Wunder" (true miracles) that are pronounced in the same way. Shown are two inflatable dummies: the figure from Munch's painting "The Cry" and a "love doll." ● Plakat für eine Ausstellung des Künstlers und Theoretikers Prof. Dr. Bazon Brock im Deutschen Historischen Museum Berlin, in der verschiedene Objekte aus den Museumsshops der Welt gezeigt werden. Abgebildet sind zwei aufblasbare Gummipuppen, eine "Love Doll" und die Figur aus dem Gemälde «Der Schrei» von Edvard Munch. ▲ Affiche d'une exposition de l'artiste et théoricien Bazon Brock au Musée d'Histoire de Berlin, présentant divers objets des boutiques de musées du monde entier. Le visuel montre deux poupées gonflables, une «Love Doll» et «Le Cri» d'Edvard Munch.

PAGE 98 #216 ART DIRECTOR/DESIGNER/PHOTOGRAPHER/ILLUSTRATOR: Armin Lindauer CLIENT: Bert Dürkop ■ Poster for four artists presenting their work in four different exhibitions under the title "Four in the space/room." The directive was to present the four exhibitions on the same poster with the possibility of changing dates and locations for each exhibition. ● Plakat für vier Künstler, die ihre Arbeiten in vier verschiedenen Ausstellungen unter dem Titel «Vier im Raum» zeigen. Hier ging es darum, die vier Ausstellungen mit einem Plakat anzukündigen, das eine Möglichkeit bieten musste, die wechselnden Informationen über Ort und Zeit einzudrucken. ▲ Affiche de quatre artistes présentant leurs travaux lors de quatre expositions différentes sous le titre «Quatre dans l'espace». Il s'agissait de présenter les quatre expositions sur une seule et même affiche permettant de changer les dates et les lieux d'exposition.

PAGE 99 #217 ART DIRECTOR/ DESIGNER/PHOTOGRAPHER/ILLUSTRATOR: Andrey Logvin AGENCY: Logvin Design CLIENT: Design Association of Russia

PAGE 99 #218 ART DIRECTOR/ DESIGNER/PHOTOGRAPHER/ILLUSTRATOR/AGENCY: Valery Viter

PAGE 100 #219, 220 DESIGNER: Shigeo Katsuoka AGENCY: Shigeo Katuoka Design Studio CLIENT: In-house

PAGE 101 #221 DESIGNER: Shigeo Katsuoka AGENCY: Shigeo Katsuoka Design Studio PHOTOGRAPHER/ILLUSTRATOR: Fernand Léger CLIENT: In-house

PAGE 101 #222 DESIGNER: Shigeo Katsuoka AGENCY: Shigeo Katsuoka Design Studio CLIENT: In-house

PAGE 101 #223 DESIGNER: Shigeo Katsuoka AGENCY: Shigeo Katsuoka Design Studio ART: Vincent Van Gogh CLIENT: In-house

PAGE 101 #224 DESIGNER: Shigeo Katsuoka AGENCY: Shigeo Katsuoka Design Studio PHOTOGRAPHER/ILLUSTRATOR: Adolphe Cassandre CLIENT: In-house

PAGE 102 #225-227 ART DIRECTORS/ DESIGNER/PHOTOGRAPHER: Makoto Saito CREATIVE DIRECTOR/PRODUCER: Ruki Matsumoto AGENCY: Makoto Saito Design Office Inc. CLIENT: Ba-Tsu Company, Ltd.

PAGE 103 #228 ART DIRECTOR/ DESIGNER/AGENCY: Tadanori Yokoo CLIENT: Issey Miyake Ltd.

PAGE 103 #229 ART DIRECTOR: Grand So DESIGNERS: Grand So, Kwok Chi Man, Au Tai Pui AGENCY: Masterline Communications Ltd. PHOTOGRAPHER: David Lo COPYWRITERS: Grand So, Johnson Cheng COMPUTER ILLUSTRATION: Simon Lam CLIENT: Wah Shing Sport Trading Company ■ Poster created to promote brand awareness for the client's sunglasses and sports goggles in Hong Kong. The red and black colors were picked to convey power and strength. ● Plakat für die Sonnen- und Sportbrillen eines Herstellers aus Hongkong. Die Farben Rot und Schwarz stehen hier für Kraft und Stärke. ▲ Affiche pour les lunettes de soleil et de sport d'un fabricant de Hongkong. Le rouge et le noir symbolisent la force et la puissance.

PAGE 104 #230, 231 ART DIRECTOR: Brian Collins DESIGNERS: Glenn Setty, Brian Collins AGENCY: FCB Promotion & Design PHOTOGRAPHER/ILLUSTRATOR: Dah Len COPYWRITER: Brian Bacino CLIENT: Levi Strauss & Company

PAGE 105 #232-234 ART DIRECTOR: Brian Collins DESIGNER: Gaby Brink AGENCY: FCB Promotion & Design PHOTOGRAPHER: Daniel Desouza CLIENT: Levi Strauss & Company

PAGE 105 #235-237 ART DIRECTOR: Brian Collins DESIGNER: Sharon Werner

AGENCY: FCB Promotion & Design ILLUSTRATOR: Eidwr Snorri COPYWRITER: Jeff Mueller CLIENT: Levi Strauss & Company

PAGE 105 #238 ART DIRECTOR: Brian Collins DESIGNERS: Brian Collins, Glenn Setty AGENCY: FCB Promotion & Design PHOTOGRAPHER/ILLUSTRATOR: Dahlen COPYWRITER: Brian Bacino CLIENT: Levi Strauss & Company

PAGE 105 #239 ART DIRECTOR: George Chadwick DESIGNER: Eric Rindall AGENCY: FCB Promotion & Design PHOTOGRAPHER/ILLUSTRATOR: Bybee Studios COPYWRITER: Damon Allred CLIENT: Levi Strauss & Company

PAGE 105 #240 ART DIRECTOR: Brian Collins DESIGNERS: Brian Collins, Glenn Setty AGENCY: FCB Promotion & Design COPYWRITER: Damon Allred CLIENT: Levi Strauss & Company

PAGE 106 #241 ART DIRECTORS: Keiji Minokura, Yasuhiko Shimura, Keiichiro Fukushima DESIGNER: Keiichiro Fukushima AGENCY: McCann-Erickson Inc. ILLUSTRATOR: Taka Kobayashi COPYWRITER: Akihiko Kawai CLIENT: Casio Computer Company, Ltd. ■ The creative execution called for sensitivity and balance between toughness and fashionability to communicate the product's qualities. ● Der nackte Körper eines Mannes und Schlamm sind Dinge, die mit Gefühl gehandhabt werden müssen, um eine Balance des Ausdrucks von Widerstandsfähigkeit und Anpassungsfähigkeit herzustellen. Ziel war es, die Widerstandsfähigkeit und schmutzabweisenden Eigenschaften der Produkte zum Ausdruck zu bringen. ▲ Le corps d'un homme nu et la boue étaient des thèmes à traiter avec sensibilité afin d'obtenir un équilibre entre capacité de résistance et faculté d'adaptation. Il s'agissait d'illustrer la solidité et les caractéristiques exceptionnelles du produit.

PAGE 106 #242 ART DIRECTOR: Kenzo Izutani DESIGNERS: Kenzo Izutani, Aki Hirai AGENCY: Kenzo Izutani Office Corporation PHOTOGRAPHERS: (statue) Kohji Ochiai, Yasuyuki Amazutsumi (dogs) ARTIST: (statue) Katsura Funakoshi COPYWRITER: Hiromitsu Koike CLIENT: Parco

PAGE 106 #243, 244 ART DIRECTORS/ DESIGNERS:/PHOTOGRAPHERS: Torsten Suter, Marcus Regensburger AGENCY: Lemon Design CLIENT: In-house

PAGE 107 #245 ART DIRECTOR/DESIGNER: Makoto Saito AGENCY: Makoto Saito Design Office Inc. PHOTOGRAPHER: Kazumi Kurigami COPYWRITER: Hiroaki Tsukamoto PRODUCER: Masato Igarashi CLIENT: International Trading Co. Ltd.

PAGE 107 #246 ART DIRECTOR/DESIGNER: Howard Brown AGENCY: Urban Outfitters CLIENT: In-house ■ One in a series of posters incorporated into various aspects of a fashion retailer's merchandising and design. ● Beispiel aus einer Reihe von Plakaten, die zum Merchandising und Auftritt eines Modeladens gehören. ▲ Affiche extraite d'une série consacrée au merchandising et à l'identité visuelle d'un magasin de mode.

PAGE 108 #247-252 ART DIRECTOR: Seichi Ohashi DESIGNERS: Seichi Ohashi, Taeko Sagara AGENCY: Les Mains Inc. PHOTOGRAPHERS/ILLUSTRATORS: Yoshiharu Asayama, Naoki Turuta, Toshiaki Takeuchi COPYWRITERS: Naomi Nishihara, Ichiro Sugitani CLIENT: TMD Company, Ltd. ■ Seasonal posters created for a fashion department store. ● Saisonale Plakate eines Modekaufhauses. ▲ Affiches saisonnières d'un magasin de mode.

PAGE 109 #253 ART DIRECTOR/DESIGNER: Norio Kudo AGENCY: Magna Inc. Advertising/Beam X 10 Inc. PHOTOGRAPHER: Takahito Sato COPYWRITER: Yuko Tanaka CLIENT: Nakayama Company, Ltd. ■ Poster for a fashion brand displayed in shops. ● Ladenplakat für eine Modemarke. ▲ Affiche de magasin pour une marque de vêtements.

PAGE 110 #254 ART DIRECTOR: Bob Meagher PRINT PRODUCER: Jenny Schoenherr AGENCY: The Martin Agency PHOTOGRAPHER: Michael Waine COPYWRITER: Joe Nagy CLIENT: Moto Europa ■ "It's like a trailer hitch for your jeans." ● «Wie eine Anhängerkupplung für Deine Jeans.» ▲ «C'est comme un attelage pour tes jeans.»

PAGE 110 #255 CREATIVE DIRECTORS: Mike Hughes, Ron Huey ART DIRECTOR: Bob Meagher PRINT PRODUCER: Jenny Schoenherr AGENCY: The Martin Agency PHOTOGRAPHER: Mark Scott COPYWRITER: Joe Nagy CLIENT: Moto Europa ■ "All those in favor of Wrangler shirts, raise your hand." ● «Alle, die für Wrangler-Hemden sind, Hand hochheben.» ▲ «Que tous ceux qui sont pour les chemises Wrangler lèvent la main.»

PAGE 111 #256-258 ART DIRECTORS: Terence Reynolds AGENCY: R&D / The Richards Group PHOTOGRAPHER: Richard Reens COPYWRITER: Todd Tilford CLIENT: Wearabout ■

Point-of-purchase posters designed to convey an "anti-establishment" image for the client. • *Ladenplakate, die das Anti-Establishment-Image von Wearabout untermauern sollen.* ▲ *Affiches de magasin visant à renforcer l'image anticonformiste de Wearabout.*

PAGE 112 #259 ART DIRECTORS: *Luiz Toledo, Walter Miranda* AGENCY: *DDB Needham* PHOTOGRAPHERS/ILLUSTRATORS: *Cássio Vasconcelos; Ugo Rossiti* COPYWRITER: *Luiz Toledo* CLIENT: *Valdemar Iódice*

PAGE 112 #260 ART DIRECTORS: *Luiz Toledo, Diego Zaragoza* AGENCY: *DDB Needham Brazil* PHOTOGRAPHER/ILLUSTRATOR: *J.R. Duran* COPYWRITER: *Luiz Toledo* CLIENT: *Valdemar Iódice*

PAGE 112 #261, 262 ART DIRECTORS: *Luiz Toledo, Walter Miranda* AGENCY: *DDB Needham* PHOTOGRAPHERS/ILLUSTRATORS: *Cássio Vasconcelos, Ugo Rossiti* COPYWRITER: *Luiz Toledo* CLIENT: *Valdemar Iódice*

PAGE 113 #263-266 ART DIRECTOR: *Barbara Longiardi* AGENCY: *Matite Giovanotte* PHOTOGRAPHER: *Werther Scudellari* COPYWRITERS: *Massimo E. Arrigoni, Antonella Bandoli* CLIENT: *Nike Italy* ■ *The agency had to focus on the verbal message which had to refer to the sport category and embody the client's spirit–irony and irreverence–in its typical style–innovative and technological. The use of witty and young language, as well as headlines "joking" with the shoes below, proved the right tools for an effective message.* • *Im Mittelpunkt stand hier die verbale Botschaft, die sich mit der Sportart befassen und dem ironischen, respektlosen Ton des Auftraggebers entsprechen musste. Die witzige, junge Sprache erwies sich als das richtige Kommunikationsmittel.* ▲ *Elément-clé de l'affiche, le message qui devait se référer au sport en question et reprendre le ton ironique et irrévérencieux propre à la marque. Le langage jeune et branché s'est révélé un moyen de communication judicieux.*

PAGE 114 #267 ART DIRECTOR/DESIGNER/PHOTOGRAPHER/ILLUSTRATOR: *Lanny Sommese* AGENCY: *Sommese Design* ■ *This poster promotes an annual summer festival of the visual and performing arts.* • *Plakat für ein jährlich stattfindendes Sommerfestival der visuellen und darstellenden Künste.* ▲ *Affiche d'un festival d'été annuel consacré aux arts visuels et aux arts du temps.*

PAGE 114 #268 ART DIRECTOR: *Megan Barra* DESIGNER/PHOTOGRAPHER/ILLUSTRATOR: *Aletha Reppel* AGENCY: *Trinity Design* CLIENT: *Festival International de Louisiane* ■ *This poster was created for a multicultural visual and performing arts festival which celebrates the cultural connections between French Louisiana and the Francophone world. The collage is comprised of elements taken from masks used to celebrate carnival in Haiti, Brazil, New Orleans, and Basile, Louisiana.* • *Das hier angekündigte multikulturelle Festival der visuellen und darstellenden Künste ist den kulturellen Verbindungen von Louisiana zur frankophonen Welt gewidmet. Die Collage besteht aus Teilen von Karnevalsmasken aus Haiti, Brasilien, New Orleans und Basile in Louisiana.* ▲ *Affiche créée pour un festival multiculturel consacré aux relations de la Louisiane avec le monde francophone. Le collage se compose de parties de masques de carnaval provenant de Haïti, du Brésil, de la Nouvelle-Orléans et de Basile, en Louisiane.*

PAGE 114 #269 ART DIRECTOR/ DESIGNER *Garry Emery* AGENCY/PHOTOGRAPHY: *Emery Vincent Design* CLIENT: *Melbourne International Festival of the Arts* ■ *A Matisse-inspired image was used to convey the ideas of performing arts, festivity, and creativity. The image also needed to be strong, simple, dynamic and memorable.* • *Von Matisse inspiriertes Plakat für ein internationales Kulturfestival in Melbourne. Das Bild sollte stark, einfach, dynamisch und einprägsam sein.* ▲ *Affiche inspirée de Matisse, créée pour le festival international des arts de Melbourne. L'image devait être forte, simple et dynamique.*

PAGE 115 #270 DESIGNER: *Raduf Karray* CLIENT: *Chambre de Commerce de SFAX*

PAGE 115 #271 ART DIRECTOR/ DESIGNER: *Slavimir Stojanović* AGENCY: *S. Team Bates Saatchi & Saatchi Advertising Balkans* PHOTOGRAPHER *Ivan Sijak* CLIENT: *Oliver Belopeta, Skopje Jazz Festival* ■ *The Skopje Jazz Festival has been organized every year for the past fifteen years by one man on a limited budget. The poster is about how to make something out of nothing.* • *«Das Jazz-Festival in Skopje wurde in den letzten 15 Jahren von einem einzigen Mann, Oliver Belopeta, mit einem sehr kleinen Budget auf die Beine gestellt. Thema des Plakates: wie man aus nichts etwas macht.* ▲ *«Depuis 15 ans, le festival de jazz de Skopje est organisé par un seul homme, Oliver Belopeta, qui ne dispose que d'un petit budget.*

Thème de l'affiche: comment faire quelque chose à partir de rien.

PAGE 115 #272 DESIGNER/PHOTOGRAPHER/ILLUSTRATOR: *Ron Kellum* AGENCY: *Ron Kellum Inc.* CLIENT: *Tramps Productions* ■ *The designer chose the Fender Stratocaster electric guitar as the primary image, an electric guitar readily identified with practitioners of electric and urban blues styles. After converting photos to line art, they were xeroxed and moved during the process to achieve a gritty street feel and to evoke a sense of energy associated with the city and music. Spray-painted color accents reinforced the urban theme, while a bold and simple color scheme echo the feeling and structure of the music.* • *Im Mittelpunkt steht hier eine elektrische Gitarre der Marke Fender Stratocaster, die allgemein mit Vertretern eines urbanen Blues-Stil assoziiert wird. Nachdem die Photos in Strichvorlagen konvertiert worden waren, wurden sie photokopiert und dabei bewegt, um den gewünschten Effekt zu erzielen: das Gefühl von Strasse und Energie, die mit der Stadt und der Musik verbunden wird. Aufgesprayte Farbakzente verstärkten das Stadthema, während die kräftige, schlichte Farbpalette Atmosphäre und Struktur der Musik wiedergibt.* ▲ *Au centre, une guitare électrique de la marque Fender Stratocaster, habituellement associée au blues urbain. Les photos ont été converties en documents au trait, puis photocopiées et bougées pour obtenir l'effet désiré: rendre l'atmosphère de la rue et l'énergie associée à la ville et à la musique. Des couleurs bombées renforcent le thème urbain, tandis que la palette de couleurs franches et simples évoquent le style de la musique.*

PAGE 116 #273 ART DIRECTOR/ DESIGNER: *Burt Kleeger* AGENCY: *Burt Kleeger Inc.* PHOTOGRAPHER: *Dennis Marten* COMPUTER ILLUSTRATOR: *Burt Kleeger* CLIENT: *Miramax Films* ■ *Poster created for the film "Mighty Aphrodite," a story about the redemption of a prostitute. The art is a combination of photography and computer illustration. The design principle followed was "less is more."* • *Plakat für den Film "Mighty Aphrodite", der von der Bekehrung eines Strassenmädchens handelt. Der Designer arbeitete mit einer Kombination von Photographie und Computer-Illustration und beschränkte sich auf das Wesentliche.* ▲ *Affiche du film «Mighty Aphrodite» de Woody Allen, l'histoire d'une prostituée qui change de vie. Le graphiste a combiné une photographie et une illustration réalisée sur ordinateur, et s'est limité à l'essentiel.*

PAGE 116 #274 ART DIRECTOR/ DESIGNER: *Werner Schauer* AGENCY: *Casa Nova Corporate Communications* PHOTOGRAPHER/ILLUSTRATOR: *Archiv* CLIENT: *Transit Film GmbH* ■ *Image poster for a company selling copyrights for the pre-WWII UFA movies.* • *Image-Plakat für eine Firma, die die Copyrights für Filme der ehemaligen UFA verkauft.* ▲ *Affiche institutionnelle pour une société qui vend les droits des films de l'ex-UFA.*

PAGE 116 #275 ART DIRECTOR: *Tony Veazey* DESIGNER: *Marcus Haslam* AGENCY: *Fahrenheit Design Partnership* PHOTOGRAPHER: *David Stewart* CLIENT: *Shed Films* ■ *Poster for the short film "Cabbage."* • *Plakat für den Kurzfilm «Cabbage».* ▲ *Affiche du court-métrage «Cabbage».*

PAGE 116 #276 ART DIRECTOR/DESIGNER: *Rick Biedel* AGENCY: *Studio Xl* PHOTOGRAPHER: *Don Penny* CLIENT: *IFP*

PAGE 117 #277 ART DIRECTOR/DESIGNER: *Istvan Orosz* AGENCY: *Utisz BT* PHOTOGRAPHER/COPYWRITER: *Istvan Orosz* CLIENT: *Pannonia Films*

PAGE 118 #278 ART DIRECTOR/DESIGNER: *Jose Serrano* AGENCY: *Mires Design* PHOTOGRAPHER: *Tracy Sabin* CLIENT: *Industry Pictures* ■ *The poster was created to promote a new film company. It and the logo were executed in a style reminiscent of the WPA era.* • *Plakat für eine neue Filmgesellschaft. Plakat und Logo erinnern an den Stil der 30er Jahre in den USA.* ▲ *Affiche d'une nouvelle société de production cinématographique. Le style de l'affiche et le logo rappellent l'ère de la WPA.*

PAGE 118 #279 ART DIRECTOR: *Dana Arnett* DESIGNERS: *Curt Schreiber, Fletch Martin* AGENCY: *VSA Partners* PHOTOGRAPHER/ILLUSTRATOR: *Scott Shigley* CLIENT: *Potlatch Corporation* ■ *This poster was part of a campaign to promote Ben Day, a film about the world's greatest designer. The poster uses cues from the film's style and mood to build interest and anticipation.* • *Werbung für einen Film über Ben Day, den «grossartigsten Designer der Welt». Das Plakat entspricht in Stil und Stimmung dem Film.* ▲ *Affiche promotionnelle du film sur Ben Day, le «plus grand designer de tous les temps», évoquant le genre et l'atmosphère du film.*

PAGE 119 #280-283 ART DIRECTOR/ DESIGNER: *Fons M. Hickmann* AGENCY: *FONS* CLIENT: *Stummfilm-Tage Graz* ■ *These posters, part of a series on the poetry of images, technology, and typography, visualize the mechanics of communication through the* *decoding of signs up to clear phrasing and back to silence. The portrait of actress Henny Porten was computer-manipulated.* ● *«Als Augen noch sprechen konnten», Plakatserie für ein Stummfilmfestival. Die Plakate veranschaulichen Kommunikations-mechanismen durch Dekodierung von Schriftzeichen bis hin zur klaren Formulierung und zurück. In jedem der Plakate steckt die gleiche Information, jedoch braucht jedes eine eigene Lese- und Betrachtungszeit. Als Bildgrundlage diente ein Porträt von Henny Porten, das im Computer manipuliert wurde.* ▲ *«Quand les yeux pouvaient encore par-ler.» Série d'affiches réalisée pour un festival du cinéma muet. Les affiches illustrent les mécanismes de la communication par le décodage de signes jusqu'à la formulation de phrases claires et cohérentes pour revenir ensuite à la première phase, le silence. Chaque affiche présente la même information, mais requiert une autre approche pour saisir les différents symboles. Le portrait de l'actrice Henny Porten a été retravaillé sur ordinateur.*

PAGE 120 #284 ART DIRECTOR: *Richard Uccello* DESIGNERS: *Mark Terranova, Richard Uccello* AGENCY: *Ted Bertz Graphic Design, Inc.* PHOTOGRAPHER: *Joe Baraban* CLIENT: *Aetna Life Insurance & Annuity Company* ■ *"The average vacation lasts two weeks. The average retirement lasts nearly twenty years. Which do you spend more time planning?" The directive was to increase awareness of the client's retirement plan, thereby increasing contri-butions to and participation in the retirement plan.* ● *«Ferien dauern durchschnittlich zwei Wochen. Die durchschnittliche Pensionszeit zwanzig Jahre. Wofür investieren Sie mehr Zeit mit der Planung?» Hier geht es um das Rentensystem einer Versicherungsgesellschaft.* ▲ *«La durée moyenne des vacances est de deux semaines. Celle de la retraite, de vingt ans. Combien de temps consacrez-vous à la planification de ces deux périodes de votre vie?» Affiche d'une compagnie d'assurance proposant un plan de retraite.*

PAGE 120 #285-287 ART DIRECTOR: *Tham Khai Meng* AGENCY: *Batey Ads Singapore* PHOTOGRAPHER/ILLUSTRATOR: *Wee Khim* COPYWRITER: *Tim Evill* CLIENT: *United Overseas Bank Group* ■ *The agency wanted to emphasize that the client's account looks after the customer's money and does all the work so there is no need to worry.* ● *«Um sich zu entspannen, suchen sich manche einen stillen Teich.» «Um sich zu entspannen, wälzen sich manche in warmem Schlamm.» «Um sich zu entspannen, lauschen manche dem Rauschen des Meeres.» Die Botschaft dieses Plakates für eine Bankengruppe: Sie küm-mert sich um die Anlagen ihrer Kunden, so dass diese sich keine Sorgen machen müssen.* ▲ *«Pour se relaxer, certains se rendent au bord des étangs tranquils.» «Pour se relaxer, certains se vautrent dans des bains de boue.» «Pour se relaxer, certains écoutent le bruit de la mer. Affiche pour une banque. Le message: la banque s'occupe de faire fructifier l'argent de ses clients qui peuvent dormir tranquille.*

PAGE 121 #288 ART DIRECTOR/AGENCY: *Sedivy Graphic Design* ILLUSTRATOR: *Lubomír Sedivy* CLIENT: *Sedivy Vik, Graphic Design*

PAGE 121 #289 ART DIRECTORS: *Steve Chalson (Miller Brewing Company), Lee Leissring, Bill Leissring* DESIGNERS: *Lee Leissring, Bill Leissring* AGENCY: *Team Design, Inc.* PHOTOGRAPHY: *William Hawkes Studio* CLIENT: *Miller Brewing Company* ■ *These posters were created to appeal to the young beer drinker.* ● *An junge Biertrinker gerichtetes Plakat.* ▲ *Affiche ciblant les jeunes amateurs de bière.*

PAGE 121 #290 ART DIRECTOR/ DESIGNER/ILLUSTRATOR: *David Lance Goines* AGENCY: *St. Hieronymus Press, Inc.* CLIENT: *Chez Panisse Café & Restaurant*

PAGE 121 #291 ART DIRECTOR: *Mark Marinozzi* DESIGNER: *Dawn Janney* AGENCY: *DesignTribe* PHOTOGRAPHER: *Skip Liepke* CLIENT: *Island Coffee Company* ■ *"I Wahi Kope Nau? (Would you like some coffee?)" The agency wanted to create a new identity to increase brand presence of the client's coffee in stores, restaurants, and coffee roasters. The Hawaiian dancer rising from the coffee's steam evokes both a cultural message of the island's heritage and a marketing message of the product's quality.* ● *«Möchten Sie Kaffee haben?» Hier ging es um die Förderung einer Kaffeemarke in Läden, Restaurants und Kaffeeröstereien. Die aus dem Kaffeedampf entsteigende hawaiische Tänzerin signal-isiert die Herkunft des Kaffees aus einem klassischen Anbauland und seine Qualität.* ▲ *«Voulez-vous un café?» Promotion d'une marque de café dans les magasins, les restau-rants et les torréfactions. La silhouette de la danseuse hawaïenne évoquée par la vapeur du café indique la provenance du produit et ses qualités.*

PAGE 122 #292-294 ART DIRECTOR: *Jack Anderson* DESIGNERS: *Jack Anderson, Lisa Cerveny, Suzanne Haddon* AGENCY: *Hornall Anderson Design Works, Inc.* PHOTOGRAPHER/ILLUSTRATOR: *Mits Katayama, Abe Girvin* CLIENT: *Jamba Juice* ■ *Point-of-purchase posters. The directive was to distinguish the client from its competitors. In doing so, the look needed to be festive without appearing trendy, and needed to appeal to young and old alike as well as communicate that the client is an authority on juice and*

nutrition. The agency used playful yet sophisticated images, a palette of bright colors, and Bembo and Meta typefaces for their friendly look and legibility. ● *Ladenplakate für einen Saft- und Lebensmittelhersteller, der sich positiv von der Konkurrenz abheben wollte. Die Plakate sollten Alt und Jung gleichermassen ansprechen, was mit spielerischen und doch anspruchsvollen Bildern, einer Palette von leuchtenden Farben und den gut lesbaren Bembo- und Meta-Schriften gelang.* ▲ *Affiches de magasin pour un fabricant de jus de fruits et de produits alimentaires, visant aussi bien un public jeune que plus âgé. L'agence a utilisé des images à la fois ludiques et sophistiquées, une palette de couleurs vives et les polices de caractères Bembo et Meta faciles à lire.*

PAGE 122 #295-297 ART DIRECTOR/ DESIGNER: *Jon Wyville* AGENCY: *McConnaughy Stein Schmidt Brown* COPYWRITER: *Kevin Lynch* CLIENT: *Sophie's Perogis To-Go* ■ *"Sophie's Perogis to go. So authentically Polish, they're Polish." The challenge was to make the design as stupid as the copy. It was successful!* ● *«Sophie's Perogis To Go. So authentisch polnisch, sie sind polnisch.» Hier ging es darum, das Design so dumm wie den Text zu machen. Es war ein voller Erfolg!* ▲ *«Sophie's Perogis To-Go. Tellement polonais qu'ils sont polonais.» L'objectif était de créer un graphisme aussi stupide que le texte. Mission accomplie!*

PAGE 122 #298 ART DIRECTOR: *Thomas Pakull* DESIGNERS: *Ove Gley, Stefan Zschaler* AGENCY: *Jung von Matt Werbeagentur* PHOTOGRAPHER/ILLUSTRATOR: *Stephan Försterling* CLIENT: *Mineralbrunnen AG* ■ *Poster for a soft drink.* ● *Plakat für ein Erfrischungsgetränk.* ▲ *Affiche pour un soda.*

PAGE 122 #299 ART DIRECTORS: *David Turner, Bruce Duckworth* DESIGNER: *Jeff Fassnacht* AGENCY: *Turner Duckworth* PHOTOGRAPHER/ILLUSTRATOR: *Stan Musilek* CLIENT: *McKenzie River Corp.*

PAGE 122 #300 ART DIRECTOR: *Thomas Pakull* DESIGNERS: *Ove Gley, Stefan Zschaler* AGENCY: *Jung von Matt Werbeagentur* PHOTOGRAPHER/ILLUSTRATOR: *Stephan Försterling* CLIENT: *Mineralbrunnen AG* ■ *Poster for a soft drink.* ● *Plakat für ein Erfrischungsgetränk.* ▲ *Affiche pour un soda.*

PAGE 123 #301 ART DIRECTOR/ DESIGNER/PHOTOGRAPHER: *Larry Kunkel* AGENCY: *Larry Kunkel Studio* CLIENT: *Celestial Arts*

PAGE 124 #302-304 ART DIRECTOR: *Todd Tilford, Eric Tilford* AGENCY: *Core / R&D / The Richards Group* PHOTOGRAPHER/ILLUSTRATOR: *James Schwartz, Michael Eastman* COPYWRITER: *Todd Tilford* CLIENT: *Schlafly* ■ *Series of posters created to launch the client's new bottled beer. Rather than positioning it as another microbrew, the agency sought to promote the brewer as bringing back the pre-prohibition, brew-pub way of brewing beer.* ● *Plakatreihe für die Lancierung eines neuen, abgefüllten Biers. Schlafly wird hier als Brauerei dargestellt, die ihr Bier wie die Wirtshäuser in den Tagen vor der Prohibition braut* ▲ *Série d'affiches pour le lancement d'une nouvelle bière en bouteille. Schlafly est présentée comme une brasserie qui fabrique sa bière selon une recette origi-nale, comme le faisaient les aubergistes avant la prohibition.*

PAGE 124 #305-307 ART DIRECTOR: *Carlos Silverio* AGENCY: *DPZ Propaganda* PHOTOGRAPHER: *Felipe Hellmeister* COPYWRITER: *Rui Branquinho* CLIENT: *Palace Brands*

PAGE 125 #308 ART DIRECTOR/ DESIGNER: *Pavel Benes* AGENCY: *Graphic Design Pavel Benes, E.D.A.* CLIENT: *In-house*

PAGE 125 #309 ART DIRECTORS: *Bob Meagher, Mike Hughes* AGENCY: *The Martin Agency* COPYWRITER: *Mike Hughes* CLIENT: *The Coca-Cola Company* ■ *"The most popular drink on the planet is now the most popular drink off the planet."* ● *«Das beliebteste Getränk auf dem Planeten ist jetzt das beliebteste Getränk ausserhalb des Planeten.»* ▲ *«La boisson la plus appréciée sur terre est désormais la boisson la plus appréciée dans l'espace.»*

PAGE 126 #310-313 DESIGNER: *Karlheinz Müller* AGENCY: *Heye & Partner* PHOTOGRAPHER/ILLUSTRATOR: *Markus Lange* COPYWRITER: *Martin Kießling* CLIENT: *McDonald's* ■ *"Great to see what they do with my eggs." "Second street at the left." "With the taste of freedom and adventure." "Tastes just right"* ● *«Toll, was die aus meinen Eiern machen.» «Zweite Gassi links.» «Mit dem Geschmack von Freiheit und Abenteuer.» «Schmeckt wie angegossen.»* ▲ *«C'est fou ce qu'ils font avec des œufs!» «La deuxième à gauche.» «Le goût de la liberté et de l'aventure.» «Du sur mesure.»*

PAGE 127 #314-316 ART DIRECTORS: *Ralph Taubenberger, Beate Gronemann* DESIGNERS: *Susanne Schaal* AGENCY: *Heye & Partner* COPYWRITER: *Otward Buchner* CLIENT: *Bad Brambacher Mineralquellen*

PAGE 127 #317 ART DIRECTORS: *Marcello Serpa, Valdir Bianchi, Luiz Sanchez* AGENCY: *Almap/BBDO* PHOTOGRAPHER/ILLUSTRATOR: *Alexandre Catan* COPYWRITER: *Alexandre Gama, Atila Francocci* CLIENT: *Miller Co.* ■ The task was to create a niche in a competitive Brazilian beer market. The client was introducing something rare in the market: a product differential–the beer isn't pasteurized, so it has characteristics of the fresh tap beer, called "Chopp" in Brazil. The agency decided to introduce the client similarly with a desired Chopp that has restricted distribution. The creative solution was to show a typical Chopp glass topped with the client's cap, presenting a fresh beer on tap, but accessible and portable. ● Hier ging es um die Einführung eines ganz speziellen Biers im stark umkämpften brasilianischen Biermarkt. Es handelt sich um ein nicht pasteurisiertes Bier, das dadurch die Eigenschaften von frisch gezapftem Bier besitzt, in Basilien «Choop» genannt. Deshalb wird hier ein typisches Choop-Glas mit der Verschlusskappe des Auftraggebers gezeigt: ein Bier, so frisch wie gezapft, das aber überall erhältlich ist und sich transportieren lässt. ▲ Affiche destinée au lancement d'une bière spéciale sur le marché de la bière brésilien très disputé. Il s'agit d'une bière non pasteurisée, possédant les qualités d'une bière pression appelée «choop» au Brésil. C'est pourquoi le visuel présente une chope avec la capsule de la marque. Cette bière, aussi fraîche qu'une bière pression, est commercialisée partout et facile à emporter.

PAGE 127 #318 ART DIRECTOR: *Marcello Serpa* AGENCY: *Almap/BBDO* PHOTOGRAPHER/ILLUSTRATOR: *J.R. Duran, Cassio Vasconcelos* COPYWRITER: *Alexandre Gama, Atila Francocci* CLIENT: *Pepsico & Co.*

PAGE 127 #319 ART DIRECTORS: *Marcello Serpa, Valdir Bianchi, Luiz Sanchez* AGENCY: *Almap/BBDO* PHOTOGRAPHER/ILLUSTRATOR: *Alexandre Catan* COPYWRITER: *Alexandre Gama, Atila Francocci* CLIENT: *Miller Co.*

PAGE 128 #320 CREATIVE DIRECTORS: *Eric Tilford, Todd Tilford* ART DIRECTOR: *Eric Tilford* AGENCY: *R&D The Richards Group* PHOTOGRAPHER/ILLUSTRATOR: *Richard Reens* COPYWRITER: *Todd Tilford* CLIENT: *Calido Chili Traders* ■ "Pain is good." ● «Schmerz ist gut.» ▲ «Quand la douleur est bonne.»

PAGE 128 #321 ART DIRECTORS: *Todd Tilford, Eric Tilford* AGENCY: *Core / R&D / The Richards Group* PHOTOGRAPHER: *Richard Reens* COPYWRITER: *Todd Tilford* CLIENT: *Calido Chili Traders* ■ Point of purchase poster to promote the brand's hottest hot sauce. ● Ladenplakat als Werbung für die schärfste der scharfen Saucen. ▲ Affiche de magasin pour la promotion d'une sauce extraforte.

PAGE 128 #322 ART DIRECTORS: *Debbie Smith Read, Steven Addis* DESIGNER: *Debbie Smith Read* AGENCY: *Addis Design* PHOTOGRAPHER/ILLUSTRATOR: *Robert Evans* CLIENT: *Bell-Carter Foods Inc.* ■ This poster was created as part of a brand repositioning program. Although the client is the oldest national brand of canned olives, its image was dated. The agency overcame this while still evoking the brand's rich heritage. The fruit crate imagery imbues the brand with a fresh appeal. ● Das Plakat gehört zu einem Programm für die Neupositionierung der ältesten nationalen Marke für Olivenkonserven, die mittlerweile etwas veraltet wirkte. Während hier die Tradition des Produktes hervorgehoben wird, sorgt das Bild der Fruchtkiste für einen frischen Eindruck des Produktes. ▲ Affiche réalisée dans le cadre d'un programme de repositionnement de la plus ancienne marque d'olives en boîte. Il s'agissait de toiletter l'image de la marque tout en évoquant la longue tradition du produit. Le visuel joue sur la fraîcheur.

PAGE 128 #323 ART DIRECTOR: *Alberto Gonzalez* DESIGNER: *Morgan Daniels* AGENCY: *Pulsar Advertising* CLIENT: *Lulu's Dessert Factory* ■ "More fun for your spoon." ● «Mehr Spass für Ihren Löffel.» ▲ «Plus de joie dans votre cuillère.»

PAGE 128 #324 ART DIRECTORS: *Alexander Bartel, Markus Lange* DESIGNER: *Karlheinz Müller* AGENCY: *Heye & Partner* PHOTOGRAPHER/ILLUSTRATOR: *Markus Lange* COPYWRITER: *Martin Kießling* CLIENT: *McDonald's*

PAGE 129 #325 CREATIVE DIRECTOR: *Antony Redman* ART DIRECTORS: *Scott Lambert, Mark Ringer* AGENCY: *Batey Ads Singapore* PHOTOGRAPHER/ILLUSTRATOR: *Lester Lefkowitz* COPYWRITERS: *Mark Ringer, Scott Lambert* CLIENT: *Beaujolais Wine Bar* ■ The client, a popular wine bar, wanted to capitalize on Jacques Chirac's nuclear testing. The affordability of this establishment was also emphasized. ● Der Auftraggeber, eine beliebte Weinbar, wollte sich Jacques Chiracs Atomtests zunutze machen. Gleichzeitig werden die durchaus freundlichen Preise des Etablissements hervorgehoben. ▲ Le client, un bar à vins réputé, a voulu tirer profit des tests nucléaires français. Parallèlement, l'accent est mis sur les prix raisonnables de l'établissement.

PAGE 130 #326 ART DIRECTOR: *Jerry Ketel* AGENCY: *Leopold Ketel & Partners* PHOTOGRAPHER: *Steve Bloch* COPYWRITER: *Leslee Dillon* CLIENT: *Table Lamp & Chair* ■ "Man without a chair." In an effort to publicize the need for good furniture, the agency decided to show the absence of furniture. ● «Mann ohne Stuhl.» Um die Notwendigkeit guter Möbel zu verdeutlichen, wird hier das Fehlen des Möbels gezeigt. ▲ «Homme sans chaise.» Pour souligner l'importance d'un mobilier de qualité, l'agence joue sur l'absence de meubles.

PAGE 130 #327-328 ART DIRECTOR/ DESIGNER: *Jürgen Pilger* AGENCY: *Pilger Harden* PHOTOGRAPHER: *Heinpeter Schreiber* ARTIST: *Victor Bonato* COPYWRITER: *Claus Harden* CLIENT: *Wiesner Hager Möbel GmbH* ■ These posters created for a furniture manufacturer were meant for architects and the trade. The artist created two objects of art entitled "Chairs" for the posters. A limited and signed edition was sent to selected clients. ● Die Plakate eines Möbelherstellers richten sich an Architekten und den Handel. Auf den Rückseiten befindet sich eine Übersicht des gesamten Programms. Für die Plakate wurden eigens zwei Kunstobjekte entworfen. Eine limitierte und signierte Auflage wurde an ausgewählte Kunden verschickt. ▲ Affiches d'un fabricant de meubles visant les architectes et le commerce. La ligne complète figure au dos des affiches. L'artiste a spécialement créé deux objets d'art intitulés «Chaises». Une édition signée et limité a été offerte aux bons clients.

PAGE 131 #329 ART DIRECTOR: *John Bricker* DESIGNER: *Patricia Glover* AGENCY: *Gensler* PHOTOGRAPHER/ILLUSTRATOR: *Doug Rosa* COPYWRITER: *Dan Fogelson* CLIENT: *Carnegie* ■ The poster was based on a single chair with a simple design. The budget for the poster, collateral materials and direct mail was small so the agency made the elements of the poster adaptable to the other pieces by changing the background color. ● Thema des Plakates ist ein einziger, sehr schlichter Stuhl. Die Elemente des Plakates wurden wegen des sehr kleinen Budgets auch für andere Werbemittel eingesetzt, wobei jeweils die Hintergrundfarbe verändert wurde. ▲ En raison du budget limité, les éléments de cette affiche ont été utilisés pour d'autres supports publicitaires, seule la couleur du fond changeant.

PAGE 132 #330, 331 ART DIRECTOR/ DESIGNER/ILLUSTRATOR: *Siegmar Münk* AGENCY: *Münkillus* CLIENT: *Self-promotion*

PAGE 133 #332 ART DIRECTOR: *Supon Phornirunlit* DESIGNER: *Steve Morris* AGENCY: *Supon Design Group* PHOTOGRAPHER/ILLUSTRATOR: *Greg Desantis* CLIENT: *Museum of Junk*

PAGE 134 #333 DESIGNER: *Gary Blakeley* AGENCY: *Aitken Blakeley* CLIENT: *Self-promotion* ■ This illustration was created for a promotional piece to showcase the agency's design and illustration. The illustration of the Leica IIF was rendered with minute detail, using Adobe Illustrator and Dimensions. ● Illustration als Eigenwerbung eines Design- und Illustrations-Studios. Die Leica IIF wurde bis ins kleinste Detail mit Hilfe der Software Adobe Illustrator originalgetreu wiedergegeben. ▲ Illustration autopromotionnelle d'une agence spécialisée dans le design et l'illustration. Grâce au logiciel Adobe Illustrator, la reproduction de l'appareil photo Leica IIF a pu être rendue fidèlement.

PAGE 134 #334 ART DIRECTORS/ DESIGNERS: *Jon Simonsen, John Muller* AGENCY: *Muller & Co.* PHOTOGRAPHER/ILLUSTRATOR: *Mike Regnier* CLIENT: *Illustration Academy* ■ This poster attempts to get art students interested in a six-week program through use of an outstanding visual. ● Mit Hilfe eines hervorragenden Bildes wird hier versucht, müde Studenten für einen sechswöchigen Kursus zu interessieren. ▲ Affiche visant à motiver des étudiants d'écoles d'art fatigués à participer à un cours de six semaines au moyen d'un visuel accrocheur.

PAGE 135 #335 ART DIRECTOR/ DESIGNER: *Henrik Barends* AGENCY: *Studio Barends & Pijnappel* PHOTOGRAPHER/ILLUSTRATOR: *Hans Dukkers* CLIENT: *Maria Austria Instituut* ■ Announcement for an exhibition on fashion photographer Hans Dukkers in Amsterdam. ● Ankündigung einer Ausstellung des Modephotographen Hans Dukkers in Amsterdam. ▲ Affiche de l'exposition du photographe de mode Hans Dukkers à Amsterdam.

PAGE 135 #336 DESIGNER: *Lisa Cromer* AGENCY: *Uffindell & West* PHOTOGRAPHER/ILLUSTRATOR: *London Transport Museum* CLIENT: *London Transport* ■ This poster is part of an information pack developed to communicate the importance of design to London Transport. The poster and pack targets design students and schools and encourages visitors to the Transport Museum. ● Das Plakat gehört zu einem Informationspaket über die Bedeutung von gutem Design für die Verkehrsbetriebe London Transport. Es richtet sich an Design-Studenten und Schulen und lädt zum Besuch des Transport Museums ein. ▲ Affiche réalisée dans le cadre d'une campagne d'information sur l'importance d'un bon design pour les entreprises de transports londoniennes. L'affiche s'adresse aux étudiants en design et aux écoles, et les invite à venir visiter le Musée des transports.

PAGE 136 #337 ART DIRECTOR: *Jennifer Morla* DESIGNERS: *Jennifer Morla, Craig Bailey* AGENCY: *Morla Design, Inc.* CLIENT: *Bacchus Press* ■ *This promotional poster commemorates the Mexican Museum. It incorporates early 20th century wood block type, lotteria imagery, the quintessential portrayal of Our Lady of Guadalupe, and a Benday portrait of Frida Kahlo owned by the museum.* ● *Plakat für das Mexikanische Museum mit Holzschnitt-Buchstaben vom Anfang des Jahrhunderts, dem Porträt «Unserer lieben Frau von Guadalupe» und einem Benday-Porträt von Frida Kahlo, das sich im Besitz des Museums befindet.* ▲ *Affiche pour le Musée mexicain réalisée avec des caractères en bois du début du siècle, le portrait de «Notre-Dame de Guadeloupe» et celui de Frida Kahlo peint par Benday qui appartient au musée.*

PAGE 136 #338 ART DIRECTOR/ DESIGNER: *Neil Becker* AGENCY: *Becker Design* PHOTOGRAPHER: *Joanne Peterson* CLIENT: *Milwaukee Public Museum* ■ *This poster was inspired by a visit to the vault of the Milwaukee Public Museum. The designer had to choose from approximately 100 glass pieces, and finally decided on the amber decanter from Bohemia because of its simple, classic shape, its etching, and the quality of light that it refracted.* ● *Für dieses Plakat des Milwaukee Public Museums konnte der Gestalter unter ca. 100 Glasgegenständen aus den Beständen des Museums auswählen. Er entschied sich für die bernsteinfarbene Karaffe aus Böhmen wegen ihrer schlichten, klassischen Form, den Ätzungen und den dadurch entstehenden speziellen Lichtbrechungen.* ▲ *Pour cette affiche du Milwaukee Public Museum, le graphiste a dû faire une sélection parmi une centaine d'objets en verre appartenant au musée. Son choix s'est porté sur une carafe de Bohème qu'il a retenue pour sa forme pure et classique, ses beaux motifs gravés et la qualité de la lumière réfléchie.*

PAGE 136 #339 ART DIRECTOR: *Mike Dempsey* DESIGNERS: *Neil Walker, Paula Snell* AGENCY: *CDT Design Limited* CLIENT: *Design Museum* ■ *This poster was created to announce a major exhibition at the Design Museum devoted to the use of plastic in design.* ● *Ankündigung einer Ausstellung im Londoner Design Museum, deren Thema hervorragend gestaltete Kunststoffgegenstände sind.* ▲ *Affiche d'une grande exposition du Musée du design à Londres consacrée à l'utilisation du plastique en design.*

PAGE 136 #340 ART DIRECTOR: *Emanuele Santi* AGENCY: *Stawicki* PHOTOGRAPHER /ILLUSTRATOR: *Christopher Tech* CLIENT: *Künstler für Artenschutz*

PAGE 137 #341 ART DIRECTOR/ DESIGNER/AGENCY: *Uwe Loesch* CLIENT: *Ruhrlandmuseum Essen* ■ *"Instead of." Poster for an exhibition entitled "The wall of the city of Essen before industrialization."* ● *"Instead of" (anstatt) – Plakat für eine Ausstellung im Ruhrlandmuseum über die Stadtmauer von Essen vor der Industrialisierung.* ▲ *«Instead of» (au lieu de) – Affiche d'une exposition intitulée «Les murs de la ville d'Essen avant l'industrialisation».*

PAGE 138 #342 DESIGNERS: *Vladimir Tsesler, Sergej Voitshenko* AGENCY: *Art Studio* CLIENT: *Liniagrafic*

PAGE 138 #343 ART DIRECTOR: *Mary Macenka (Seattle Symphony)* DESIGNER: *Bruce Hale* AGENCY: *Bruce Hale Design* ILLUSTRATOR: *Marsha Burns* CLIENT: *Seattle Symphony* ■ *Because the Seattle Symphony is breaking ground for a new concert hall in the heart of the city, the agency wanted to create imagery that reflected the move forward.* ● *Die Bemühungen des Symphonie-Orchesters von Seattle um einen neuen Konzertsaal im Herzen der Stadt sind Thema dieses Plakates.* ▲ *Thème de l'affiche: les efforts entrepris par l'orchestre symphonique de Seattle pour une nouvelle salle de concerts au cœur de la ville.*

PAGE 139 #344 ART DIRECTORS: *Norman Moore, Tommy Steele* DESIGNER: *Norman Moore* AGENCY: *Design/Art, Inc.* PHOTOGRAPHER: *Lorraine Day* CLIENT: *Capitol Records* ■ *The client wanted a more abstract, impressionistic look than the typical live album, so the main image was manipulated and blurred in Photoshop. The client also wanted to show other star performers so the colorful strip of small live shots was added.* ● *Um den vom Kunden gewünschten Look zu erzielen, der abstrakter und impressionistischer als bei Live-Plattenhüllen sein sollte, wurde das zentrale Bildmotiv im Photoshop manipuliert und verzerrt. Der farbenfrohe Streifen mit kleinen Life-Photos wurde eingefügt, weil auch andere Stars gezeigt werden sollten.* ▲ *Pour créer un effet plus abstrait et plus impressionniste que celui des pochettes de disques live, l'image centrale a été manipulée avec Photoshop. La bande aux couleurs vives présentant de petites photos de scène a été ajoutée afin de présenter d'autres stars.*

PAGE 139 #345 ART DIRECTOR/ DESIGNER: *Norman Moore* AGENCY: *Design/Art, Inc.* PHOTOGRAPHER: *Brothers Quay* CLIENT: *RCA Records* ■ *This design uses the musician's portrait combined with frame grabs from an animated video that was then distorted and altered.* ● *Das Porträt des Künstlers wurde mit Ausschnitten aus einem Video kombiniert, die verzerrt und manipuliert wurden.* ▲ *Le portrait de l'artiste a été combiné avec des extraits d'une vidéo qui ont été manipulés.*

PAGE 139 #346 ART DIRECTORS: *Norman Moore, Richard Frankel* DESIGNER: *Norman Moore* AGENCY: *Design/Art, Inc.* PHOTOGRAPHER: *Michel Comte* CLIENT: *A & M Records* ■ *This CD design was created for a greatest hits album. Because the agency had already designed the album cover, new photos were picked and adapted to the design elements.* ● *Plakat für eine CD mit Hits. Da die Agentur bereits die CD-Hülle gestaltet hatte, wurden neue Photos ausgewählt und den Designelementen angepasst.* ▲ *Affiche créée pour un CD des plus grands tubes. Comme l'agence avait déjà réalisé la pochette, de nouvelles photos ont été sélectionnées et adaptées aux éléments du design.*

PAGE 139 #347 ART DIRECTOR/ DESIGNER: *Norman Moore* AGENCY: *Design/Art, Inc.* CLIENT: *RCA Records* ■ *Design created to promote a successful single. Since the sleeve was already designed, the agency adapted and elaborated on the style with abstracts and color to give it a new disco/club dance feel.* ● *Werbung für eine erfolgreiche Single-Platte. Die CD-Hülle lieferte die Basis für den Stil, der verstärkt auf das Disco-Publikum ausgerichtet wurde.* ▲ *Publicité pour un single à succès. Le style de la pochette du CD a été repris et adapté à un public disco.*

PAGE 140 #348 ART DIRECTOR: *Thomas G. Fowler* DESIGNERS: *Karl S. Maruyama, Samuel Toh* AGENCY: *Tom Fowler, Inc.* ILLUSTRATOR: *Samuel Toh* CLIENT: *Connecticut Grand Opera & Orchestra* ■ *Poster announcing an upcoming performance of "La Traviata." When translated it means "The Fallen Woman," hence the image of the bed with a reclining heart. The final act takes place in Violetta's bedroom where she collapses in her lover's arms and dies.* ● *Ankündigung einer Aufführung von «La Traviata». Das Bild des Bettes mit dem Herzen bezieht sich auf den letzten Akt, in dem Violetta in den Armen ihres Geliebten stirbt.* ▲ *Affiche annonçant une représentation de «La Traviata». L'image du lit et du cœur se réfère au dernier acte, lors duquel Violetta meurt dans les bras de son prétendant.*

PAGE 140 #349 ART DIRECTOR/ DESIGNER/ILLUSTRATOR: *Thomas G. Fowler* AGENCY: *Tom Fowler, Inc.* COMPUTER REFINEMENT: *Samuel Toh* CLIENT: *Connecticut Grand Opera & Orchestra* ■ *Poster promoting an upcoming performance of Carmina Burana, a choral masterpiece derived from 13th century suggestive secular poems. Hence, the monk with an amusing grin on his face.* ● *Plakat für eine Aufführung der Carmina Burana. Die amüsierte Mimik des Mönches ist eine Anspielung auf die säkulare Natur der aus dem 13. Jahrhundert stammenden Vaganten-Lieder.* ▲ *Affiche pour une représentation des Carmina Burana. La mimique amusée du moine évoque le caractère de la collection de pièces vocales d'inspiration profane composées au XIIᵉ siècle.*

PAGE 140 #350 ART DIRECTOR/ DESIGNER: *Jeffery Fey* AGENCY: *Capitol Records* ILLUSTRATOR: *Michael Wilson* CLIENT: *In-house* ■ *This in-store poster was created to promote the most recent CD release from a critically acclaimed singer-songwriter. The design process was purposely low-tech and the poster was printed on inexpensive newsprint, tying it conceptually with the stark and lo-fi nature of the music.* ● *Ladenplakat für eine neue CD eines Sängers und Song-Schreibers. Das Plakat wurde auf billigem Zeitungspapier gedruckt, und das Design war bewusst einfach, um der schlichten Musik gerecht zu werden.* ▲ *Affiche de magasin pour le nouveau CD d'un chanteur-compositeur, imprimée sur un papier journal bon marché. La simplicité du design est en accord avec le genre musical.*

PAGE 140 #351 ART DIRECTOR/ DESIGNER: *Marc Brunner* AGENCY: *Büro Destruct* CLIENT: *Kulturzenturum Wasserwerk*

PAGE 141 #352 ART DIRECTOR/ DESIGNER: *Allen Weinberg* AGENCY: *Sony Music* PHOTOGRAPHER: *Karen Kuetta* CLIENT: *Sony Classical*

PAGE 141 #353 ART DIRECTOR/ DESIGNER: *Jon Simonsen* AGENCY: *Muller & Co.* ILLUSTRATOR: *Jon Simonsen* CLIENT: *Kansas City Blues & Jazz Festival* ■ *This poster was designed as a commemorative piece used to tie the festival in with Kansas City's rich blues and jazz heritage.* ● *Plakat zur Erinnerung an das Kansas City Blues & Jazz Festival, wobei die Jazz- und Blues-Tradition der Stadt hervorgehoben wird.* ▲ *Affiche commémorant la riche tradition de la ville de Kansas City dans les domaines du blues et du jazz.*

PAGE 142 #354 ART DIRECTOR/ DESIGNER: *Mirko Ilic´* AGENCY: *Mirko Ilic´ Corp.* PHOTOGRAPHER/ILLUSTRATOR: *Rajko Bizjak* CLIENT: *Helidon* ■ *This poster was created for the Slovenian group Buldozer Noc´ to promote their new album "Noc´/Night. The title has a symbolic meaning as the record was produced during wartime in ex-*

Yugoslavia. The designer tried to create from the word Noc´ a black object, a "thing" pressing on the landscape and breaking a flower. The word "night" can be written in various forms in the different languages of former Yugoslavia, but the designer intentionally omitted any form of accentuation, therefore giving it a universal meaning and avoiding any identification with any ethnicity. ■ *Plakat für ein neues Album der slovenischen Gruppe Buldozer Noc mit dem Titel «Noc» (Nacht). Dieser Titel hat symbolische Bedeutung, denn die Aufnahmen entstanden während des Krieges in Ex-Jugoslawien. Aus dem Wort «Noc» machte der Designer ein schwarzes Objekt, ein «Ding», das sich auf die Landschaft drückt und eine Blume bricht. Bewusst verzichtete der Gestalter beim Wort Noc auf Akzente, die in den verschiedenen Sprachen Ex-Jugoslawiens unterschiedlich sind, um eine bestimmte ethnische Zuordnung zu vermeiden.* ▲ *Affiche pour un nouvel album du groupe slovène Buldozer Noc, intitulé «Noc» (nuit). Ce titre a une signification symbolique, les prises de vues ayant été réalisées durant la guerre en ex-Yougoslavie. Le graphiste a fait du mot «Noc» un objet noir, une «chose» qui écrase la nature et brise une fleur. Il a volontairement renoncé aux accents qui ne sont pas les mêmes dans les différentes langues de l'ex-Yougoslavie afin que le mot «Noc» ne se réfère à aucune ethnie particulière.*

PAGE 142 #355 ART DIRECTOR/ DESIGNER: *Allen Weinberg* AGENCY: *Sony Music* PHOTOGRAPHER/ILLUSTRATOR: *Mark Hanauer* CLIENT: *In-house*

PAGE 142 #356 ART DIRECTOR/ DESIGNER: *Ine Ilg* AGENCY: *Büro für Gestaltung, Kommunikation und Kultur* PHOTOGRAPHER/ILLUSTRATOR: *Karlheinz Bechholz* CLIENT: *GKB*

PAGE 142 #357 ART DIRECTOR/ DESIGNER: *Ine Ilg* AGENCY: *Büro Für Gestaltung, Kommunikation und Kultur* PHOTOGRAPHER/ILLUSTRATOR: *Karlheinz Bechholz* CLIENT: *Kunterbunt E.V.* ■ *The typographic structure of this poster was developed from the rhythm of Fats Domino's music.* ● *Die typographische Struktur dieses Plakates wurde vom Rhythmus der Musik Fats Dominos inspiriert.* ▲ *La structure typographique de cette affiche s'inspire de la musique de Fats Domino.*

PAGE 143 #358 AGENCY: *Zero Defects* CLIENT: *Thoughtographic*

PAGE 143 #359 ART DIRECTOR: *Michael Cronan* DESIGNERS: *Michael Cronan, Joseph Stitzlein, Tom Dennis* AGENCY: *Cronan Design* CLIENT: *Dallas Society of Visual Communications* ■ *This poster announces two functions. The bowling nuns refer to a design lecture by Michael Cronan and Karin Hibma and the buzzsaws refer to a rock and roll performance by Adjam and the Fuzztones.* ● *Die kegelnden Nonnen in diesem Plakat beziehen sich auf einen Vortrag von Michael Cronan und Karin Hibma, während die Kreissägen auf ein Rock-and-Roll-Konzert von Adjam and the Fuzztones hinweisen.* ▲ *Les nonnes jouant aux quilles font référence à une conférence de Michael Cronan et de Karin Hibma, les scies circulaires, à un concert rock d'Adjam and the Fuzztones.*

PAGE 144 #360 ART DIRECTORS/ DESIGNERS: *Micah Hahn, Jeff MacDuffie* AGENCY: *Jeff & Mike* CLIENT: *Self-promotion* ■ *Limited edition of forty non-commissioned silkscreen posters created for the performance of the band Foreskin 500. The designers wanted to achieve a "spy" look for this poster because they felt this would reflect the band's sound and attitude. They were on a limited budget and deadline, so they used a narrow format to get two posters out of each sheet of paper. For the logo, they altered the Jackson 5 logo off the "Dancing Machine" LP. The "J" was changed to an "F" and the logo was finished off with Helvetica.* ● *Siebdruckplakat in limitierter Auflage für eine Vorstellung der Band Foreskin 500. Der James-Bond-Look entspricht nach Meinung der Gestalter dem Stil und der Musik der Band. Das kleine Format machte es möglich, zwei Plakate auf einmal zu drucken. Das «F» des Logos wurde aus dem «J» des Jackson-5-Logos für die LP «Dancing Machine» heraus entwickelt.* ▲ *Sérigraphie en édition limitée pour un concert du groupe Foreskin 500. Le look «espion» correspond au style et à la musique du groupe. Le petit format a permis d'imprimer deux affiches à la fois et de limiter ainsi les coûts. Le «F» du logo s'inspire du «J» des Jackson 5 figurant sur le 33 tours «Dancing Machine».*

PAGE 144 #361 DESIGNER: *Jeff Matz* AGENCY: *Larkin Meeder & Schweidel* PHOTOGRAPHER/ILLUSTRATOR: *Jeff Matz* CLIENT: *Figurehead Records* ■ *The directive was to create a poster that would promote two different performances at two different locations on the same evening. The solution included a separate and complete image for each show, while packaging them together by emphasizing the date.* ● *Plakat für die Ankündigung von zwei Konzerten, die am selben Abend an verschiedenen Orten stattfanden. Die Lösung bestand in einem separaten Bild für jede Veranstaltung, wobei das Datum zum verbindenden Element wurde.* ▲ *Affiche annonçant deux concerts donnés le*

même soir à des endroits différents. La solution consista à créer deux images distinctes, la date – mise en évidence – faisant office de lien.

PAGE 145 #362 ART DIRECTOR: *Kenzo Izutani* DESIGNERS: *Kenzo Izutani, Aki Hirai* AGENCY: *Kenzo Izutani Office Corporation* PHOTOGRAPHER/ILLUSTRATOR: *Yasuyuki Amazutsumi* CLIENT: *Yougey, Inc.*

PAGE 145 #363 ART DIRECTOR: *Stefan Sagmeister* DESIGNERS: *Stefan Sagmeister, Veronica Oh* AGENCY: *Sagmeister Inc.* PHOTOGRAPHER/ILLUSTRATOR: *Timothy Greenfield Sanders* CLIENT: *Lou Reed/Warner Brothers* ■ *This poster announces Lou Reed's new album. Since the lyrics are extremely personal, the agency showed this by writing the lyrics directly over his face.* ● *Ankündigung eines neuen Albums von Lou Reed. Die Texte sind sehr persönlich und wurden deshalb auf sein Gesicht geschrieben.* ▲ *Affiche pour un nouvel album de Lou Reed. Les textes, très personnels, ont été écrits sur son visage.*

PAGE 145 #364 ART DIRECTOR/ DESIGNER: *Rik Besser* AGENCY: *Besser Joseph Partners* PHOTOGRAPHER: *Terry Heffernan* CLIENT: *National Resophonic Guitars*

PAGE 145 #365 ART DIRECTOR/ DESIGNER: *Steve Sandstrom* AGENCY: *Sandstrom Design* PHOTOGRAPHER/ILLUSTRATOR: *Ward Schumaker* COPYWRITER: *Steve Sandoz* CLIENT: *KINK Radio* ■ *Poster promoting outdoor summer concerts. Because of a limited budget, a single concept needed to be developed to promote three different concerts. The design was used for posters, advertising, t-shirts, banners and a painted wall mural.* ● *Plakat für Sommerkonzerte im Freien. Wegen des beschränkten Budgets musste das Konzept für drei verschiedene Konzerte anwendbar sein. Der Entwurf wurde für Plakate, T-Shirts, Transparente und ein Wandbild verwendet.* ▲ *Affiche pour des concerts d'été en plein air. En raison du budget limité, le même concept devait s'appliquer à trois concerts. Le design a été utilisé pour des affiches, des tee-shirts, des bannières et une peinture murale.*

PAGE 146 #366, 367 ART DIRECTOR/ DESIGNER/ILLUSTRATOR: *Niklaus Troxler* AGENCY: *Niklaus Troxler Grafik Studio* CLIENT: *Jazz In Willisau*

PAGE 146 #368 ART DIRECTOR/ DESIGNER/ILLUSTRATOR: *David Lance Goines* AGENCY: *St. Hieronymus Press Inc* CLIENT: *Napa Valley Wine Auction*

PAGE 146 #369 ART DIRECTOR/ DESIGNER: *David Lance Goines* AGENCY: *St. Hieronymus Press, Inc.* CLIENT: *Berkeley Symphony Orchestra*

PAGE 146 #370 ART DIRECTOR: *Alli Truch* DESIGNER/LOGO DESIGN: *Jennifer Roddie* AGENCY: *Elektra Entertainment* ILLUSTRATOR: *Dan Winters* CLIENT: *Clutch* ■ *For a consistent point-of-purchase identity, it was crucial to link this poster with the client's second album package due to the introduction of the band's new Arabic-influenced logo. It was thematically important to maintain the atmosphere of an "alien presence" as well as reveal the band members' identities.* ● *Wegen der Einführung eines neuen, arabisch inspirierten Logos der Band war es wichtig, mit diesem Ladenplakat für einen homogenen Auftritt in Verbindung mit dem zweiten Album der Gruppe zu sorgen. Thematisch sollte die Atmosphäre einer «ausserirdischen Präsenz» beibehalten werden.* ▲ *En raison du nouveau logo du groupe d'inspiration arabe, il était important de créer avec cette affiche de magasin une image cohérente en accord avec le deuxième album du groupe. Il s'agissait de créer une atmosphère suggérant une «présence extra-terrestre».*

PAGE 147 #371 DESIGNER/AGENCY: *Ninja V. Oertzen* PHOTOGRAPHER: *Jan Kornstaedt* CLIENT: *Entertainment Support*

PAGE 148 #372 ART DIRECTORS: *David Gauger, Lori Murphy* DESIGNER: *Laura Levy* AGENCY: *Gauger & Silva Associates* COPYWRITER: *David Gauger* CLIENT: *Commercial Bank of San Francisco* ■ *"Free samples, inquire within." This poster served as a promotional piece for a business bank with a single location in San Francisco's financial district. The concept was tied into a direct mail campaign offering a free sample (a dollar bill) to promote business loans, and flyers with quarters attached handed out by a bank guard in front of the bank. The objective was to gain new customers while differentiating the bank from its larger, less personal competitors.* ● *«Kostenloses Muster. Fragen Sie drinnen.» Werbung für eine Bank mit nur einer Niederlassung in San Franciscos Finanzdistrikt. Das Konzept wurde im Rahmen einer Direct-Mail-Kampagne entwickelt, in der ein kostenloses Muster (eine 1-Dollar-Note) angeboten wird, um für Unternehmenskredite zu werben. Vor der Bank wurden Handzettel mit 25-Cent-Stücken verteilt. Mit dieser Aktion sollten neue Kunden mit dem Argument geworben werden, dass der Service dieser Bank persönlicher als der ihrer grösseren Konkurrenten ist.* ▲ *«Echantillon gratuit. Demandez à l'intérieur.» Publicité pour une banque ayant une seule succursale dans le quartier des* *affaires de San Francisco. Développé dans le cadre d'une campagne de mailing, le concept prévoit d'offrir un échantillon gratuit (un billet d'un dollar) dans le but de proposer des crédits aux entreprises. Devant la banque, un gardien distribuait des flyers comportant des pièces de 25 cents. La banque entendait gagner ainsi de nouveaux clients en se montrant plus personnelle que les grandes banques de la place.*

PAGE 148 #373, 374 ART DIRECTOR/ DESIGNER: *Clive Cochran* AGENCY: *Mithoff Advertising Inc.* PHOTOGRAPHER/ILLUSTRATOR: *Clive Cochran* CLIENT: *Hanley Paint Manufacturing Co., Inc.* ■ *"It can hide, but it won't run." "Foul weather friend." The agency needed to create awareness of the client's product in a crowded advertising venue, and to make the most of a modest media and production budget. The solution was to use simple graphics rendered in bold, eye-catching colors. The graphics were silkscreened without incurring expensive separation and four-color process printing costs. Layered paint swatch shapes and the logo treatment emphasize the nature of the product.* ● *«Sie deckt ab, tropft aber nicht.» «Schlechtwetter-Freund.» Die Aufgabe bestand darin, das Farbensortiment des Kunden effizient mit einem niedrigen Budget zu bewerben. Die Lösung bestand im Einsatz einfacher Graphik in kräftigen, auffälligen Farben. Siebdruck erwies sich als das günstigste Verfahren. Die Darstellung von Farbmustern und das Logo unterstreichen den Charakter des Produktes.* ▲ *«Son couvrant est parfait et elle ne coule pas.» «L'amie du mauvais temps.» Publicité petit budget pour un fabricant de peintures. L'affiche combine graphisme simple et couleurs vives. La sérigraphie s'est révélée la technique la moins onéreuse. La représentation d'échantillons de couleur et le logo soulignent les caractéristiques du produit.*

PAGE 149 #375 ART DIRECTOR: *Paula Scher* AGENCY: *Pentagram Design Inc.* PHOTOGRAPHER: *Michael Bierut* CLIENT: *Ambassador Arts Inc/Champion*

PAGE 149 #376 ART DIRECTOR: *Paula Scher* AGENCY: *Pentagram Design Inc.* PHOTOGRAPHER: *Yaron Vardimon* CLIENT: *Ambassador Arts Inc/Champion*

PAGE 149 #377 ART DIRECTOR: *Paula Scher* AGENCY: *Pentagram Design Inc.* PHOTOGRAPHER: *Paul Davis* CLIENT: *Ambassador Arts Inc/Champion*

PAGE 149 #378 ART DIRECTOR: *Paula Scher* AGENCY: *Pentagram Design Inc.* PHOTOGRAPHER: *Pierre Mendell* CLIENT: *Ambassador Arts Inc/Champion*

PAGE 149 #379 ART DIRECTOR: *Paula Scher* AGENCY: *Pentagram Design Inc.* PHOTOGRAPHER: *Seymour Chwast* CLIENT: *Ambassador Arts Inc/Champion*

PAGE 149 #380 ART DIRECTOR: *Paula Scher* AGENCY: *Pentagram Design Inc.* PHOTOGRAPHER/ILLUSTRATOR: *Rosemarie Tissi* CLIENT: *Ambassador Arts Inc/Champion*

PAGE 149 #381 ART DIRECTOR: *Paula Scher* AGENCY: *Pentagram Design Inc.* ILLUSTRATOR: *Rosemarie Tissi* CLIENT: *Ambassador Arts Inc/Champion*

PAGE 149 #382 ART DIRECTOR: *Paula Scher* AGENCY: *Pentagram Design Inc.* PHOTOGRAPHER/ILLUSTRATOR: *Woody Pirtle* CLIENT: *Ambassador Arts Inc/Champion*

PAGE 149 #383 ART DIRECTOR: *Paula Scher* AGENCY: *Pentagram Design Inc.* PHOTOGRAPHER/ILLUSTRATOR: *Woody Pirtle* CLIENT: *Ambassador Arts Inc./Champion*

PAGE 150 #384 ART DIRECTOR: *Akio Okumura* DESIGNER: *Mitsuo Ueno* AGENCY: *Packaging Create Inc.* CLIENT: *Musa Co. Ltd.*

PAGE 150 #385 ART DIRECTOR: *Akio Okumura* DESIGNER: *Mitsuo Ueno* AGENCY: *Packaging Create Inc.* PHOTOGRAPHER: *Nob Fukuda* CLIENT: *Oji Paper Co. Ltd.*

PAGE 150 #386 ART DIRECTORS: *Charles S. Anderson, Todd Piper Hauswirth* DESIGNER: *Todd Piper Hauswirth* AGENCY: *Charles S. Anderson Design Company* PHOTOGRAPHER/ILLUSTRATOR: *Darrell Eager* CLIENT: *French Paper Company*

PAGE 150 #387 ART DIRECTOR: *Phil Hamlett* DESIGNER: *Matt Rollins* AGENCY: *Executive Arts* PHOTOGRAPHER: *Michael Lamonica* COPYWRITER: *Paul Roberts* CLIENT: *Potlatch Corp.*

PAGE 151 #388-391 ART DIRECTORS: *Yoshinari Nishimura, Iwao Matsuura* DESIGNER: *Kamikura Atsushi* AGENCY: *Iwao Matsuura Design Office Co., Ltd.* CALLIGRAPHER: *Yoshinari Nishimura* CLIENT: *Takeo Co., Ltd.*

PAGE 152 #392 ART DIRECTORS: *William Thompson, Tim Girvin* DESIGNER: *William Thompson* CALLIGRAPHER: *Tim Girvin* AGENCY: *William Thompson Photographs* PHOTOGRAPHER/ILLUSTRATOR: *William Thompson* CLIENT: *Jackson Hole Mountain Guides* ■ *Poster originally designed for Jackson Hole Mountain Guides as a promotion and "for sale" poster now utilized as the agency's Self-promotion.* ● *Plakat für Bergführer, die «Jackson Hole Mountain Guides». Es wurde auch zum Verkauf angeboten und dient dem Studio ebenfalls als Eigenwerbung.* ▲ *Affiche pour des guides de montagne, les «Jackson Hole Mountain Guides», destinée à la vente. L'agence s'en servit également pour sa propre publicité.*

PAGE 152 #393 DESIGNER: *Joe Goodwin* AGENCY: *May & Company* PHOTOGRAPHER/ILLUSTRATOR: *Michele Clement* CLIENT: *Dallas Art Directors Club* ■ *Poster promoting a slide show and lecture by photographer Michele Clement.* ● *Plakatwerbung für eine Diavorführung und einen Vortrag des Photographen Michele Clement.* ▲ *Affiche pour une projection de diapos et une conférence du photographe Michele Clement.*

PAGE 153 #394 ART DIRECTORS: *Scott Mires, José Serrano* AGENCY: *Mires Design* PHOTOGRAPHER: *Carl VanderSchuit* CLIENT: *VanderSchuit Studio* ■ *The agency chose an approach akin to that of European fashion advertising.* ● *Hier wird im Stil europäischer Modewerbung für Teigwaren geworben.* ▲ *Publicité pour des pâtes dans l'esprit d'une publicité de mode européenne.*

PAGE 153 #395 ART DIRECTOR/ DESIGNER/PHOTOGRAPHER: *Elke Zimmermann* AGENCY: *Fotostudio Zimmermann* CLIENT: *In-house*

PAGE 153 #396, 397 ART DIRECTOR: *Roger Gould* DESIGNER: *Tim Powers* AGENCY: *Gould Design* PHOTOGRAPHER: *Craig Vander Lende* CLIENT: *Wace USA/The Etheridge Company* ■ *The client wanted a poster promoting its capabilities in high-fidelity color imaging and printing to a national audience of graphic designers. The strategy was to create a compelling image that would exemplify the client's capabilities without the use of words or even a logo. The toy robots, loaned by a local collector, were selected for their broad appeal and their suitability to the photographer's expertise in the light-painting technique.* ● *Dieses Plakat ist an Graphiker gerichtet und soll die Qualität der Farblithos und Reproduktionen des Kunden demonstrieren. Die von einem Sammler ausgeliehenen Spielzeugroboter wurden ausgewählt, weil sie einerseits ein breites Publikum ansprechen und andererseits ideale Objekte für eine Demonstration der Light-Painting-Technik des Photographen waren.* ▲ *Destinée aux graphistes, cette affiche devait illustrer la qualité des lithos couleur et des reproductions du client. La solution consista à choisir une image accrocheuse qui se passe de tout texte et de logo. Les robots empruntés à un collectionneur présentent un double avantage: d'une part, ils s'adressent à un large public et, d'autre part, ils permettent d'illustrer à merveille la technique du light-painting appliquée par le photographe.*

PAGE 154 #398-400 DESIGNER: *Hans Teensma* AGENCY: *Impress Inc.* PHOTOGRAPHER/ILLUSTRATOR: *Alan Epstein* CLIENT: *Magnani & McCormick* ■ *This poster utilizes images and type to show the expanded range possible on an eight-color press.* ● *Bei diesem Plakat geht es um die Demonstration der Möglichkeiten einer Acht-Farben-Druckpresse.* ▲ *Affiche illustrant les possibilités d'une presse huit couleurs.*

PAGE 154 #401-403 ART DIRECTOR: *Lars Rune Nilsson* AGENCY: *TBWA* PHOTOGRAPHER: *Ole Christiansen, Kenneth Rimm* COPYWRITER: *Soren Wedderkopp* CLIENT: *Nikon/DFA* ■ *"You don't take pictures; they are given to you." "Your camera is your weapon." "All your pictures expose yourself." These posters were part of an image campaign for Nikon. The goal was to make Nikon more personal and less technically oriented, and to appeal to customers who live and breathe for photography.* ● *«Man macht keine Aufnahmen; sie werden einem gegeben.» «Deine Kamera ist deine Waffe.» «Alle deine Bilder sprechen von dir.» Das Plakat gehört zu einer Image-Kampagne für Nikon. Ziel war es, Nikon statt eines technischen ein persönliches Image zu geben und ein Publikum anzusprechen, für das Photographie das Leben bedeutet.* ▲ *«On ne prend pas de photos; elles nous sont données.» «Ton appareil, c'est ton arme.» «Toutes tes images parlent de toi.» Affiche réalisée dans le cadre d'une campagne Nikon. L'objectif était de conférer une image plus personnelle que technique à la marque et d'interpeller les mordus de la photographie.*

PAGE 155 #404 DESIGNER: *Vater Unde Sohn* AGENCY: *Todd Haiman Studio* PHOTOGRAPHER: *Todd Haiman* CLIENT: *Self-promotion*

PAGE 155 #405 DESIGNER: *Ricki Conrad Design* AGENCY: *William Thompson Photographs* PHOTOGRAPHER/ILLUSTRATOR: *William Thompson* CLIENT: *Ranier Color of Seattle* ■ *"Landscapes of a Western Mind #231." This poster was conceived as as Self-*

promotion of the photographer as well as for the client. The image is from a photographic series which the photographer has been working on for 20 years. It was substantially modified by digital imaging techniques. ● Das Plakat wurde als Eigenwerbung eines Photographen und als Werbung für einen Farbenhersteller eingesetzt. Es gehört zu einer Photoserie, mit der sich der Photograph seit 20 Jahren befasst. Die Aufnahme wurde digital erheblich verfremdet. ▲ Affiche autopromotionnelle pour un photographe, utilisée comme publicité par un fabricant de couleurs. Extraite d'une série sur laquelle le photographe travaille depuis 20 ans, l'image, retravaillée sur ordinateur, a subi d'importantes modifications.

PAGE 156 #406 ART DIRECTOR/ DESIGNER/PHOTOGRAPHER: *Roger Cook* AGENCY: *Cook And Shanosky Associates, Inc.* CLIENT: *Middle East Peace* ■ The agency aligned two powerful symbols to show that peace is sought by both sides of the Middle East conflict. ● Mit den beiden eindrucksvollen Symbolen soll verdeutlicht werden, dass sich beide Seiten des Konfliktes im Mittleren Osten um Frieden bemühen. ▲ Les deux symboles, très forts, devaient montrer que les deux parties impliquées dans le conflit au Moyen-Orient travaillent à la paix.

PAGE 156 #407 ART DIRECTORS/ DESIGNERS/COPYWRITERS: *Sue Schaffner, Carrie Moyer* AGENCY: *Dyke Action Machine (DAM)* PHOTOGRAPHER: *Carrie Moyer* ILLUSTRATOR: *Sue Schaffner* CLIENT: *Irish Lesbian & Gay Organization* ■ "I'd rather fight than switch." As a public art group consisting of only two people working part-time with limited outside funding, the design problem was producing an effective but inexpensive poster campaign. The goal was to motivate as many peole as possible to participate in a direct action protest. The strategy was to insert lesbian images into a recognizably mainstream commercial context. The slogan from the 1970s Carlton cigarette campaign was used. The slogan's new meaning was an effective tool for inspiring activists and their supporters, which was evident by the overwhelming response of participants. ● «Ich kämpfe lieber als mich umzustellen.» Der Slogan, der bei diesem Plakat für eine irische Lesben- und Schwulen-Organisation eine neue Bedeutung erhält, stammt aus einer Carlton-Zigarettenwerbung aus den siebziger Jahren. Mit dem Plakat, das wenig kosten durfte, aber wirksam sein musste, sollten soviele Menschen wie möglich zur Teilnahme an einer Demonstration bewegt werden. Die Verflechtung von Lesbenbildern mit Mainstream-Werbung erwies sich als äusserst erfolgreich. ▲ «Je préfère me battre que de changer!» Emprunté à une publicité des cigarettes Carlton des années 70, le slogan de cette affiche pour une organisation irlandaise de lesbiennes et d'homosexuels prend une autre signification. Cette affiche réalisée à moindres frais devait attirer de nombreux participants à une manifestation. La combinaison d'images de lesbiennes et d'une publicité mainstream s'est révélée très efficace.

PAGE 156 #408 ART DIRECTOR/ DESIGNER: *Les Soos* AGENCY: *Ranscombe & Co* PHOTOGRAPHER/ILLUSTRATOR: *Steve Jackson* COPYWRITER: *Jim Ranscombe* CLIENT: *Coalition of Canadian Advertising Agencies Against Nuclear Testing* ■ "Nuke de Brie." The agency had to find an icon that immediately said "French" and "nuclear" to tell people to boycott French products. It was necessary to communicate the relationship between what is in the shopping cart and what is happening in the South Pacific that is far from appetizing. ● Ein Aufruf zum Boykott französischer Produkte wegen der Atomtests im Pazifik. «Nuke de Brie» - das Wort «nuklear» in Kombination mit dem Namen eines allgemein bekannten französischen Käses. ▲ Affiche appelant à boycotter les produits français en raison des tests nucléaires dans le Pacifique. «Nuke de Brie» – jeu de mots avec le terme «nucléaire» et le nom du fameux fromage.

PAGE 156 #409 ART DIRECTOR/ DESIGNER/COPYWRITER: *Kenichi Samura* AGENCY: *Number One Design Office* PHOTOGRAPHER/ILLUSTRATOR: *Mitsuo Shibata* CLIENT: *JAGDA* ■ "We still have too many nuclear weapons. For what? For who?" ● «Wir haben noch immer zuviele Atomwaffen. Für was? Für wen?» ▲ «Nous avons toujours trop d'armes atomiques. Pour quoi faire? Pour qui?»

PAGE 157 #410 ART DIRECTOR/ DESIGNER: *Yukichi Takada* AGENCY: *CID Lab* CLIENT: *Japan Graphic Designers Association* ■ This poster was designed with the theme of "Peace and Environment," in memory of the 50th anniversary of World War II. The agency utilized a remote view of the solar system to emphasize the precious nature of the Earth and humans and the sterility of fighting among the species on the blue planet. ● Plakat zum Thema «Frieden und Umwelt» als Erinnerung an das Ende des 2. Weltkrieges vor 50 Jahren. Hier wird die Kostbarkeit der Natur unseres Planeten und des menschlichen Lebens einerseits und die Kälte des Krieges andererseits zum Ausdruck gebracht. ▲ Affiche sur le thème «Paix et Environnement» commémorant la fin de la Deuxième guerre mondiale. Elle montre, d'une part, à quel point la nature et la vie humaine sont précieuses et, de l'autre, l'horreur de la guerre.

PAGE 158 #411 ART DIRECTOR/ DESIGNER: *Laurie Ann Meghan Murphy* PHOTOGRAPHER: *Jacques Brédy* ■ This poster was created to increase awareness of racism and how it affects young children. ● Thema dieses Plakates ist der Rassismus und seine Auswirkung auf Kinder. ▲ Thème de l'affiche: le racisme et ses répercussions sur les enfants.

PAGE 158 #412 ART DIRECTOR/ DESIGNER: *Fons Hickmann* AGENCY: *FONS* CLIENT: *In-house*

PAGE 158 #413 ART DIRECTOR/ DESIGNER: *Yossi Lemel* AGENCY: *Lemel Glazer* CLIENT: *In-house* ■ Personal criticism against the functioning of the UN during the war in the former Yugoslavia and a cynical comment on the impotence in the 50th anniversary of the organization. ● Eine persönliche Kritik des Einsatzes der UN-Truppen während des Krieges im ehemaligen Jugoslawien - ein zynischer Kommentar zum 50jährigen Bestehen der UNO. ▲ Critique personnelle de l'intervention des troupes des Nations unies durant la guerre de l'ex-Yougoslavie, un commentaire cynique pour le 50e anniversaire de l'ONU.

PAGE 158 #414 ART DIRECTOR/ DESIGNER: *Yossi Lemel* AGENCY: *Lemel Glazer* CLIENT: *Amnesty International Israeli Section* ■ This poster was part of a campaign to increase Israeli awareness of Amnesty International and to recruit new members. ● Das Plakat gehört zu einer Kampagne, mit der in Isreal um Aufmerksamkeit und neue Mitglieder für Amnesty International geworben wird. ▲ Affiche réalisée pour une campagne en Israël destinée à sensibiliser l'opinion et à gagner de nouveaux membres pour Amnesty International.

PAGE 159 #415 ART DIRECTOR/ DESIGNER: *Katsu Nagaishi* AGENCY: *Nagaishi Office* PHOTOGRAPHER/ILLUSTRATOR: *Kazuhiko Sonoki* COPYWRITER: *Fumi Kaneko* CLIENT: *FM Fukuoka*

PAGE 159 #416 ART DIRECTOR/COPYWRITER: *David Tartakover* AGENCY: *Tartakover Design* PHOTOGRAPHER/ILLUSTRATOR: *Oded Klein* CLIENT: *Self-promotion* ■ Every Jewish New Year, the designer creates a personal greeting poster. In 1995, the atmosphere in Israel was saturated with violence to a point that the image of the revolver on the poster seemed inevitable. Two months after the poster was produced, Prime Minister Rabin was assassinated. ● Jedes Jahr veröffentlicht der Designer ein Plakat zum Neuen Jahr der Juden. 1995 war die Atmosphäre in Israel derart von Gewalt geprägt, dass der Revolver das richtige Symbol zu sein schien. Zwei Monate nach der Herstellung des Plakates wurde Premierminister Rabin ermordet. ▲ Chaque année, le graphiste réalise une affiche pour le Nouvel-An juif. En 1995, le climat était si tendu en Israël qu'une arme s'est imposée comme symbole. Deux mois après la création de l'affiche, le Premier ministre Rabin était assassiné.

PAGE 159 #417 ART DIRECTOR: *Jurek Wajdowicz* DESIGNERS: *Lisa LaRochelle, Jurek Wajdowicz* AGENCY: *Emerson Wajdowicz Studios* PHOTOGRAPHER: *Victor Mello* CLIENT: *United Nations Office for Project Services* ■ "New perspectives for education." This poster was created as part of an ongoing series of "Progress Haiti." It represents confidence and hope in educational possibilities for the youth in Haiti within the framework of development programs in proverty-stricken areas. ● «Neue Perspektiven für die Ausbildung.» Das Plakat gehört zu einer Serie, deren Thema die Ausbildungsmöglichkeiten für die Jugend Haitis im Rahmen eines Entwicklungsprogramms für die Armen ist. ▲ «Nouvelles perspectives pour l'éducation.» Affiche extraite d'une série sur les possibilités de formation offertes aux jeunes Haïtiens dans le cadre d'un programme de développement destiné aux régions défavorisées.

PAGE 160 #418-420 ART DIRECTOR/ DESIGNER/PHOTOGRAPHER: *Finn Nygaard* AGENCY: *Finn Nygaard Graphic Design* CLIENT: *FS-TRYK* ■ "Sign Through the Time." Posters with different examples of sign printed in dry offset. ● «Zeichen der Zeiten.» Eine Plakatserie. ▲ «Signes des temps.» Série d'affiches imprimées en offset.

PAGE 161 #421 ART DIRECTORS/ DESIGNERS: *Nancy Skolos, Thomas Wedell* AGENCY: *Skolos/Wedell* PHOTOGRAPHER/ILLUSTRATOR: *Thomas Wedell* CLIENT: *Reynolds-Dewalt Printing*

PAGE 161 #422 ART DIRECTOR/ DESIGNER: *Paul Sych* AGENCY: *Faith* PHOTOGRAPHER/ILLUSTRATOR: *Derek Shapton* CLIENT: *Annan & Sons Trade Lithography / Faith* ■ This background image was first commissioned for an Absolut Vodka ad. The concept was "It's not the bottle, but what's in the bottle." The ad agency ultimately did not use the ad, but the designer used the shot and added the word "Smashed" as a parody of his experience. The poster was used as a self-promotional piece and as a promotional piece for a printing company. ● Die Basis dieses Plakates ist ein

Entwurf für eine Absolut-Wodka-Anzeige, der aber von der Werbeagentur als zu vulgär und direkt empfunden und deshalb abgelehnt wurde. Der Designer benutzte das Motiv daraufhin als Eigenwerbung, der er im Sinne der gemachten Erfahrung des Wort "Smashed" (zerschmettert) hinzufügte. Es wurde ausserdem von der Druckerei als Werbung verwendet. ▲ A l'origine, le concept était destiné à une publicité Absolut Vodka, mais l'agence de publicité le refusa, le trouvant trop vulgaire et trop direct. Le graphiste l'utilisa ensuite pour sa propre publicité en y ajoutant le mot «smashed» (démoli), clin d'œil à ce qu'il venait de vivre. L'imprimerie l'a également utilisé à des fins publicitaires.

PAGE 162 #423 ART DIRECTOR/ DESIGNER/COPYWRITER: *Norio Kudo* AGENCY: *Magna Inc. Advertising* PHOTOGRAPHER/ILLUSTRATOR: *Masato Okamura, Akio Tomari* CLIENT: *Nishiki Printing Co.*

PAGE 162 #424 CREATIVE DIRECTOR/COPYWRITER: *Masumi Katayori* ART DIRECTOR/ DESIGNER: *Kazuhito Sato* AGENCY: *Magna Inc. Advertising* PHOTOGRAPHER/ILLUSTRATOR: *Takashi Iwakiri* CLIENT: *Nishiki Printing Co., Ltd.*

PAGE 162 #425 ART DIRECTOR/ DESIGNER/ILLUSTRATOR: *Brian Boyd* AGENCY: *The Richards Group* CLIENT: *Williamson Printing* ■ *"If the annual's late, the relationship's expired. We get it." This poster was created for a printing company.* ● *«Wenn das Jahrbuch zu spät herauskommt, verlieren wir den Auftrag. Wir verstehen.» Plakat für eine Druckerei.* ▲ *«Si la publication annuelle sort trop tard, nous perdons le client. C'est tout vu.» Affiche pour une imprimerie.*

PAGE 162 #426 ART DIRECTOR/ DESIGNER: *Andrey Logvin* AGENCY: *Logvin Design* CLIENT: *Liniagrafic Print Company*

PAGE 163 #427 ART DIRECTOR/ DESIGNER: *Lisa Reynolds* AGENCY: *Gill Design* PHOTOGRAPHER/ILLUSTRATOR: *Brad Newton* CLIENT: *Graphic Press* ■ *The client wanted a promotional campaign that would generate a high level of recall among designers and advertisers. The agency focused on a strategic function and created a series of posters that also served as a wall calendar. A large format was utilized to command attention and to provide ample opportunity to illustrate print and pre-press capabilities.* ● *Das Plakat ist Teil einer Werbekampagne für eine Druckerei, die sich an Graphiker und Werber richtet. Es entstand eine Reihe von grossformatigen Plakaten, die als Wandkalender konzipiert waren und somit einen hohen Aufmerksamkeitsgrad erzielten. Gleichzeitig boten sie der Druckerei die Möglichkeit, ihr Können in der Druck- und Druckvorstufe zu demonstrieren.* ▲ *Affiche réalisée pour la campagne d'une imprimerie et destinée aux graphistes et aux publicitaires. L'agence créa également une série d'affiches faisant office de calendrier mural qui eurent beaucoup de succès. Le grand format des affiches permit à l'imprimerie d'illustrer son savoir-faire dans les domaines presse et pré-presse.*

PAGE 163 #428 AGENCY/DESIGN: *Gilchi, Tokoshashin Seihan* PHOTOGRAPHER: *Takashi Iwakiri* CLIENT: *Tanaka Sangyo Co. Ltd.*

PAGE 164 #429 ART DIRECTOR/ DESIGNER: *Klas Björkman* AGENCY: *Björkman & Mitchell Ab* PHOTOGRAPHER/ILLUSTRATOR: *K.W. Gullers* COPYWRITER: *Stefan Edström* CLIENT: *Ljungbergs Printing* ■ *Summer vacation announcement.* ● *Ankündigung von Sommerferien.* ▲ *Affiche annonçant les grandes vacances.*

PAGE 165 #430 ART DIRECTOR/DESIGNER: *Michael Kimmerle* AGENCY: *Wagner Siebdruck GmbH* PHOTOGRAPHER/ILLUSTRATOR: *Bernhard Widmann* CLIENT: *In-house*

PAGE 165 #431 ART DIRECTOR/DESIGNER: *Michael Kimmerle* AGENCY: *Wagner Siebdruck GmbH* TEXT: *Johannes Itten* CLIENT: *In-house*

PAGE 165 #432 ART DIRECTOR/DESIGNER: *Peter Steiner* AGENCY: *Wagner Siebdruck GmbH* CLIENT: *In-house*

PAGE 165 #433 ART DIRECTOR/DESIGNER: *Peter Steiner* AGENCY: *Wagner Siebdruck GmbH* CLIENT: *In-house*

PAGE 166 #434, 435 ART DIRECTOR/DESIGNER: *Michael Ancevic* AGENCY: *Hoffman York & Compton* COPYWRITER: *David Hanneken, Michael Ancevic* CLIENT: *Jensen* ■ *This poster campaign needed to draw attention to a line of car audio products while staying within a very limited budget. The agency decided to use a graphic, "in-your-face" design with hard-hitting headlines.* ● *Thema dieser Plakatkampagne ist eine Reihe von Audio-Geräten für Autos. Das Budget war sehr klein, und die Agentur verliess sich deshalb auf die Wirkung der stark graphisch geprägten Bilder und der packenden Slogans.* ▲ *Campagne publicitaire*

pour des appareils audio pour voitures. L'agence respecta les impératifs budgétaires en optant pour des images graphiques fortes et des slogans très directs.

PAGE 167 #436 CREATIVE DIRECTOR: *Alex Bogusky* ART DIRECTORS: *Tony Calcao, Markham Cronin* AGENCY: *Crispin & Porter Advertising* COPYWRITER: *Scott Linnen* CLIENT: *Shimano American*

PAGE 167 #437 CREATIVE DIRECTOR: *Antony Redman* ART DIRECTORS: *Scott Lambert* AGENCY: *Batey Ads Singapore* PHOTOGRAPHER/ILLUSTRATOR: *William Chan* COPYWRITER: *Mark Ringer* CLIENT: *Fei Fah Drug Store* ■ *"Cheeky Grin: For the Relief of Constipation." Over-indulgence in food and irregular eating habits can sometimes lead to unsavory side effects. The herbal properties of the client's product can help solve the dilemma, yet the problem is so delicate, the agency had to handle it in a simple, fun way that would bring a smile.* ● *«Cheeky Grin hilft bei Verstopfung.» Übermässiges und unregelmässiges Essen kann zu unerfreulichen Nebenwirkungen führen, ein häufiges Problem in Singapur, wo Essen ein nationaler Zeitvertreib ist. Die pflanzlichen Wirkstoffe im Produkt des Auftraggebers helfen bei dem Dilemma. Das etwas delikate Thema sollte auf einfache, humorvolle Art behandelt werden.* ▲ *«Cheeky Grin aide en cas de constipation.» Des repas irréguliers ou trop riches peuvent avoir des conséquences fâcheuses, un problème courant à Singapour où manger est un passe-temps national. La publicité vante les vertus de ce produit à base de plantes sur un ton qui se veut simple et humoristique.*

PAGE 167 #438 ART DIRECTOR: *George Vargas* AGENCY: *Batey Ads Singapore* PHOTOGRAPHER: *Shaun Pettigrew* COPYWRITER: *Peter Moyse* CLIENT: *The Jamu Centre* ■ *"High potency for men." Poster for a natural supplement that increases libido, fertility, and vitality in men—important factors in Asia.* ● *Plakat für einen natürlichen Wirkstoff, der die Potenz, Fruchtbarkeit und Vitalität von Männern steigern soll.* ▲ *Publicité pour un produit asiatique à base de plantes aux vertus aphrodisiaques et destiné aux hommes.*

PAGE 167 #439 ART DIRECTOR/ DESIGNER: *Tom Kim* AGENCY: *McConnaughy Stein Schmidt Brown* PHOTOGRAPHER/ILLUSTRATOR: *David Emmite* COPYWRITER: *Dave Loew* CLIENT: *Bungie Software* ■ *The agency wanted to advertise the computer game by showing attitude, but without using sophomoric phrases like. The agency tried to arouse morbid curiosity. The poster was sent to customers, distributors, and also ran as an ad in computer magazines.* ● *Werbung für ein Computerspiel. Anstatt sich darüber auszulassen, wie süchtig das Spiel macht, wollte die Agentur die Art von morbider Neugier wecken, die Leute z.B. dazu bringt, bei einem Autounfall einfach hinschauen zu müssen. Das Plakat wurde an Kunden und Händler abgegeben und erschien auch als Anzeige in Computermagazinen.* ▲ *Publicité pour un jeu électronique. Plutôt que de dire que ce jeu rend accro, l'agence a voulu éveiller une sorte de curiosité malsaine, comme celle qui fait que les gens regardent quand il y a un accident. L'affiche a été distribuée aux clients et aux commerçants et a également été publiée dans des magazines spécialisés.*

PAGE 168 #444, 445 CREATIVE DIRECTOR/COPYWRITER: *Antony Redman* ART DIRECTOR: *Andrew Clarke* AGENCY: *Batey Ads Singapore* PHOTOGRAPHER/ILLUSTRATOR: *Tomek Sikora* CLIENT: *Sony Singapore* ■ *Since the Walkman is a product known for fun and makes you want to walk, the agency decided to show the uncanny effect it has on on legs that can't be controlled. This was used to create visually striking, humurous ads that would appeal to the core youth market.* ● *Ein Walkman macht Spass und Lust aufs Gehen. Die unheimliche Wirkung des Walkman auf die Beine ist deshalb das Thema des Plakates, das sich mit viel Humor an das junge Publikum wendet.* ▲ *Un walkman, c'est fun et ça donne envie de bouger. Les jambes en mouvement sur l'affiche sont un clin d'œil humoristique à l'adresse des jeunes.*

PAGE 169 #446 ART DIRECTOR: *Seymour Chwast* DESIGNER: *James Victore* AGENCY: *Victore Design Works* CLIENT: *Earth Day* ■ *"Dead Duck/Exxon."* ● *Ein Kommentar zur Exxon-Ölkatastrophe.* ▲ *Un commentaire sur la catastrophe écologique causé par la compangie pétrolière Exxon.*

PAGE 169 #447 ART DIRECTOR/DESIGNER: *Gianni Bortolotti* AGENCY: *Studio Gianni Bortolotti & C. Sas* CLIENT: *ANIEP* ■ *The theme posed by the client was to express the value of sport as a means to help in the social integration of handicapped people using the opportunity of the 1996 Olympic games in Atlanta. The message is centered on the analogy between the rings of the Olympic symbol and the wheels in the handicapped symbol, thereby creating a graphic composition by a reduction to essence.* ● *Die Bedeutung von Sport für die soziale Integration von Behinderten ist Thema dieses Plakates. Der Gestalter nahm Bezug auf die Olympischen Spiele 1996 in Atlanta und verband die olympischen Ringe mit den Rädern im Symbol für Behinderte, eine graphische Komposition, die auf das Wesentliche reduziert ist.* ▲ *Affiche consacrée à l'importance du* sport dans l'intégration sociale des handicapés. Elle s'inspire des Jeux olympiques de 1996 à Atlanta et combine les anneaux olympiques avec les roues d'une chaise roulante, symbole des handicapés, dans une composition réduite à l'essentiel.

PAGE 170 #448 ART DIRECTOR: *Jan Wilker* DESIGNER: *Karsten Schweizer* AGENCY: *Büro für alles Kreaktive und Verrückte* PHOTOGRAPHER: *Armin Buhl* CLIENT: *Self promotion*

PAGE 171 #449-452 ART DIRECTOR: *Kris Jenson* AGENCY: *Cramer Krasselt* PHOTOGRAPHER: *Jeff Salzer Photography* COPYWRITER: *Tom Dixon* CLIENT: *Society of St. Francis* ■ *These posters were designed to focus attention on the "putting to sleep": of animals at animal shelters. Stark, powerful visuals coupled with straightforward headlines were used.* ● «*Die meisten Tierheime sind wirklich human. Sie schläfern die Tiere ein, bevor sie sie verbrennen.*» «*Die meisten Tierheime können nur 3 von 10 Tieren platzieren. Der Rest wird hier platziert.*» «*Unser Tierheim arbeitet ein bisschen anders als andere. Für Spätzünder: Wir töten keine Tiere, um sie dann in Verbrennungsöfen zu werfen.*» «*Im Gegensatz zu manchen anderen Kulturen essen wir weder Hunde noch Katzen. Warum rösten wir dann so viele von ihnen?*» *Die Plakate befassen sich mit der Tötung von Haustieren, ein schwerwiegendes Problem, das hier mit eindrucksvoller Graphik und unmissverständlichen Headlines und Texten angepackt wird. Dabei werden die Leser darauf hingewiesen, dass es eine Alternative gibt.* ▲ «*La plupart des refuges pour animaux sont très humains. Ils endorment les bêtes avant de les incinérer.*» «*La plupart des chenils n'arrivent à placer que trois bêtes sur dix. Les autres finissent leur vie ici.*» «*Notre refuge est un peu différent des autres. Nous ne tuons pas les animaux pour les incinérer.*» «*Contrairement à d'autres cultures, nous ne mangeons ni les chiens ni les chats. Alors pourquoi en grillons-nous autant?*» *Affiches sur l'euthanasie pour les animaux domestiques, un grave problème rendu ici avec des visuels forts, des headlines et des textes sans équivoque. Le message indique qu'il existe une alternative.*

PAGE 172 #453 ART DIRECTOR/ DESIGNER: *Kum-Jun Park* AGENCY: *Cheil Communications Inc.* PHOTOGRAPHER/ILLUSTRATOR: *Hoo-Man Park* COPYWRITER: *Joon-Young Bae* CLIENT: *Korean Alliance to Defeat Aids*

PAGE 173 #454-457 AGENCY: *After Hours Creative* PHOTOGRAPHERS: *Bob Carey, Bruce Racine, Sue Bennett, Rick Gayle* DESIGN AND PHOTOGRAPHY SERVICES: *Courtesy of Heritage Graphics* CLIENT: *Gay Men's Sex Project* ■ *These posters were posted in places where gay and bi-sexual men would see them. The posters couldn't be threatening or patronizing, and tried to make safer sex seem fun, the norm, and a desirable practice. The agency figured if it could grab the audience's attention with the sexual nature of the posters, viewers would be drawn to them enough to read the copy. The idea of safer sex was reinforced by including a photo of a condom with the more graphic images. The agency felt it was vital to acknowledge that gay men are sexual, and that if they are going to have sex, it should be safer sex.* ● «*Schmackhafte Kleinigkeiten mit Cremefüllung sind zu Ihrem Schutz immer eingepackt.*» «*Einlass nur mit angemessener Bekleidung.*» «*Wenn er sich Hals über Kopf...*» «*Helfen Sie ihm, seinen Kopf zu gebrauchen.*» *Die Plakate wurden an Orten ausgehängt, wo homosexuelle und bisexuelle Männer sie sehen würden, bevor sie Sex haben. Es ging darum, das Thema spielerisch und humorvoll anzupacken und sicheren Sex als etwas Wünschenswertes und Selbstverständliches darzustellen. Wichtig war dabei auch, die Sexualität von homo- und bisexuellen Männern als etwas ganz Normales zu behandeln.* ▲ «*Ces délicieuses mignardises fourrées sont toujours emballées pour votre sécurité.*» «*Tenue correcte exigée à l'entrée.*» «*S'il se précipite...*» «*Aidez-le à utiliser sa tête.*» *Affiches placardées dans des endroits fréquentés par des homosexuels et des bisexuels. L'objectif était d'aborder ce thème de manière ludique et humoristique et de présenter le «safe sex» comme quelque chose de souhaitable et d'évident. L'homosexualité et la bisexualité devaient aussi apparaître comme une chose normale.*

PAGE 174 #458, 459 CREATIVE DIRECTORS: *Antony Redman, Graham Fink* ART DIRECTORS: *Antony Redman, Derrick Seah* AGENCY: *Batey Ads Singapore* PHOTOGRAPHER/ILLUSTRATOR: *Charles Liddall* COPYWRITERS: *Antony Redman Ian Batey, Jim Aitchinson* TYPOGRAPHY: *Antony Redman, Martin Lim* CLIENT: *Asian Pals of The Planet* ■ *Despite Monsoonal rainfalls, water is becoming a scarce commodity in Asia due to wastage, lack of controls and rapid industrialization. The designer wanted to communicate that the water wasted in the home can be reduced if it is treated with respect.* ● *Trotz der mit dem Monsun einsetzenden Regenzeit wird das Wasser in Asien knapp. Die Gründe sind Verschwendung, mangelnde Kontrolle und rapide Industrialisierung. Hier sollte zum Ausdruck gebracht werden, dass der Privatverbrauch von Wasser reduziert werden kann, wenn die Menschen begreifen, wie kostbar es ist.* ▲ *Malgré les moussons, l'eau devient rare en Asie. Ce phénomène est dû au gaspillage, aux contrôles déficients et à l'industrialisation rapide. Le message du graphiste: la consommation domestique peut être réduite si l'être humain comprend à quel point l'eau est précieuse.*

PAGE 174 #460, 461 ART DIRECTOR: *Tom Lichtenheld* AGENCY: *Fallon McElligott* ILLUSTRATOR: *Buck Holzmer* COPYWRITER: *Sally Hogshead* CLIENT: *Cease Fire* 460) *"This is how many safety regulations our government imposes on the product that kills over 5000 American children a year."* 461) *"By your child's first year, she can squeeze your finger with seven pounds of pressure. Approximately the same amount needed to squeeze the trigger of a gun." The directive was to convince people that buying and owning a gun is more a threat to your family than protection.* ● (460) «*Hier sehen Sie, wieviele Sicherheitsvorschriften unsere Regierung für das Produkt erlässt, mit dem pro Jahr über 5000 amerikanische Kinder getötet werden.*» (461) «*Wenn Ihr Kind ein Jahr alt ist, kann es Ihren Finger mit einer Krafteinwirkung von ca. 7 Pfund drücken. Ungefähr die gleiche Kraft ist notwendig, um den Abzug einer Handfeuerwaffe zu ziehen.*» *Hier ging es darum, die Bevölkerung zu überzeugen, dass der Kauf und Besitz von Waffen eher Bedrohung als Schutz für die Familie darstellt.* ▲ 460) «*C'est le nombre de prescriptions de sécurité qu'impose notre gouvernement pour cet objet qui tue chaque année plus de 5000 enfants américains.*» 461) «*A l'âge d'un an, votre enfant peut écraser vos doigts avec une force équivalant à 7 livres. La même force est nécessaire pour appuyer sur la gâchette d'une arme.*» *Le but de ces affiches était de convaincre l'opinion que l'achat et la détention d'armes représentent une menace pour la sécurité des familles.*

PAGE 174 #462 CREATIVE DIRECTORS: *Antony Redman, Jim Aitchinson* ART DIRECTOR: *Antony Redman* AGENCY: *Batey Ads Singapore* PHOTOGRAPHER: *Charles Liddall* COPYWRITERS: *Antony Redman, Ian Batey, Jim Aitchinson* TYPOGRAPHY: *Antony Redman, Martin Lim* CLIENT: *Asian Pals of the Planet* ■ *Despite Monsoonal rainfalls, water is becoming a scarce commodity in Asia due to wastage, lack of controls and rapid industrialization. The designer wanted to communicate that the water wasted in the home can be reduced if it is treated with respect.* ● *Trotz der mit dem Monsun einsetzenden Regenzeit wird das Wasser in Asien knapp. Die Gründe sind Verschwendung, mangelnde Kontrolle und rapide Industrialisierung. Hier sollte zum Ausdruck gebracht werden, dass der Privatverbrauch von Wasser reduziert werden kann, wenn die Menschen begreifen, wie kostbar es ist.* ▲ *Malgré les moussons, l'eau devient rare en Asie. Ce phénomène est dû au gaspillage, aux contrôles déficients et à l'industrialisation rapide. Le message du graphiste: la consommation domestique peut être réduite si l'être humain comprend à quel point l'eau est précieuse.*

PAGE 174 #463 AGENCY: *Fallon McElligott* CLIENT: *Children's Defense Fund* ■ *"Congratulations. You've just brought more violence into your home than ABC, CBS and NBC combined."* ● «*Herzlichen Glückwunsch. Sie haben gerade mehr Gewalt ins Haus gebracht als (die TV-Sender) ABC, CBS und NBC zusammen.*» ▲ «*Toutes nos félicitations! Vous avez réussi à amener encore plus de violence chez vous que les trois chaînes de télévision ABC, CBS et NBC réunies.*»

PAGE 176 #464 ART DIRECTOR: *Mike Scricco* DESIGNER: *Jeff Lin* AGENCY: *Keiler & Co.* COPYWRITER: *Doretta Wildes* CLIENT: *Connecticut Art Directors Club* ■ *"Do it for love. Do it for money." The directive was to motivate students to enter a statewide design competition. The main challenge was encouraging participation despite scant reception in previous years due to the usual pressures of the academic year and the latent fears that prohibit many young designers from exposing themselves to unknown and potentially unforgiving critics. The poster also had to compete for attention on densely populated campus bulletin boards. The agency decided to use a photograph that depicts in exaggerated form the intensively competitive arena that students fear they are entering while simultaneously including words of encouragement.* ● «*Tun Sie's aus Liebe, tun Sie's für Geld.*» *Mit diesem Plakat sollten Studenten zur Teilnahme an einem landesweiten Design-Wettbewerb ermuntert werden. Angesichts der eher mageren Teilnehmerzahl im vergangenen Jahr, die auf die schulische Belastung einerseits und die latente Angst vor strengen Juries andererseits zurückzuführen ist, musste das Plakat sehr überzeugend wirken und sich zudem an den dicht behängten schwarzen Brettern der Universitäten durchsetzen. Das bewusst übersteigerte Motiv des Plakates nimmt Bezug auf die Konkurrenzängste, während gleichzeitig mit Worten zur Teilnahme ermutigt wird.* ▲ «*Faites-le par amour, faites-le pour de l'argent.*» *Affiche visant à encourager les étudiants à participer à un concours de design national. Un défi de taille au vu de la maigre participation au concours précédent, les exigences étant élevées et les étudiants craignant la sévérité notoire du jury. L'affiche devait se démarquer au milieu des nombreuses petites annonces et communications du tableau d'affichage. Cette image forte symbolise la peur de la concurrence tandis que le texte encourage à participer.*

PAGE 176 #465 ART DIRECTOR/ DESIGNER: *Anne-Mette Hansen* CLIENT: *Council for Greater Safety in Traffic* ■ *Poster on the subject of traffic safety. It won second prize in a competition sponsored by the Danish Council for Greater Safety in Traffic.* ● *Sicherheit im Verkehr ist Thema dieses Plakates. Es erhielt den zweiten Preis in einem Wettbewerb*

des dänischen Verbandes für grössere Verkehrssicherheit. ▲*Affiche de la sécurité routière, récompensée par le deuxième prix d'un concours organisé par une association danoise pour plus de sécurité sur les routes.*

PAGE 177 #466 ART DIRECTOR: *Kika Matos* DESIGNER: *James Victore* AGENCY: *Victore Design Works* CLIENT: *NAACP/LDF* ■ *"The Death Penalty Mocks Justice."* ● *«Die Todesstrafe verhöhnt die Rechtsprechung.»* ▲ *«La peine de mort tue la justice.»*

PAGE 177 #467 DESIGNER/AGENCY: *Homayoun Mahmoudi*

PAGE 177 #468 DESIGNER: *Andrew Pogson* AGENCY: *BBDO Hong Kong Ltd.* CLIENT: *Hong Kong Aids Foundation Hong Kong Aids Foundation Hotline*

PAGE 177 #469 ART DIRECTOR/ DESIGNER/ILLUSTRATOR: *Tadanori Yokoo* CLIENT: *JAGDA* ■ *Poster for the International Design Center, Nagoya, Japan.* ● *Plakat für das internationale Design-Zentrum in Nagoya, Japan.* ▲*Affiche pour le Centre international de design de Nagoya au Japon.*

PAGE 178 #470, 471 AGENCY: *Dentsu Y+R* DESIGNER: *Yusuaki Tamura*

PAGE 178 #472, 473 ART DIRECTOR: *Dave Robb* DESIGNER: *Shawn Eichenauer* AGENCY: *Riester* PHOTOGRAPHER/ILLUSTRATOR: *Bob Carey (472) Dan Vermillion (473)* COPYWRITER: *Amy Dominy* CLIENT: *Arizona Dept. of Health Services* ■ *"Birth defects can come in all shapes and sizes."* ● *«Geburtsschäden gibt es in allen Formen und Grössen.»* ▲ *«Il existe toutes sortes de malformations à la naissance.»*

PAGE 179 #474, 475 ART DIRECTOR/ DESIGNER/PHOTOGRAPHER: *Claudio Alessandri* AGENCY: *Alessandri GmbH* CLIENT: *Aids Hilfe Austria*

PAGE 180 #476 ART DIRECTOR: *Garry Emery* AGENCY: *Emery Vincent Design* CLIENT: *Self-promotion* ■ *This poster was aimed at the corporate community and announces the launch of a publication about corporate identity.* ● *Das Plakat, das die Lancierung einer Publikation über Firmenerscheinungsbilder bekannt gibt, richtet sich an Unternehmen.* ▲*Affiche réalisée pour le lancement d'une publication sur les images institutionnelles destinée aux entreprises.*

PAGE 180 #477 ART DIRECTOR/ DESIGNER/ILLUSTRATOR: *Scott Easley* AGENCY: *Maelstrom Studios* CLIENT: *Marvel Comics*

PAGE 181 #478-481 ART DIRECTOR: *Casey Grady* AGENCY: *McCann Amster Yard* COPYWRITER: *Fred Stesney* CLIENT: *Chief Executive Magazine*

PAGE 182 #482 ART DIRECTORS/ DESIGNERS: *Jacques Koeweiden, Paul Postma* AGENCY: *Koeweiden Postma Associates* ILLUSTRATOR: *Rob V/D Vet* COPYWRITER: *Peter Hansen* CLIENT: *Creative Review Magazine* ■ *This poster was produced for a special issue of Creative Review magazine focussing on advertising and design in Amsterdam. The idea was to depict Amsterdam as a city of internationally oriented creativity.* ● *Das Plakat wurde für eine Sonderausgabe der Zeitschrift Creative Review entworfen, deren Thema Werbung und Design in Amsterdam war. Die Idee war, Amsterdam als eine Stadt darzustellen, die sich durch international ausgerichtete Kreativität auszeichnet.* ▲*Affiche créée pour une édition spéciale du magazine Creative Review, sur le thème de la publicité et du design à Amsterdam. L'idée était de présenter Amsterdam comme une capitale internationale de la créativité.*

PAGE 183 #483 ART DIRECTOR: *Howard Brown* DESIGNERS: *Mike Calkins, Howard Brown* AGENCY: *Urban Outfitters* CLIENT: *In-house* ■ *The theme for this fall print campaign was "science project." The posters were inspired by the "boomer-era graphics" and share a repeat pattern in the half circles on the left and right sides of each poster–apparent when two or more posters are displayed side by side.* ● *Das Plakat für ein Modegeschäft bezieht sich auf die Nachkriegszeit, als die USA einen Baby-Boom erlebten. Wenn zwei oder mehrere Plakate zusammen ausgehängt werden, formen die Halbkreise links und rechts auf den Plakaten zu einem Muster.* ▲*Le thème de cette campagne réalisée en automne 1995 pour un magasin de mode était un projet scientifique. Lorsqu'une ou plusieurs affiches sont placardées côte-à-côte, les demi-cercles à gauche et à droite des affiches forment un motif.*

PAGE 183 #484 ART DIRECTOR: *Howard Brown* DESIGNERS: *Mike Calkins, Howard Brown* AGENCY: *Urban Outfitters* CLIENT: *In-house* ■ *The theme for this fall print campaign was "post modernism." The copy and images are a play on merchandising con-*

cepts. ● *Thema dieser Kampagne im Herbst 1995 war der Postmodernismus. Text und Bilder beziehen sich auf Merchandising-Konzepte.* ▲*Le thème de cette campagne de 1995 était le postmodernisme. Textes et images jouent avec les concepts du merchandising.*

PAGE 184 #485, 486 ART DIRECTOR/DESIGNER: *Jimmy Olson* AGENCY: *McConnaughy Stein Schmidt Brown* COPYWRITER: *Jim Schmidt* CLIENT: *Oscar Isberian Rugs* ■ *The client wanted this particular rug displayed prominently, so the designer opted for an elegant look that would soften the tone of the lines as well as show off the rugs.* ● *«Allah ist in den Details.» «Endlich etwas aus dem Mittleren Osten, das nicht mit seiner gesamten Umgebung beisst.»* Hier ging es darum, einen bestimmten Teppich in den Vordergrund zu stellen, was durch zurückhaltendes Design erreicht wurde.* ▲ *«Allah est dans les détails.» «Enfin quelque chose du Moyen-Orient qui n'est pas en désaccord avec son environnement.» Le client désirait qu'un tapis particulier figure au premier plan, ce qui a été obtenu au moyen d'un design élégant et discret.*

PAGE 184 #487, 488 ART DIRECTOR/PHOTOGRAPHER/ILLUSTRATOR: *Minato Ishikawa* DESIGNER: *Kayoko Akiyama* PRODUCER: *Ruki Mastumoto* AGENCY: *Minato Ishikawa Associates Inc.* CLIENT: *Farmer's Table* ■ *These posters were designed for the tenth anniversary of a store in Tokyo.* ● *Plakat zum zehnjährigen Bestehen eines Ladens in Tokio.* ▲*Affiche créée pour le 10ᵉ anniversaire d'un magasin de Tokyo.*

PAGE 185 #489-491 ART DIRECTOR/DESIGNER: *Kristin Koniarek* AGENCY: *CreaTeam Werbeagentur GmbH & Co. KG* CLIENT: *PlusCity* ■ *Posters promoting a shopping center. "Full fun ahead, guys." "Follow me discretely, guys." "Let's go, boys." "Something's happening there."* ● *Plakatkampagne für ein grosses Einkaufszentrum.* ▲ *«Plein cap sur le plaisir, les gars!» «Suivez-moi discrètement, les gars.» «Allons-y, les gars!» «Il y a quelque chose qui se passe là-bas.» Campagne d'affichage pour un centre commercial.*

PAGE 186 #492-497 ART DIRECTOR: *Adam Greiss* DESIGNERS: *Adam Greiss, Nana Kobayashi* AGENCY: *Adam Greiss Design/Booms Creative, Inc.* PHOTOGRAPHER: *David Mansure Photography* CLIENT: *Jamaica Center Improvement Association* ■ *Bus shelter poster series. Each poster contains a word that pertains to the photograph and simultaneously sums up a particular retail category.* ● *Eine für Bushaltestellen bestimmte Plakatreihe. Jedes Plakat enthält ein Wort, das sich auf das Photo bezieht und bezeichnet gleichzeitig eine bestimmte Einzelhandelskategorie.* ▲*Série d'affiches conçues pour les abribus. Sur chacune d'entre elles figure un mot qui se réfère à l'image et désigne en même temps un type de commerce de détail.*

PAGE 187 #498, 499 DESIGNER: *Frank Kofsuske* AGENCY: *Em Dash/Daniel Proctor Photography* PHOTOGRAPHER: *Daniel Proctor* CLIENT: *Pottery Barn*

PAGE 188 #500 ART DIRECTOR: *Howard Brown* DESIGNERS: *Mike Calkins, Howard Brown* AGENCY: *Urban Outfitters* CLIENT: *In-house* ■ *The theme for this fall print campaign was "science project." The posters were inspired by the "boomer era" science kiosks and share a repeat pattern in the half circles on the left and right sides of each poster–apparent when two or more posters are displayed side by side.* ● *Das Plakat für ein Modegeschäft bezieht sich auf die Nachkriegszeit, als die USA einen Baby-Boom erlebten. Wenn zwei oder mehrere Plakate zusammen ausgehängt werden, formen die Halbkreise links und rechts auf den Plakaten zu einem Muster.* ▲*Le thème de cette campagne réalisée en automne pour un magasin de mode était un projet scientifique. Lorsqu'une ou plusieurs affiches sont placardées côte-à-côte, les demi-cercles à gauche et à droite des affiches forment un motif.*

PAGE 188 #501 ART DIRECTOR: *Howard Brown* DESIGNERS: *Mike Calkins, Howard Brown* AGENCY: *Urban Outfitters* CLIENT: *In-house* ■ *The theme for this fall print campaign was "post modernism." The copy and images are a play on merchandising concepts.* ● *Thema dieser Kampagne im Herbst war der Postmodernismus. Text und Bilder beziehen sich auf Merchandising-Konzepte.* ▲*Le thème de cette campagne de était le postmodernisme. Textes et images jouent avec les concepts du merchandising.*

PAGE 189 #502-507 ART DIRECTOR: *Antony Redman* AGENCY: *Batey Ads Singapore & Chan Aitchinson Partnership* PHOTOGRAPHER/ILLUSTRATOR: *Antony Redman* COPYWRITERS: *Antony Redman, Jim Aitchinson* CLIENT: *D Corner* ■ *A single-outlet Nike dealer competing against bigger retailers wanted high-ground positioning. The agency tried to create cutting-edge work that would appeal to Singapore's young, affluent Nike buyers. Posters were used in-store and circulated to customers free.* ● *Werbung für ein Geschäft, das ausschliesslich Nike-Artikel führt. Es galt, sich gegenüber grösseren Geschäften durchzusetzen und die junge, wohlhabende Nike-Kundschaft Singapurs anzusprechen. Die Plakate wurden im Laden ausgehängt und als Geschenk an Kunden*

abgegeben. ▲ *Publicité pour un point de vente Nike. L'objectif était de se démarquer des grands magasins et d'attirer les jeunes gens aisés de Singapour. Les affiches ont été placardées dans le magasin et offertes aux clients.*

PAGE 190 #508-509 ART DIRECTOR: *Satoshi Kato* DESIGNER: *Hideki Kawasoe* AGENCY: *McCann-Erickson Inc.* ILLUSTRATOR: *Shintaro Shiratori* COPYWRITER: *Toshiya Mozoguchi* CLIENT: *People Co., Ltd.* ■ *"A good choice–don't forget to shed off that extra fat for the summer." "A good choice–how would you like a fitness plan to shut the guys up?" The directive for these posters was to communicate the effect earned by joining the fitness club. The comparison of one sharp and one rounded pencil and the differently shaped bottles relate the point visually. The representation of the human body is executed by making the pencil color similar to human skin color, and by bringing out the soft textures of the bottles.* ● *«Eine gute Wahl – vergiss nicht, das überflüssige Fett zum Sommer runterzubringen.» «Eine gute Wahl – wie würde Ihnen ein Fitness-Plan gefallen, der den Jungs den Mund stopft.» Hier wird für einen Fitness-Club geworben, wobei den Mitgliedern ein schöner Erfolg in Bezug auf Figurprobleme in Aussicht gestellt wird.* ▲ *«Un bon choix - pense à éliminer toute cette graisse avant l'été!» «Un bon choix - que diriez-vous d'un programme de remise en forme pour clouer le bec à tous ces mecs?» Publicité pour un club de remise en forme, promettant des résultats probants aux personnes soucieuses de leur ligne.*

PAGE 191 #510 ART DIRECTOR/DESIGNER: *Gregg A. Floyd* AGENCY: *GAF Advertising/Design* PHOTOGRAPHER/ILLUSTRATOR: *Greg Blomberg* DIGITAL ILLUSTRATION: *David Obar* COPYWRITER: *Jennie Stevens* CLIENT: *Signgrafx* ■ *"And you think you know what a sign looks like? Look again." The agency wanted to create immediate awareness of a digital printing shop among key audience segments: graphic designers, art directors, and ad agencies. The campaign's thrust was to position the company as innovative and knowlegeable. The image combines a recognizable icon associated with creativity (the eye) and cactus needles to produce a startling provocative graphic image that will command attention.* ● *«Und du denkst, du weisst, wie ein Zeichen aussieht. Sieh' nochmal hin.» Das Plakat für einen digitalen Druckladen richtet sich an Graphiker, Art Direktoren und Werbeagenturen, wobei der Auftraggeber als innovativ und kompetent dargestellt werden sollte. Das Auge wurde als Symbol für Kreativität eingesetzt, während die Kaktusstacheln für die nötige Aufmerksamkeit sorgen sollten.* ▲ *«Et tu crois savoir à quoi ressemble un signe? Regarde encore une fois.» Cette affiche pour un magasin d'impression numérique, qui désirait se profiler comme novateur et professionnel, s'adresse aux graphistes, aux directeurs artistiques et aux agences de publicité. L'œil symbolise la créativité, et les piquants du cactus devaient attirer l'attention.*

PAGE 193 #511, 512 ART DIRECTOR/DESIGNER/ILLUSTRATOR: *Günter Schmidt* CLIENT: *W. Nonhoff/Uhrmacherei* ■ *Poster advertising for a clock workshop. The black-and-white design is intended to emphasize the mechanical work and the service–not the product sale.* ● *Plakat für eine Uhrmacherei. Im Mittelpunkt stehen Handwerk und Service und nicht der Verkauf des Produktes.* ▲ *Affiche pour un fabricant de montres. L'emphase est mise sur le mouvement de la montre et le service à la clientèle, et non sur la vente.*

PAGE 192 #513, 514 CREATIVE DIRECTOR: *Antony Redman* ART DIRECTOR: *George Vargas* AGENCY: *Batey Ads Singapore* PHOTOGRAPHER: *Rodney Schaffer* COPYWRITER: *Peter Moyse* CLIENT: *Dottys* ■ *"If nothing else, you can have great hair." Poster campaign created for a budget-conscious hairdresser marketed to inner-city youth with a street mentality. The agency opted to emphasize these factors in a dark/wry way.* ● *«Wunderschönes Haar können Sie jedenfalls haben.» Plakatkampagne für einen preisgünstigen Coiffeur, der sich an Jugendliche von der Strasse richtet. Der Ton des Plakates ist entsprechend trocken.* ▲ *«A défaut d'autre chose, tu peux quand même avoir de beaux cheveux.» Affiche pour un coiffeur pratiquant de petits prix pour les jeunes de la rue.*

PAGE 193 #515 ART DIRECTOR/DESIGNER/ILLUSTRATOR: *Günter Schmidt* CLIENT: *W. Nonhoff/Uhrmacherei* ■ *Poster advertising for a clock workshop. The black-and-white design is intended to emphasize the mechanical work and the service–not the product sale.* ● *Plakat für eine Uhrmacherei. Im Mittelpunkt stehen Handwerk und Service und nicht der Verkauf des Produktes.* ▲ *Affiche pour un fabricant de montres. L'emphase est mise sur le mouvement de la montre et le service à la clientèle, et non sur la vente.*

PAGE 192 #516 CREATIVE DIRECTOR: *Antony Redman* ART DIRECTOR: *George Vargas* AGENCY: *Batey Ads Singapore* PHOTOGRAPHER: *Rodney Schaffer* COPYWRITER: *Peter Moyse* CLIENT: *Dottys* ■ *"If nothing else, you can have great hair." Poster campaign created for a budget-conscious hairdresser marketed to inner-city youth with a street mentality. The agency opted to emphasize these factors in a dark/wry way.* ● *«Wunderschönes Haar können Sie jedenfalls haben.» Plakatkampagne für einen preisgünstigen Coiffeur, der sich an Jugendliche von der Strasse richtet. Der Ton des Plakates ist entsprechend*

trocken. ▲ *«A défaut d'autre chose, tu peux quand même avoir de beaux cheveux.» Affiche pour un coiffeur pratiquant de petits prix pour les jeunes de la rue.*

PAGE 194 #517 ART DIRECTOR/DESIGNER: *Jack Harris* AGENCY/CLIENT: *Harris Design, Inc.* PHOTOGRAPHER/ILLUSTRATOR: *Jack Harris* ■ *The agency wanted to create a leave-behind self-promotion that would demonstrate the firm's conceptual skills and commitment to design and service. The result was a limited edition silkscreen poster with service as its theme.* ● *Siebdruckplakat in limitierter Auflage zum Thema Service. Es dient der Eigenwerbung eines Design-Studios, das auf seine Leistungen in der Entwicklung von Konzepten und den umfassenden Service aufmerksam machen will.* ▲ *Sérigraphie. Edition limitée sur le thème du service à la clientèle. Cette publicité d'une agence de design souligne son savoir-faire dans l'élaboration de concepts et la qualité de ses services.*

PAGE 195; IMAGES 518, 519 ART DIRECTOR: *Shyam Madiraju* AGENCY: *Euro RSCG Ball Partnership* PHOTOGRAPHER: *Rensis Ho* COPYWRITER: *Keiron Simpson* CLIENT: *Cinemate*

PAGE 195 #520 ART DIRECTOR: *John Coffman* AGENCY: *Solomon Turner Advertising* PHOTOGRAPHER: *Ted Wright* CLIENT: *Coffman Brothers Inc.* ■ *This image icon is used on all the client's trucks, large equipment, employee uniforms, promotional material and outdoor signage.* ● *Die Ikone wird auf allen Wagen, grossen Geräten, Uniformen der Angestellen, Werbematerial und der Aussenbeschilderung des Kunden verwendet.* ▲ *Cette icône figure sur tous les véhicules, les équipements, les uniformes des employés, le matériel publicitaire et la signalétique du client.*

PAGE 195 #521 ART DIRECTOR: *Lisa Wilkerson* AGENCY: *Barkley & Evergreen* COPYWRITER: *Jennifer Brocker* CLIENT: *La Petite Academy* ■ *To create awareness of the client as an ideal place for childcare, a fairytale/storybook approach was utilized.* ● *Der märchenartige Stil dieses Plakates soll vermitteln, dass Kinder bei La Petite Academy bestens aufgehoben sind.* ▲ *Affiche inspirée des livres d'enfants, indiquant que La Petite Academy est le meilleur endroit pour y faire garder ses enfants.*

PAGE 196 #522 ART DIRECTOR/DESIGNER: *Cherie Valentine* AGENCY: *Wyse Advertising, Inc.* PHOTOGRAPHER: *Cherie Valentine, Bruce Sereta* COPYWRITER: *Pamela Blossom* CLIENT: *Hunter Jumper Classic* ■ *To build excitement and awareness for the Hunter Jumper Classic, the agency wanted to represent the style and control which unite the horse and rider, producing an illusion of effortless grace.* ● *Pferd und Reiter und die scheinbar mühelose Anmut des Reitens sind Thema dieses Plakates.* ▲ *Le cheval et le cavalier – une équipe en parfaite symbiose – sont le thème de cette affiche pour un concours hippique.*

PAGE 196 #523 ART DIRECTOR: *Bill Merriken* AGENCY: *Michael Schwab Studio* PHOTOGRAPHER/ILLUSTRATOR: *Michael Schwab* CLIENT: *Polo Retail Corporation* ■ *This poster served a posted advertisement and the imagery also appeared on retail items. The agency wanted to portray an image of polo without using the typical action shots of galloping horses. It also wanted to portray a certain intrigue and attitude. This image was also used for the Polo Ralph Lauren Classic in Minneapolis, MN 1996.* ● *Dieses Plakat diente als Werbung und wurde auch für Produkte, die bei dem Anlass erhältlich waren, verwendet. Die Agentur verzichtete bei der Darstellung des Polo-Sports auf die üblichen Action-Aufnahmen galoppierender Pferde zugunsten einer bestimmten Faszination und Haltung. Das Bild wurde auch für das Polo Ralph Lauren Classic in Minneapolis 1996 verwendet.* ▲ *Affiche d'un match de polo utilisée comme publicité et pour les produits vendus lors de la manifestation. L'agence a renoncé aux chevaux galopants et autres images classiques du polo, préférant jouer sur la fascination et l'attitude. Cette affiche a également été utilisée pour le Polo Ralph Lauren Classic à Minneapolis en 1996.*

PAGE 197 #524-526 ART DIRECTOR/DESIGNER/COPYWRITER: *Gary Goldsmith* AGENCY: *Goldsmith/Jeffrey* PHOTOGRAPHER: *Steve Hellerstein* CLIENT: *Everlast Activewear* ■ *"Nails"; "Bicep"; "Beer Can"* ● *«Nägel» «Bizeps» «Bierdose».* ▲ *«Clous» «Biceps» «Canette de bière»*

PAGE 198 #527 ART DIRECTOR: *Pierre-Yves Tinguely* DESIGNER: *Johann Terrettaz* AGENCY: *Tinguely Concept* PHOTOGRAPHER/ILLUSTRATOR: *David Schenker* CLIENT: *Nidecker Snowboards* ■ *This poster targeted race snowboarders and had to translate a technical sensibility.* ● *Das Plakat ist an Snowboard-Profis gerichtet und stellt deshalb Technik in den Mittelpunkt.* ▲ *Affiche destinée aux pros du snowboard, mettant la technique au premier plan.*

PAGE 198 #528 ART DIRECTOR/DESIGNER: *Johann Terrettaz* AGENCY: *Tinguely Concept* ILLUSTRATOR: *Wojciech* CLIENT: *Nidecker Snowboards* ■ *This poster created for a snow-*

board company targeted "freeriders." The agency tried to portray the mystical communion of the rider with his/her environment. ● *Das Plakat für einen Snowboard-Hersteller richtete sich an die Freistil-Gruppe. Thema war die geheimnisvolle Zwiesprache zwischen Snowboarder und ihrer/seiner Umgebung.* ▲ *Affiche d'un fabricant de snowboards s'adressant aux adeptes du «freestyle». Thème de l'affiche: la communion entre le snowboarder et son environnement.*

PAGE 199 #529 ART DIRECTORS: *Christian Dekant, Rüdiger Götz* DESIGNER: *Christian Dekant* AGENCY: *Stubenrauch & Simon* COPYWRITER: *Stefan Frier* CLIENT: *Fichtel & Sachs*

PAGE 199 #530 ART DIRECTOR: *Will Roth* CREATIVE DIRECTOR: *Kerry Casey* COPYWRITER: *Derek Pletch* PHOTOGRAPHER: *Curtis Johnson* AGENCY: *Carmichael Lynch* CLIENT: *Schwinn*

PAGE 200 #531 ART DIRECTOR/DESIGNER: *Craig Barez* AGENCY: *Nike, Inc.* PHOTOGRAPHER/ILLUSTRATOR: *Craig Barez* CLIENT: *Defasco*

PAGE 200 #532 ART DIRECTORS: *Tracy Wong, Michael Ivan Boychuk* DESIGNER: *Michael Ivan Boychuk* AGENCY: *Wongdoody* ILLUSTRATOR: *Michael Ivan Boychuk, Wy'east Color* CLIENT: *Seattle Supersonics* ■ *The directive for this poster was to portray the "explosiveness" of NBA superstar Shawn Kemp. The agency felt his playing style was analogous to a massive electrical storm.* ● *Hier ging es darum, die «Explosivität» des NBA-Superstars Shawn Kemp zum Ausdruck zu bringen. Sein Stil wird dabei mit einem massiven elektrischen Sturm gleichgesetzt.* ▲ *L'objectif était de montrer l'explosivité de Shawn Kemp, superstar de la NBA. Son style est comparé à un orage chargé d'électricité.*

PAGE 201 #533 ART DIRECTOR: *Michele Melandri* DESIGNERS: *Michele Melandri, Morgan Thomas* AGENCY: *Nike, Inc.* PHOTOGRAPHER/ILLUSTRATOR: *Morgan Thomas* COPYWRITER: *Stanley Hainsworth* CLIENT: *In-house* ■ *The agency decided to use the look of a boxing poster to represent the friendly rivalry between the two tennis players.* ● *Um die freundschaftliche Rivalität zweier Tennisspieler darzustellen, wurde bei diesem Plakat auf Boxplakate zurückgegriffen.* ▲ *Image s'inspirant des affiches de matches de boxe, illustrant la rivalité fair-play entre deux joueurs de tennis.*

PAGE 201 #534 ART DIRECTOR/DESIGNER: *Ron Dumas* AGENCY: *Nike, Inc.* PHOTOGRAPHER/ILLUSTRATOR: *Richard Corman* COPYWRITER: *Bob Lambie* CLIENT: *In-house* ■ *The directive was to develop a poster featuring Sergi Fedorov from the Detroit Redwings. The poster introduced Nike's debut into ice hockey with a signature skate.* ● *Das Plakat verkündet Nikes Einstieg in das Eishockey- bzw. Schlittschuhgeschäft. Gezeigt ist Sergi Fedorov von den Detroit Redwings.* ▲ *Affiche annonçant l'arrivée de Nike dans le monde du hockey sur glace et du patinage. L'image montre Sergi Fedorov des Detroit Redwings.*

PAGE 202 #535-538 ART DIRECTOR/ DESIGNER: *Irene Kugelmann* AGENCY: *Wieden & Kennedy Amsterdam* PHOTOGRAPHER/ILLUSTRATOR: *Max Vadukul* COPYWRITER: *John Park* CLIENT: *Nike*

PAGE 202 #539 CREATIVE DIRECTOR: *Dan Wieden* ART DIRECTOR: *John C. Jay* DESIGNER: *Iman Pao* AGENCY: *Wieden & Kennedy* PHOTOGRAPHER *John Huet* COPYWRITER: *Jimmy Smith* CLIENT: *Nike* ■ *Poster from "Trash Talk," one component of a New York City multimedia campaign which celebrated New York's love for basketball. The campaign ran only in New York.* ● *Das Plakat ist Teil einer Multimedia-Kampagne, in der es um die Vorliebe der New Yorker für Basketball ging. Die Kampagne lief ausschliesslich in New York.* ▲ *Affiche réalisée dans le cadre d'une campagne multimédia sur la passion des New-Yorkais pour le basket. Cette campagne se limitait à la ville de New York.*

PAGE 203 #540 ART DIRECTOR: *Michael Tiedy* DESIGNER: *Derek Welch* AGENCY: *Nike Image Design* PHOTOGRAPHER/ILLUSTRATOR: *Cliff Watts* CLIENT: *In-house* ■ *This poster was created to commemorate Nikepark, a venue at Centennial Park in Atlanta during the 1996 Olympics. The goal was to illustrate and celebrate the multitude of Nike athletes and the sports in which they compete.* ● *Plakat als Erinnerung an Nikepark, einen Austragungsorte der Olympischen Spiele 1996 in Atlanta. Ziel war es, die Vielzahl der Nike-Athleten und der von ihnen ausgeübten Sportarten darzustellen.* ▲ *Affiche en souvenir du Nikepark, lieu de rencontre durant les Jeux olympiques d'Atlanta en 1996. Il s'agissait de présenter la pléiade d'athlètes Nike et les disciplines qu'ils pratiquent.*

PAGE 204 #541 ART DIRECTOR/DESIGNER: *Michele Melandri* AGENCY: *Nike Inc* PHOTOGRAPHER/ILLUSTRATOR: *Tony Dizinno* CLIENT: *In-house* ■ *Tennis balls incorporating each of the four country flags that host a grand slam event determined the corner*

placement and red, white, and blue color scheme. "The Agassi Rules" are rules Andre Agassi follows to win each event. ● *Die Flaggen auf den Tennisbällen gehören zu den vier Ländern, in denen der Grand Slam ausgetragen wird. «The Agassi Rules» sind Regeln, die André Agassi befolgt, um die Turniere zu gewinnen.* ▲ *Les drapeaux figurant sur les balles de tennis sont ceux des quatre pays qui disputent le Grand Slam. «The Agassi Rules» sont les règles qu'applique André Agassi pour gagner un match.*

PAGE 204 #542 ART DIRECTOR: *Jeff Weithman* DESIGNERS: *Jeff Weithman, Webb Blevins* AGENCY: *Nike Inc.* PHOTOGRAPHER/ILLUSTRATOR: *Bradford Johnson* COPYWRITER: *Neil Webster* CLIENT: *In-house* ■ *"Your vision just got faster." This poster was designed to accompany free eyewear given to Hollywood celebrities and musicians prior to its actual release. It had to be quick, to-the-point, and entertaining. It also had to educate about the technical aspects of the product in an engaging way.* ● *«Ihre Sehfähigkeit ist einfach schneller geworden.» Das Plakat entstand im Zusammenhang mit der kostenlosen Abgabe von Brillen an Hollywood-Berühmtheiten und Musiker vor der tatsächlichen Markteinführung der Produkte. Das Plakat sollte leicht verständlich und unterhaltend sein und dabei auf ansprechende Art über die technischen Aspekte des Produktes informieren.* ▲ *«Votre vue est devenue plus rapide.» Affiche conçue dans le cadre d'une promotion de lunettes offertes à des stars d'Hollywood et à des musiciens avant le lancement effectif du produit sur le marché. Elle devait présenter les caractéristiques techniques du produit de façon claire et séduisante.*

PAGE 205 #543-545 ART DIRECTOR/ DESIGNER: *Tim Bade* PRODUCTION MANAGER: *Bill Mammorella* AGENCY: *The Marlin Company* PHOTOGRAPHER/ILLUSTRATOR: *Kirk Worden* COPYWRITERS: *Joe Totten, Michael Stelzer* CLIENT: *Southwest Area Special Olympics* ■ *"Because they can." This campaign was created to support the image of the Southwest Area Special Olympics. They pay tribute to actual athletes and their special talents and portray them as heroes in their field. These athletes differ from professionals because they choose to play their games for fun and not for hype and commercialism that tends to drive most sports.* ● *«Weil sie's können.» Das Plakat gehört zu einer Image-Kampagne für die Southwest Area Special Olympics, in der Athleten und ihre speziellen Talente im Mittelpunkt stehen. Diese Athleten unterscheiden sich von den Profis, weil ihre Motivation Spass am Sport ist und nicht Ruhm oder der Kommerz, der heute die meisten Sportarten regiert.* ▲ *«Parce qu'ils en sont capables.» Affiche réalisée dans le cadre d'une campagne pour les Southwest Area Special Olympics, lors desquels les athlètes démontrent leurs talents. Ceux-ci se différencient des professionnels dans la mesure où ils font passer le sport et le plaisir avant la gloire et l'argent.*

PAGE 205 #546-548 ART DIRECTOR: *Becky Shaeffer* AGENCY: *Sietsema Engel* PHOTOGRAPHER: *Carl Cedergren* COPYWRITER: *Jay Kaskel* CLIENT: *Calhoun Cycle* ■ *The objective was to let people know the client rented tandem bicycles. The agency took a rather risqué approach because of the hip, urban, generation-x neighborhood where the bike shop was located.* ● *«Möchtest Du vorne oder hinten?» «Es wird das Fahren auf dem Rücksitz empfohlen.» «Bitte, was immer Du tust, lass keinen fliegen.» Dieser etwas gewagte Approach des Plakates für einen Verleih von Tandem-Fahrrädern trägt dem Publikum der Umgebung Rechnung, das vor allem aus ausgeflippten, Generation-X-Stadtmenschen besteht.* ▲ *«Tu veux aller devant ou derrière?» «Conduite à l'arrière recommandée.» «Fais ce que tu veux, mais ne nous plante pas!» Affiche d'un magasin de location de tandems adaptée à la population de son environnement urbain, des jeunes avides de sensations fortes.*

PAGE 206 #549-550 AGENCY: *Ogilvy and Mather* CLIENT: *Neil Pryde*

PAGE 206 #551 ART DIRECTOR: *Vasiliy Tsygankov* DESIGNER: *Igor Gurovich* AGENCY: *Ima-Press Publishers* CLIENT: *Orion Cup*

PAGE 206 #552 ART DIRECTOR/DESIGNER/ILLUSTRATOR: *Finn Nygaard* AGENCY: *Finn Nygaard Graphic Design* CLIENT: *Helsingør Handball Club* ■ *"Applause for fifty years in division handball."* ● *«Applaus für fünfzig Jahre Handball in der ersten Liga.»* ▲ *«Une ovation pour cinquante ans de handball en première division.»*

PAGE 207 #553 ART DIRECTOR: *Ted Bertz* DESIGNER: *Dawn Droskoski* AGENCY: *Ted Bertz Graphic Design, Inc.* CLIENT: *Middlesex County Chamber of Commerce* ■ *This poster commemorates the 1995 Head of the Connecticut Regatta.* ● *Plakat als Erinnerung an die Head-of-Connecticut-Regatta im Jahre 1995.* ▲ *Affiche souvenir de la régate Head of the Connecticut disputée en 1995.*

PAGE 207 #554 ART DIRECTOR: *R. Morrison* DESIGNER: *Ted Wright* AGENCY: *Ted Wright Illustration/Design* ILLUSTRATOR: *Ted Wright* CLIENT: *US Olympic Committee* ■ *The* *directive was to create a bold, colorful graphic that captured the excitement and splendor of the Olympics held in Atlanta, Georgia.* ● *Hier ging es darum, mit einem ausdrucksvollen, farbenfrohen Plakat Begeisterung und Glanz der Olympischen Spiele 1996 in Atlanta zu vermitteln.* ▲ *Affiche visant à donner une image forte et dynamique des Jeux olympiques d'Atlanta en 1996.*

PAGE 208 #555 ART DIRECTOR/DESIGNER: *Lex Reitsma* CLIENT: *De Nederlandse Opera* ■ *This poster fits in with the highly graphic set design of the Wozzeck production it promotes. The set design included three-dimensional black houses of various sizes in front of an enveloping yellow backcloth. The typography completes the silhouette of the house.* ● *Dieses Plakat für eine Wozzeck-Aufführung nimmt Bezug auf das stark graphisch geprägte Bühnenbild, zu dem dreidimensionale schwarze Häuser in verschiedenen Grössen vor einem gelben Prospekt gehören. Die Typographie vollendet die Silhouette des Hauses, das der Soldat und Aussenseiter Wozzeck betreten möchte.* ▲ *Affiche pour une représentation de Wozzeck inspirée du graphisme des décors, qui comprennent des maisons noires tridimensionnelles de différentes tailles se détachant sur un fond jaune. La typographie souligne les contours de la maison dans laquelle le soldat Wozzeck veut entrer.*

PAGE 208 #556 ART DIRECTOR/DESIGNER: *Leo Raymundo* AGENCY: *NBBJ Graphic Design* CLIENT: *The Empty Space Theatre* ■ *Poster for a one-woman play about the life of an Englishwoman in the American wild west.* ● *Ankündigung eines Ein-Frauen-Stückes über das Leben einer aus England stammenden Frau im Wilden Westen Amerikas.* ▲ *Affiche d'un one-woman-show sur la vie d'une Anglaise dans le Far West.*

PAGE 209 #557 AGENCY: *Stasys* PHOTOGRAPHER/ILLUSTRATOR: *Stasys Eidrigevicius* CLIENT: *Teatre Odense*

PAGE 209 #558 AGENCY: *Stasys* PHOTOGRAPHER/ILLUSTRATOR: *Stasys Eidrigevicius* CLIENT: *Teatre Amufer*

PAGE 209 #559, 560 ART DIRECTOR/DESIGNER: *Harry Pearce* AGENCY: *Lippa Pearce* PHOTOGRAPHER/ILLUSTRATOR: *Andrzej Kumonski* CLIENT: *Theater Clwyd*

PAGE 210 #561 ART DIRECTOR: *Drew Hodges* DESIGNERS: *Naomi Mizusaki, Amy Guip* AGENCY: *Spot Design* PHOTOGRAPHER/ILLUSTRATOR: *Amy Guip* CLIENT: *The Booking Office* ■ *Poster created for "Rent." The agency wanted to create an "un-Broadway" Broadway show graphic. Rather than communicating the plot line, the agency decided to emphasize how it feels to experience live theater.* ● *Plakat für eine Aufführung am Broadway, das nichts vom üblichen Broadway-Stil haben sollte. Statt auf den Inhalt bzw. den Titel des Stückes einzugehen, steht das Theatererlebnis ansich im Mittelpunkt.* ▲ *Affiche d'un spectacle à Broadway qui devait se démarquer des affiches classiques. Au lieu de mettre l'accent sur le titre et le contenu de la pièce, l'agence a préféré suggérer le plaisir que procure le théâtre.*

PAGE 211 #562 ART DIRECTOR: *Paula Scher* DESIGNERS: *Paula Scher, Lisa Mazur* AGENCY: *Pentagram Design Inc* PHOTOGRAPHER/ILLUSTRATOR: *Richard Avedon* CLIENT: *The Public Theater* ■ *"Bring in 'Da Noise, Bring in 'Da Funk" is a Tony award-winning musical history of rhythm in African-American life. The Broadway ad campaign features wood typefaces, and the active image is amplified by surrounding, stark white space. In the show's poster, dancer/choreographer Savion Glover is bombarded by critics' quotes like curbside shouts–raves coming in from all sides.* ● *Hier geht es um ein mit dem Tony-Preis ausgezeichnetes Musical über die Geschichte des Rhythmus im afrikanisch-amerikanischen Leben. Es wurden Holzschnitt-Schriften verwendet, während die Wirkung des Bildes von viel weisser Fläche unterstützt wird. Im Plakat wird der Tänzer und Choreograph, Savion Glover, mit Zitaten der Kritiker von allen Seiten bombardiert.* ▲ *Comédie musicale retraçant l'histoire des rythmes afro-américains, récompensée par un Tony award. Des caractères en bois ont été utilisés pour la typographie, et les surfaces blanches renforcent l'impact de l'image. L'affiche montre le danseur et chorégraphe Savion Glover, bombardé de citations de la critique.*

PAGE 211 #563 ART DIRECTOR: *Paula Scher* DESIGNERS: *Paula Scher, Lisa Mazur* AGENCY: *Pentagram Design Inc* PHOTOGRAPHER/ILLUSTRATOR: *Carol Rosegg* CLIENT: *The Public Theater*

PAGE 212 #564 ART DIRECTOR/ DESIGNER: *David Hillman* AGENCY: *Pentagram Design Ltd.* CLIENT: *Volktheater & Feliks Buttner* ■ *Poster for a theater production of "Romeo and Juliet." An East German theater company invited a number of international poster artists to design posters for its 1995 season. Each designer was asked to focus on one play and to keep to two colors, one of them fluorescent.* ■ *Plakat für eine Aufführung von*

«Romeo und Julia». Ein ehemals ostdeutsches Theater lud einige internationale Plakatgestalter ein, die Plakate für die Saison 1995 zu entwerfen. Jeder Gestalter sollte sich auf ein Stück beschränken und mit zwei Farben arbeiten, wovon eine fluoreszierend sein musste. ▲ *Affiche pour une représentation de «Roméo et Juliette». Un ancien théâtre de l'ex-Allemagne de l'Est a invité des affichistes du monde entier à créer les affiches de la saison 1995. Chaque artiste devait se limiter à une seule affiche et travailler avec deux couleurs, dont une fluorescente.*

PAGE 213 #565 ART DIRECTOR: *Paula Scher* DESIGNERS: *Paula Scher, Lisa Mazur* AGENCY: *Pentagram Design Inc* CLIENT: *New York Shakespeare Festival/The Public Theater* ■ *This poster created for the New York Shakespeare festival borrows from the tradition of old-fashioned English theater annoucements, using only type in varying weights and sizes.* ● *Dieses Plakat für das New Yorker Shakespeare-Festival macht eine Anleihe bei alten englischen Theaterplakaten, die nur mit Schriften in verschiedenen Stärken und Grössen gestaltet wurden.* ▲ *Affiche du festival Shakespeare à New York s'inspirant des anciennes affiches de théâtre anglaises, réalisées uniquement à l'aide de caractères de différents corps.*

PAGE 213 #566 ART DIRECTOR/DESIGNER: *Jørgen Thomsen* AGENCY: *Ozean* CLIENT: *Corona Danseteater* ■ *Poster announcing the performance of a modern ballet. The title "Heavy" refers to Heavy Metal music.* ● *Ankündigung einer modernen Ballettaufführung. Der Titel «Heavy» bezieht sich auf Heavy-Metal-Musik.* ▲ *Affiche d'un ballet moderne. Le titre «Heavy» fait allusion au Heavy Metal.*

PAGE 214 #567, 568 ART DIRECTOR/DESIGNER: *Savas Cekic* AGENCY: *Valor Tasarim* PHOTOGRAPHER/ILLUSTRATOR: *Savas Cekic* CLIENT: *Istanbul City Theaters* ■ *Posters for plays entitled "Strider" by Tolstoi and "Zoo" by Edward Albee.* ● *Ankündigungen der Aufführung eines Stückes von Tolstoi und des Stückes «Zoo» von Edward Albee.* ▲ *Affiches d'une pièce de Tolstoï et de «Zoo», d'Edward Albee.*

PAGE 215 #569, 570 ART DIRECTOR: *Walter Vorjohann* AGENCY: *Büro Walter Vorjohann* PHOTOGRAPHER/ILLUSTRATOR: *Ute John* CLIENT: *Oper Frankfurt*

PAGE 215 #571 ART DIRECTOR: *Mike Dempsey* DESIGNER: *Neil Walker* AGENCY: *CDT Design Limited* PHOTOGRAPHER/ILLUSTRATOR: *Lewis Mulatero* CLIENT: *English National Opera* ■ *The directive was to produce an image for the English National Opera's production of "Tosca" which would reflect the opera on leaflets, posters, and press advertisements.* ● *Plakat für eine Aufführung von Tosca an der English National Opera. Der Entwurf sollte sich auf die Oper beziehen und sich auch für Prospekte und Anzeigen in der Presse eignen.* ▲ *Affiche pour une représentation de «La Tosca» à l'English National Opera. Le visuel devait évoquer l'opéra et se prêter aux prospectus et aux annonces presse.*

PAGE 215 #572 ART DIRECTOR: *Mike Dempsey* DESIGNER: *Neil Walker* AGENCY: *CDT Design Limited* PHOTOGRAPHER/ILLUSTRATOR: *Robin Cracknell* CLIENT: *English National Opera* ■ *The directive was to produce an image for the English National Opera's production of "Mohagonny" which would reflect the opera on leaflets, posters, and press advertisements.* ● *Plakat für eine Aufführung von «Mahagoni» an der English National Opera. Der Entwurf sollte sich auf die Oper beziehen und sich auch für Prospekte und Anzeigen in der Presse eignen.* ▲ *Affiche pour une représentation de «Mahagoni» à l'English National Opera. Le visuel devait évoquer l'opéra et se prêter aux prospectus et aux annonces presse.*

PAGE 216 #573 ART DIRECTOR/ DESIGNER/AGENCY: *K.D. Geissbühler* CLIENT: *Operhaus Zürich* ■ *"Il Trittico" consists of three operas performed on one evening on the theme of jealousy, passion and death.* ● *«Il Trittico» besteht aus drei Opern an einem Abend. Die Themen sind Neid, Leidenschaft, Tod.* ▲ *«Il Trittico» se compose de trois opéras donnés le même soir, sur les thèmes de la jalousie, de la passion et de la mort.*

PAGE 216 #574 ART DIRECTOR/ DESIGNER/AGENCY: *K.D. Geissbühler* CLIENT: *Operhaus Zürich* ■ *Announcement for the perfomance of "Samson and Delilah." The image is a symbolic rendering of the destruction of a temple.* ● *Ankündigung einer Aufführung von «Samson und Dalila». Thema des Plakates ist die symbolische Zerstörung des Tempels.* ▲ *Annonce d'une représentation de «Samson et Dalila». Thème de l'affiche: la destruction symbolique du temple.*

PAGE 216 #575 ART DIRECTOR/AGENCY: *K.D. Geissbühler* DESIGNERS: *K.D. Geissbühler, Maruan Dib* CLIENT: *Opernhaus Zürich* ■ *"Magic realm" is an opera for children. The elements of the poster refer to three-dimensional elements used on the stage.* ●

«Zauberwelt» ist eine Oper für Kinder. Die Bildelemente entsprechen Versatzstücken des Bühnenbildes. ▲ «Le monde enchanté» est un opéra pour enfants. Les éléments du visuel reprennent les décors.

PAGE 216 #576 ART DIRECTOR/DESIGNER/AGENCY: *K.D. Geissbühler* PHOTOGRAPHER/ILLUSTRATOR: *Susanne Schwiertz* CLIENT: *Opernhaus Zürich* ■ *Poster for a ballet performance.* ● *Plakat für eine Ballett-Aufführung.* ▲ *Affiche pour un ballet.*

PAGE 217 #577 DESIGNERS: *Sergey Ilyin, Irina Voloshina* AGENCY: *Grade Group* PHOTOGRAPHER/ILLUSTRATOR: *Vitaly Teplov* CLIENT: *Kukuruza* ■ *Poster for a folk group.* ● *Plakat für eine Folk-Gruppe.* ▲ *Affiche d'un groupe de folk.*

PAGE 218 #578-583 CREATIVE DIRECTOR: *Stefan Zschaler* ART DIRECTOR: *Ove Gley* AGENCY: *Jung von Matt Werbeagentur* PHOTOGRAPHER/ILLUSTRATOR: *Uwe Duettmann* CLIENT: *Gallaher International/Benson & Hedges* ■ *"Now just don't make a mistake.". "For a real good cigarette, you can do any kind of advertising." "But mother earth smokes too." "You are not just anybody. Don't smoke just anything." "He comes with, he comes without, he comes with...." "Be tolerant. Except when it is a question of your cigarette."* ● *Werbung für eine Zigarettenmarke.* ▲ *«Ne faites pas d'erreur, surtout maintenant!» «N'importe quelle forme de publicité se prête à une bonne cigarette.» «Mère Nature fume aussi.» «Vous n'êtes pas n'importe qui. Ne fumez pas n'importe quoi!» «Il vient avec, il vient sans, il vient avec...» «Soyez tolérant, sauf pour votre marque de cigarettes!» Publicités pour une marque de cigarettes.*

PAGE 219 #584 ART DIRECTOR/DESIGNER: *Tom Antista* AGENCY: *Antista Fairclough Design* PHOTOGRAPHER/ILLUSTRATOR: *Tom Antista* CLIENT: *Omni Cigarettes* ■ *Limited edition product launch poster.* ● *In limitierter Auflage produziertes Plakat für die Lancierung von einer Zigarettenmarke.* ▲ *Edition limitée réalisée pour le lancement d'une marque de cigarettes.*

PAGE 220-221 #585-590 CREATIVE DIRECTOR: *Rich Silverstein* ART DIRECTOR: *Steve Luker* DESIGNERS: *Michael Schwab, Jami Spittler* AGENCY: *Goodby, Silverstein & Partners* PHOTOGRAPHER/ILLUSTRATOR: *Michael Schwab* COPYWRITER: *Steve Simpson* CLIENT: *The Golden Gate National Parks* ■ *Posters and series of bus shelters designed to build public awareness and support for the Golden Gate National Parks. The intent was to create images with a timeless, American style–reminiscent of WPA artwork from the 1930s. The images are the cornerstone of an ongoing marketing campaign for the parks featuring the icons that visually brand the individual parks.* ● *Aufgabe dieser Plakate ist es, die Öffentlichkeit für die Golden Gate National Parks zu begeistern und ihre finanzielle Unterstützung zu gewinnen. Gewünscht war ein zeitloser Stil in Anlehnung an den amerikanischen Stil der 30er Jahre. Die Bilder mit den Ikonen, die die einzelnen Parks kennzeichnen, bilden die Grundlage für eine andauernde Kampagne.* ▲ *Affiche publicitaire pour les Golden Gate National Parks visant à encourager les dons. Le client désirait un style intemporel inspiré du style américain des années 30. Les images présentent des icônes qui symbolisent les différents parcs seront utilisées tout au long de la campagne.*

PAGE 222 #591 ART DIRECTOR/DESIGNER/PHOTOGRAPHER: *Jon Warren Lentz* CLIENT: *The Port Of San Francisco*

PAGE 223 #592 ART DIRECTOR/ DESIGNER: *Tom Poth* AGENCY: *Hixo, Inc.* PHOTOGRAPHER/ILLUSTRATOR: *Douglas Stermer* COPYWRITER: *Jackie Hutto* CLIENT: *Moody Gardens* ■ *This poster seeks to inform and attract visitors to an indoor rainforest conservancy located in Texas.* ● *Thema des Plakates ist ein Regenwald-Treibhaus in Texas. Es informiert und wirbt um Besucher.* ▲ *Affiche visant à attirer des visiteurs dans une serre tropicale située au Texas.*

PAGE 224 #593 ART DIRECTOR/DESIGNER: *Dr. Ulla Fürlinger* AGENCY/CLIENT: *Tirol Werbung* PHOTOGRAPHER/ILLUSTRATOR: *Werner Pawlok* ■ *This poster promoting the region of Tirol in Austria uses the historical figure of the "Geierwally" to evoke strength and courage. In the 19th century, a young peasant woman climbed a steep rock to save an eagle's nest, which earned her the name of "Geierwally." The figure became the protagonist of a novel, a film and a play.* ● *Das «Geierwally»-Motiv dieses Plakates steht für Tirol als Bergland, als Land der Kraft und des Mutes. Die Geierwally war eine Tiroler Bauerntochter, die im 19. Jahrhundert lebte, und sich diesen Namen durch die waghalsige Rettung eines Adlerhorstes in einer Felswand verdiente. Die literarische Ausbeutung ihres Abenteuers machte sie zu einer Roman-, Film- und Bühnenfigur.* ▲ *Affiche touristique pour le Tyrol, présenté comme un pays de montagne. Geierwally, le personnage sur l'affiche, était une fille de paysan qui vécut au XIXᵉ siècle et devint célèbre en sauvant un vautour (Geier en allemand) sur une paroi rocheuse. Cette jeune fille téméraire est devenue l'héroïne d'un roman, d'un film et d'une pièce de théâtre.*

PAGE 225 #594-596 CREATIVE DIRECTOR: *Diane Durban* DESIGNER: *John Trinanes* AGENCY: *Crispin Porter + Bogusky Design* PHOTOGRAPHER/ILLUSTRATOR: *Oscar Alonzo* CLIENT: *Travel Channel Latin America* ■ *These posters were created to communicate the "Travel Channel brand image" to media buyers, cable operators, and consumers in 17 countries.* ● *Diese Plakate richten sich an Media-Buyer, das Kabelfernsehen und das TV-Publikum in 17 Ländern, mit dem Ziel, sie auf einen Reise-Sender aufmerksam zu machen.* ▲ *Affiches pour une chaîne consacrée aux voyages s'adressant aux acheteurs de médias, aux exploitants de réseaux câblés et aux téléspectateurs de 17 pays.*

PAGE 225 #597 ART DIRECTOR/DESIGNER: *Minko T. Dimov* AGENCY: *Minko Images* CLIENT: *In-house* ■ *Self-promotional piece entitled "Montreal."* ● *Eigenwerbungsplakat mit dem Titel «Montreal».* ▲ *Publicité autopromotionnelle intitulée «Montréal».*

PAGE 226 #598-600 ART DIRECTOR: *H.J. Kristhan* DESIGNER: *Jiayang Lin (Student Project)* SCHOOL: *Hochschule Der Künste Berlin* ■ *Poster for the World Fair to take place in the year 2000 in Hanover. The theme for the students was "man, technology, ecology."* ● *Plakat für die Weltausstellung 2000 in Hannover. Es handelt sich um ein Studentenprojekt, dessen Thema «Mensch, Technologie, Ökologie» war.* ▲ *Affiche réalisée pour l'Exposition universelle de l'an 2000 à Hanovre. Ce projet d'étudiants a pour thème «L'homme, la technologie, l'écologie».*

PAGE 226 #601 ART DIRECTOR: *Kan Tai-Keung* DESIGNERS: *Kan Tai-Keung, Pamela Law* AGENCY: *Kan & Law Design Consultants* PHOTOGRAPHER/ILLUSTRATOR: *C.K. Wong* CLIENT: *Japan Typography Association* ■ *This design was originally published in Ti Magazine. Five internationally active graphic designers clarify what typography can do for the future of the world.* ● *Fünf international tätige Graphik-Designer erläutern hier, was Typographie für die Welt tun kann. Der Entwurf wurde ursprünglich in der Zeitschrift Ti veröffentlicht.* ▲ *Cinq graphistes travaillant dans le monde entier explicitent ce que la typographie peut faire pour le monde. Ce visuel a déjà paru dans Ti Magazine.*

PAGE 227 #602 ART DIRECTOR/ DESIGNER: *Beth A. Wegiel* ■ *Student project entitled "Conversation Between Stella and Blanche."* ● *Plakat im Rahmen eines Studentenprojektes mit dem Titel: «Konversation zwischen Stella und Blanche».* ▲ *Projet d'étudiants intitulé «Conversation entre Stella et Blanche».*

PAGE 228 #603, 604 ART DIRECTOR/AGENCY: *Claude Kuhn* CLIENT: *Zirkus Knie* ■ *Poster for the Swiss National Circus.* ● *Plakat für den Schweizer Nationalzirkus Knie.* ▲ *Affiche du cirque national suisse.*

BACK COVER JACKET ART DIRECTOR/ DESIGNER: *Rick Vaughn* AGENCY: *Vaughn/Weeden Creative* PHOTOGRAPHER/ILLUSTRATOR: *Greg Tucker* CLIENT: *US West*

INDICES

VERZEICHNISSE

INDEX

ILLUSTRATORS · PHOTOGRAPHERS

C O P Y W R I T E R S

(CLIENTS)

G R A P H I S   B O O K S

BOOKS	ALL REGIONS
☐ GRAPHIS ADVERTISING 97	US$ 69.95
☐ GRAPHIS ANNUAL REPORTS 5	US$ 69.95
☐ GRAPHIS BOOK DESIGN	US$ 75.95
☐ GRAPHIS BROCHURES 2	US$ 75.00
☐ GRAPHIS DESIGN 97	US$ 69.95
☐ GRAPHIS DIGITAL FONTS 1	US$ 69.95
☐ GRAPHIS LETTERHEAD 3	US$ 75.00
☐ GRAPHIS LOGO 3	US$ 49.95
☐ GRAPHIS MUSIC CDS	US$ 75.95
☐ GRAPHIS NEW MEDIA	US$ 69.95
☐ GRAPHIS NUDES (PAPERBACK)	US$ 39.95
☐ GRAPHIS PACKAGING 7	US$ 75.00
☐ **GRAPHIS PAPER SPECIFIER SYSTEM (GPS)**	US$ 495.00**
☐ GRAPHIS PHOTO 96	US$ 69.95
☐ GRAPHIS POSTER 96	US$ 69.95
☐ GRAPHIS STUDENT DESIGN 96	US$ 44.95
☐ HUMAN CONDITION PHOTOJOURNALISM 95	US$ 49.95
☐ INFORMATION ARCHITECTS	US$ 49.95
☐ WORLD TRADEMARKS (2 VOL. SET)	US$ 250.00

** ADD $4 SHIPPING PER BOOK. SHIPPING OUTSIDE US ADDITIONAL.
** ADD $30 SHIPPING/HANDLING FOR GPS.

NOTE! NY RESIDENTS ADD 8.25% SALES TAX

☐ CHECK ENCLOSED (PAYABLE TO GRAPHIS)

USE CREDIT CARDS TO PAY IN US DOLLARS.

☐ AMERICAN EXPRESS   ☐ MASTERCARD   ☐ VISA

CARD NO.   EXP. DATE

CARDHOLDER NAME

SIGNATURE

(PLEASE PRINT)

NAME

TITLE

COMPANY

ADDRESS

CITY   STATE/PROVINCE

ZIP CODE   COUNTRY

SEND ORDER FORM AND MAKE CHECK PAYABLE TO:
GRAPHIS INC, 141 LEXINGTON AVENUE, NEW YORK NY 10016-8193

BOOKS	EUROPE/AFRICA MIDDLE EAST	GERMANY	U.K.
☐ GRAPHIS ADVERTISING 97	SFR. 123.–	DM 149,–	£ 59.95
☐ GRAPHIS ANNUAL REPORTS 5	SFR. 137.–	DM 149,–	£ 59.95
☐ GRAPHIS BOOK DESIGN	SFR. 137.–	DM 149,–	£ 59.95
☐ GRAPHIS BROCHURES 2	SFR. 137.–	DM 149,–	£ 59.95
☐ GRAPHIS DESIGN 97	SFR. 123.–	DM 149,–	£ 59.95
☐ GRAPHIS DIGITAL FONTS 1	SFR. 123.–	DM 149,–	£ 59.95
☐ GRAPHIS LETTERHEAD 3	SFR. 123.–	DM 149,–	£ 59.95
☐ GRAPHIS LOGO 3	SFR. 98.–	DM 112,–	£ 42.00
☐ GRAPHIS MUSIC CDS	SFR. 137.–	DM 149,–	£ 59.95
☐ GRAPHIS NEW MEDIA	SFR. 123.–	DM 149,–	£ 59.95
☐ GRAPHIS NUDES (PAPERBACK)	SFR. 59.–	DM 68,–	£ 38.00
☐ GRAPHIS PACKAGING 7	SFR. 137.–	DM 149,–	£ 59.95
☐ GRAPHIS PHOTO 96	SFR. 123.–	DM 149,–	£ 59.95
☐ GRAPHIS POSTER 96	SFR. 123.–	DM 149,–	£ 59.95
☐ GRAPHIS STUDENT DESIGN 96	SFR. 69.–	DM 88,–	£ 39.95
☐ HUMAN CONDITION PHOTOJOURNALISM 95	SFR. 69.–	DM 78,–	£ 42.00
☐ INFORMATION ARCHITECTS	SFR. 75.–	DM 98,–	£ 39.95
☐ WORLD TRADEMARKS	SFR. 385.–	DM 458,–	£ 198.00

(FOR ORDERS FROM EC COUNTRIES V.A.T. WILL BE CHARGED IN
ADDITION TO ABOVE BOOK PRICES)

FOR CREDIT CARD PAYMENT (ALL CARDS DEBITED IN SWISS FRANCS):

☐ AMERICAN EXPRESS ☐ DINER'S CLUB ☐ VISA/BARCLAYCARD/CARTE BLEUE

CARD NO.   EXP. DATE

CARDHOLDER NAME

SIGNATURE

☐ BILL ME (ADDITIONAL MAILING COSTS WILL BE CHARGED)

(PLEASE PRINT)

LAST NAME   FIRST NAME

TITLE

COMPANY

ADDRESS   CITY

POSTAL CODE   COUNTRY

SEND ORDER FORM AND MAKE CHECK PAYABLE TO: DESIGN BOOKS
INTERNATIONAL, DUFOURSTRASSE 107, CH-8008 ZURICH/SWITZERLAND

G R A P H I S   M A G A Z I N E